Words of Life

Words of Life

A Religious and Inspirational Album
Containing Over 1,000 Quotations
from the Minds and Hearts of
Writers of Twenty Centuries

Edited by

Charles L. Wallis

Photographs by Catherine Hopkins

HARPER & ROW, PUBLISHERS
SAN FRANCISCO

Cambridge London
Hagerstown Mexico City
Philadelphia São Paulo
New York 1817 Sydney

Acknowledgment is made to the following for permission to reprint copyrighted material:

ABINGDON PRESS for extracts from *Lift Up Your Hearts* by Walter Russell Bowie, copyright © 1939, 1956 by Pierce and Washabaugh; extracts from *Sermons on the Parables of Jesus* and *Sermons for Special Days* by Charles M. Crowe; "I Will Not Hurry" from *I Have a Stewardship* by Ralph S. Cushman, copyright 1939 assigned to Abingdon Press; "At Calvary," "Sheer Joy," "The Secret," and "The Starlit Night" from *Spiritual Hilltops* by Ralph S. Cushman; *Adults at Worship* by Wallace Fridy, copyright © 1959 by Abingdon Press; *Victorious Suffering* by Carl A. Glover; "The Understanding Heart" from *Be Still and Know* by Georgia Harkness, copyright 1953 by Pierce and Washabaugh; "Basic Rules for Daily Living" from *Leaves from a Spiritual Notebook* by Thomas S. Kepler, copyright © 1960 by Abingdon Press; *The Springs of Creative Living* by Rollo May; "A Woman's Way" from *In Pastures Green* by Jane Merchant, copyright © 1959 by Abingdon Press; *Making Prayer Real* by Lynn James Radcliffe; "What Jesus Does for Me" by Robert E. Speer in *Treasury of Sermon Illustrations*, ed. by Charles L. Wallis; "Little Lights" and "Prayer for Service" from *A Poet Prays* by Violet Alleyn Storey; "And He Was Only Thirty-Three" by Violet Alleyn Storey in *Lenten-Easter Sourcebook*, ed. by Charles L. Wallis.

APPLETON-CENTURY-CROFTS for extract from *Three to Get Married* by Fulton J. Sheen, copyright 1951 by Fulton J. Sheen.

THE BOBBS-MERRILL COMPANY, INC., for extract from *Be Kind to Yourself* by Vash Young, copyright 1936 by The Bobbs-Merrill Company, Inc., © 1963 by Vash Young.

JONATHAN CAPE, LTD., for "And the Word Was Made Flesh" from *Little Plays of St. Francis* by Laurence Housman, copyright 1932 by Jonathan Cape, Ltd., published by Sidgwick & Jackson, Ltd.

CONDE NAST, INC., for extract from Sophie Kerr in *The Arts of Living* by the Editors of *Vogue*.

DODD, MEAD & COMPANY for "Veni Creator" and "Vestigia" from *Bliss Carman's Poems*, copyright 1929 by Bliss Carman; "The Land of Beyond" from *The Complete Poems of Robert Service*, copyright 1916, 1944 by Robert Service.

DOUBLEDAY & COMPANY, INC., for extracts from *Peace With God* by Billy Graham, copyright 1953 by Billy Graham; *The Secret of Happiness* by Billy Graham, copyright 1955 by Billy Graham; *Great Possessions* by David Grayson, copyright 1917 by Doubleday & Company, Inc.; "Sussex" from *Rudyard Kipling's Verse, Inclusive Edition*, reprinted by permission of Doubleday & Company, The Macmillan Company of Canada, and Mrs. George Bambridge.

E. P. DUTTON & COMPANY, INC., for "The Coming of the Trees" from *Death and General Putnam and 101 Other Poems* by Arthur Guiterman, copyright 1935 by E. P. Dutton & Company, Inc., © 1965 by Vida Lindo Guiterman; extracts from *The Conquest of Mount Everest* by John Hunt, copyright 1954 by E. P. Dutton & Company, Inc.; *Living Can Be Exciting* by Aaron N. Meckel, copyright © 1956 by E. P. Dutton & Company, Inc.; "Creeds" from *Lanterns in Gethsemane* by Willard Wattles, copyright 1918 by E. P. Dutton & Company, Inc.

WM. B. EERDMANS PUBLISHING COMPANY for extracts from *Feeling Low?*, *Thoughts Afield*, and *Through the Valley* by Harold E. Kohn.

HARCOURT, BRACE & WORLD, INC., for extracts from *The Recreating of the Individual* by Beatrice Hinkle; *Flight to Arras* by Antoine de Saint-Exupéry; "Lesson from a Sun-Dial" from *Rainbow in the Sky* by Louis Untermeyer.

HOLT, RINEHART AND WINSTON, INC., for "The Pasture," "A Prayer in Spring," "The Tuft of Flowers," "The Death of the Hired Man," "The Star-Splitter," and "Two Tramps in Mud Time" from *Complete Poems of Robert Frost*, copyright 1923, 1930, 1934, 1939 by Holt, Rinehart and Winston, Inc., 1936, 1951, © 1958, 1962 by Robert Frost, © 1964 by Lesley Frost Ballantine; extract from *Man for Himself* by Erich Fromm; "Sometimes" from *Shadow of the Perfect Rose* by Thomas S. Jones, Jr., copyright 1937, © 1965 by John L. Foley; "Tears" from *Selected Poems of Lizette Woodworth Reese*; "A Little Song of Life" from *A Wayside Lute* by Lizette Woodworth Reese.

HOUGHTON MIFFLIN COMPANY for extract from *Adam, the Baby, and the Man from Mars* by Irwin Edman; extract from "Summer" from *Complete Poetical Works of Amy Lowell*.

ALFRED A. KNOPF, INC., for extract from *The Prophet* by Kahlil Gibran, copyright 1923 by Kahlil Gibran, 1951 by Administrators C.T.A. of Kahlil Gibran Estate and Mary G. Gibran; "Heaven" from *Fields of Wonder* by Langston Hughes.

J. B. LIPPINCOTT COMPANY for "Poetry" from *Poems for Children* by Eleanor Farjeon; "Harbour Lights" from *Collected Poems of Alfred Noyes*, copyright 1941, 1947 by Alfred Noyes; extract from *The Self You Have to Live With* by Winfred Rhoades.

THE MACMILLAN COMPANY for extracts from *The Individual and His Religion* by Gordon W. Allport; *The Meaning of Right and Wrong* by Richard C. Cabot; "Another Lincoln," "Little Boys in Church," "Strange Holiness," and "Things Enough" from *Collected Poems* by Robert P. Tristram Coffin; *Early One Morning in the Spring* by Walter de la Mare; "Hold Fast Your Dreams" from *Garden Grace* by Louise Driscoll; *The Power to Become* by Lewis L. Dunningham; "Marriage" from *Collected Poems* by W. W. Gibson; "The Mystery" from *Poems* by Ralph Hodgson; *Rufus Jones Speaks to Our Time*, ed. by Harry Emerson Fosdick; *The Rediscovery of Man* by Henry C. Link; extract from *Dead Ned* and "The Seekers" from *Poems* by John Masefield; extract from "Captain Craig" and "Credo" from *Collected Poems* by Edwin Arlington Robinson; *Seven Essays* by George Sampson; *Memoirs of Childhood and Youth* by Albert Schweitzer; extracts from *Collected Poems and Plays* by Rabindranath Tagore; "The Coin" and "Grace Before Sleep" from *Collected Poems* by Sara Teasdale; *The Hope of the World* by William Temple.

(See additional acknowledgments on page 241)

LC 81-47850
ISBN 0-06-069239-1

82   83   84   85   86   10   9   8   7   6   5   4   3   2   1

CONTENTS

Preface	vii	FELLOWSHIP	73
BELIEVING	1	FRIENDSHIP	77
BIBLE	5	GOD	83
BROTHERHOOD	11	GROWTH	89
CHEERFULNESS	15	HEAVEN	95
CHRIST	21	HERITAGE	103
CHRISTMAS	31	HOME	107
CHURCH	39	HOPE	115
CONTENTMENT	47	IDEALS	119
CROSS	53	INFLUENCE	125
DEVOTION	59	INSPIRATION	129
EASTER	63	JOY	133
FAITH	69	LEARNING	139

LIFE 147

LOVE 155

MEMORIES 161

MUSIC 165

NATURE 169

OVERCOMING 177

PRAISE 183

PRAYER 187

SERVING 195

STEWARDSHIP 201

THANKSGIVING 205

TODAY 209

TRUST 215

WITNESS 219

WORK 225

WORLD HORIZONS 231

WORSHIP 237

Index of Prose Authors 242

Poetry Index 244

Index of Topics 247

PREFACE

Within the pages of this album are found heart-enlarging and faith-empowering words by which we live and grow and achieve a fuller, richer relationship and understanding with God, our neighbors, and ourselves. The forty-two words featured in the subtitles are not new words. Rather, they are time-honored and time-hallowed words which have been wrought on the anvil of experience, fashioned according to the aspiration and need of daily living, and tested by the challenges and exigencies of our common venture through time to eternity.

The words in prose and poetry have come from the pens of sensitive and discerning writers of many centuries. They convey to us the diction and syntax of timeless wisdom and insight. Here are words of reconciliation, knowledge, comfort, authority, redemption, and encouragement. These words are lamps, kindled by others, for our feet. These words are lights, illumined by inspiration and genius, for our paths.

These then are, in the language of the Gospel hymn, wonderful words of life. But they are more, for they mirror the saving grace and radiate the eternal promises of the One about whom the Evangelist bore witness: "In the beginning was the Word, and the Word was with God, and the Word was God. . . . In him was life; and the life was the light of men. . . . And the Word was made flesh, and dwelt among us, . . . full of grace and truth."

To these pages we may, if we will, bring our candles and claim a flame for our minds. To these pages we may bring our vessels and draw from deep-flowing springs waters of refreshment and peace. To these pages we may bring our faltering efforts and in the classroom of Christ learn those lessons which are essential to abundant living.

CHARLES L. WALLIS

Keuka College
Keuka Park, New York

Believing

Lord, thou hast been our dwelling place in all generations.

Before the mountains were brought forth, or ever thou hadst formed the earth and the world, even from everlasting to everlasting, thou art God.

For a thousand years in thy sight are but as yesterday when it is past, and as a watch in the night.   PSALM 90:1-2, 4

The greatest force for making people bigger and better than they are now is the belief in your heart and mine that they have infinite potential for growth. Even when they fail us, we are to continue to carry and express the mental image of what they may become. To have someone believe in you, even when you fail, is the most blessed and creative force in the universe.

LEWIS L. DUNNINGHAM

A DAILY DOZEN

1. Believe in yourself, for you are marvelously endowed.
2. Believe in your job, for all honest work is sacred.
3. Believe in this day, for every minute contains an opportunity to do good.
4. Believe in your family, and create harmony by trust and co-operation.
5. Believe in your neighbor, for the more friends you can make the happier you will be.
6. Believe in uprightness, for you cannot go wrong doing right.
7. Believe in your decisions; consult God first, then go ahead.
8. Believe in your health; stop taking your pulse, etc., etc.
9. Believe in your church; you encourage others to attend by attending yourself.
10. Believe in the now; yesterday is past recall and tomorrow may never come.
11. Believe in God's promises; He means it when He says, "I am with you always."
12. Believe in God's mercy; if God forgives you, you can forgive yourself — and try again tomorrow.

ALASTAIR MAC ODRUM

CORNERSTONE

I rejoice in my life because the lamp still glows;
I seek no thorny ways;
I love the small pleasures of life.
If the doors are too low, I bend;
If I can remove a stone from the path, I do so;
If it is too heavy, I go round it.
I find something in every day that pleases me.
The cornerstone, my belief in God, makes my
heart glad and my face shining.

GOETHE'S MOTHER

When life becomes all snarled up, offer it to our Lord and let Him untie the knots.

A BOOK OF DAYS FOR CHRISTIANS

CREDO

I cannot find my way: there is no star
In all the shrouded heavens anywhere;
And there is not a whisper in the air
Of any living voice but one so far
That I can hear it only as a bar
Of lost, imperial music, played when fair
And angel fingers wove, and unaware,
Dead leaves to garlands where no roses are.

No, there is not a glimmer, nor a call,
For one that welcomes, welcomes when he fears,
The black and awful chaos of the night;
For through it all — above, beyond it all —
I know the far-sent message of the years,
I feel the coming glory of the Light.

EDWIN ARLINGTON ROBINSON

GOD'S BOOK

The believer is the only book in which God himself writes his New Testament.

WILLIAM DELL

CREDO

Not what, but *Whom*, I do believe,
    That, in my darkest hour of need,
    Hath comfort that no mortal creed
    To mortal man may give;
Not what, but *Whom!*
    For Christ is more than all the creeds,
    And His full life of gentle deeds
    Shall all the creeds outlive.
Not what I do believe, but *Whom!*
    Who walks beside me in the gloom?
    Who shares the burden wearisome?
    Who all the dim way doth illume,
    And bids me look beyond the tomb
    The larger life to live?
Not what I do believe,
But *Whom!*
Not what,
But *Whom!*

JOHN OXENHAM

GATEWAY

The Gateway to Christianity is not through an intricate labyrinth of dogma, but by a simple belief in the person of Christ.

WILLIAM LYON PHELPS

The greatest adventures are experienced in the soul of man, not across oceans or deserts.

DAGOBERT D. RUNES

WHAT A SCIENTIST WROTE

I will frankly tell you that my experience in prolonged scientific investigations convinces me that a belief in God, a God who is behind and within the chaos of vanishing points of human knowledge, adds a wonderful stimulus to the man who attempts to penetrate into the regions of the unknown. I never make preparations for penetrating into some small province of nature hitherto undiscovered without breathing a prayer to the Being who hides his secrets from me only to allure me graciously on to the unfolding of them.

LOUIS AGASSIZ

BEYOND DOUBT

The sun, with all those planets moving round it, can ripen the smallest bunch of grapes as if it had nothing else to do. Why then should I doubt His power?

GALILEO

It was neither preaching nor praying that made a better man of me, but one or two people who believed in me better than I deserved, and I hated to disappoint them.

OWEN WISTER

BELIEVING THE BEST

I have believed the best of every man,
And find that to believe it is enough
To make a bad man show him at his best,
Or even a good man swing his lantern higher.

4

Bible

We have not followed cunningly devised fables, when we made known unto you the power and coming of our Lord Jesus Christ, but were eye-witnesses of his majesty.

For he received from God the Father honour and glory, when there came such a voice to him from the excellent glory, This is my beloved Son, in whom I am well pleased.

And this voice which came from heaven we heard, when we were with him in the holy mount.

We have also a more sure word of prophecy; whereunto ye do well that ye take heed, as unto a light that shineth in a dark place, until the day dawn, and the day star arise in your hearts:

Knowing this first, that no prophecy of the scripture is of any private interpretation.

For the prophecy came not in old time by the will of man: but holy men of God spake as they were moved by the Holy Ghost.   II Peter 1:16-21

We search the world for truth; we cull
The good, the true, the beautiful,
From graven stone and written scroll,
And all old flower-fields of the soul;
And, weary seekers of the best,
We come back laden from our quest,
To find that all the sages said
Is in the Book our mothers read.

JOHN GREENLEAF WHITTIER

THE MASTER LIGHT

For those who have lived sensibly and familiarly with the Bible for a term of years and have kept their own souls alive upon its warnings and promises, not trying to evade its tendency to deal with us at close quarters, the Bible becomes indeed the master light of all our seeing.

JOHN A. HUTTON

In this one book are the two most interesting personalities in the whole world — God and yourself. The Bible is the story of God and man, a love story in which you and I must write our own ending, our unfinished autobiography of the creature and the Creator.

FULTON OURSLER

BIBLE STATISTICS

The Bible contains 3,586,489 letters and 773,692 words.

The Bible contains 31,173 verses and 1,189 chapters.

The middle verse is Psalm 118:18.

The longest verse is Esther 8:9 and the shortest John 11:35.

AN ANCIENT PRAYER

Blessed Lord, who hast caused all Holy Scriptures to be written for our learning: grant that we may in such wise hear them, read, mark, learn, and inwardly digest them, that by patience, and comfort of thy Holy Word, we may embrace and ever hold fast the blessed hope of everlasting life, which thou hast given us in our Savior Jesus Christ.

EVERYMAN'S BOOK

The Old Testament is the history of a race, the revelation of its mind, the record of its eternal, restless search after "the things of God." If it were only that, in the hands and minds of gifted men, it would rightly deserve immortality. But it is more. For these ancient men by their wisdom, desire, and compassion, by their understanding of the power of language, and by their imagination which carried them from their bare Judean hills to the uttermost parts of the earth, have transformed a thousand years of human life into the countless centuries of man's experience. It is surely not by chance that the term "every man" occurs numberless times in both Old Testament prose and poetry. For the Old Testament is the record of the life of every man, in every age and place, throughout all the perils and the compensations of his threescore years and ten.

MARY ELLEN CHASE

I know the Bible
is inspired
because
it inspires me.

DWIGHT L. MOODY

I AM THE BIBLE

I am a library of sixty-six books.

I am the world's best seller.

I am more than a mere book. I am a force that overpowers opposing systems of thought.

I am the rock upon which civil liberties and social freedom rest.

I answer the question: Who and where is God?

I was written by minds saturated with consciousness of God.

I am published in more languages and dialects than any other book that has ever been written.

I am cherished by millions of people as being the only concretely available and infallible rule of faith and practice.

I am the Word of God as set forth by inspired prophet, law-giver, genealogist, priest, historian, poet, essayist, story-writer, moralist, seer, and theologian.

I set forth the way of life that leads to abundance and satisfaction of experience.

I tell the story of the great drama of redemption.

I inspire devotion to truth and purity of life purpose.

NORMAN E. RICHARDSON

And should my soul be torn with grief
  Upon my shelf I find
A little volume, torn and thumbed,
  For comfort just designed.
I take my little Bible down
  And read its pages o'er,
And when I part from it I find
  I'm stronger than before.

EDGAR A. GUEST

England has two books, one which she has made and one which has made her: Shakespeare and the Bible.

VICTOR HUGO

A bit of the Book in the morning,
  To order my onward way,
A bit of the Book in the evening,
  To hallow the end of the day.

MARGARET E. SANGSTER

PRAYER

Make me respect my mind so much that I dare not read what has no meaning or moral. Help me to choose with equal care my friends and my books, because they are both for life. Show me that as in a river, so in reading, the depths hold more of strength and beauty than the shallows. Teach me to value art without being blind to thought. Keep me from caring more for much reading than for careful reading; for books than the Bible. Give me an ideal that will let me read only the best, and when that is done, stop me. Repay me with power to teach others, and then help me to say from a disciplined mind a grateful amen.

CHARLES LAMB

The gospel is neither a sermon nor a treatise on religion, but a story that tells how Christianity began in something that happened, in a deed that was done, in a life that was lived.

L. P. JACKS

UNIVERSAL AND TIMELESS

Born in the East and clothed in Oriental form and imagery, the Bible walks the ways of all the world with familiar feet and enters land after land to find its own everywhere.

It has learned to speak in hundreds of languages to the heart of man.

It comes into the palace to tell the monarch that he is a servant of the Most High, and into the cottage to assure the peasant that he is a son of God.

Children listen to its stories with wonder and delight, and wise men ponder them as parables of life.

It has a word for the time of peril, a word of comfort for the time of calamity, a word of light for the house of darkness.

Its oracles are repeated in the assembly of the people, and its counsels whispered in the ear of the lonely.

The wicked and the proud tremble at its warnings, but to the wounded and penitent it has a mother's voice.

The wilderness and the solitary place have been made glad by it, and the fire on the hearth has lit the reading of its well-worn pages.

No man is poor or desolate who has this treasure for his own.

When the landscape darkens and the trembling pilgrim comes to the valley named of the shadow, he is not afraid to enter; he takes the rod and staff of Scripture in his hand and says to his friend and comrade, "Goodbye, we shall meet again." Comforted by that support, he goes toward the lonely pass as one who walks through darkness into light.

HENRY VAN DYKE

A young Christian packing his bag for a journey said to a friend, "I have nearly finished packing. All I have to put in are

a guidebook,
a lamp,
a mirror,
a microscope,
a telescope,
a volume of fine poetry,
a few biographies,
a package of old letters,
a book of songs,
a sword,
a hammer, and
a set of tools."

"But you cannot put all that into your bag," objected the friend. "Oh, yes," said the Christian. "Here it is." And he placed his Bible in the corner of the suitcase and closed the lid.

VISION OF GOD

To me the greatest thing that has happened on this earth of ours is the rise of the human race to the vision of God. That story of the human rise to what I call the vision of God is the story which is told in the Bible.

JAN CHRISTIAN SMUTS

For books are more than books, they are the life,
The very heart and core of ages past;
The reason why men lived, and worked, and died,
The essence and quintessence of their lives.

JAMES RUSSELL LOWELL

READING THE BIBLE

If a person will read three chapters every day and five chapters each Sunday, he can finish reading the entire Bible in just one year.

If he reads two chapters a day, he can finish reading the New Testament in less than twenty weeks.

If he reads only on Sunday, completing five chapters each Sunday, he will finish reading the New Testament on the fifty-second Sunday.

In one afternoon a person can begin with Luke's Gospel and at one sitting read the remainder of the New Testament and be thrilled forever with its moving story of power.

J. RICHARD SNEED

EQUILIBRIUM

Unless we form the habit of going to the Bible in bright moments as well as in trouble, we cannot fully respond to its consolations because we lack equilibrium between light and darkness.

HELEN KELLER

Hear the voice of the Bard,
Who present, past, and future sees;
Whose ears have heard
Thy Holy Word
That walked among the ancient trees.

WILLIAM BLAKE

ROAD TO CHRIST

Just as from every village in Britain there is a road which, linking on to other roads, brings you to London at last, so from every text in the Bible, even the remotest and least likely, there is a road to Christ.

JAMES S. STEWART

PERSONAL TRANSLATION

I am my neighbor's Bible:
  He reads me when we meet,
Today he reads me in my house,
  Tomorrow in the street;
He may be relative or friend,
  Or slight acquaintance be;
He may not even know my name,
  Yet he is reading me.

THE BOOK

Softly I closed the Book as in a dream
And let its echoes linger to redeem
Silence with music, darkness with its gleam.

That day I worked no more. I could not bring
My hands to toil, my thoughts to trafficking.
A new light shone on every common thing.

Celestial glories flamed before my gaze.
That day I worked no more. But, to God's praise,
I shall work better all my other days.

WINFRED ERNEST GARRISON

Brotherhood

This is the message that ye heard from the beginning, that we should love one another.

We know that we have passed from death unto life, because we love the brethren.

Hereby perceive we the love of God, because he laid down his life for us: and we ought to lay down our lives for the brethren.

Let us not love in word, neither in tongue; but in deed and in truth.

I JOHN 3:11, 14, 16, 18

OUR BROTHERHOOD

The common hopes that make us men
Were His in Galilee;
The tasks He gives are those He gave
Beside the restless sea.

Our brotherhood still rests in Him,
The Brother of us all,
And o'er the centuries we hear
The Master's winsome call.

OZORA S. DAVIS

BROTHER'S KEEPER

The spiritual interpretation of life teaches us
    that all human life is sacred;
that we are members one of another;
that the things which we have in common are
    greater than those which divide;
that each is his brother's keeper.

W. L. MACKENZIE KING

CLAIMS

All men have their troubles, their problems,
    whether we know of them or not.
All have their hopes and heartaches, their need
    of others, their feelings of frustration.
All need someone to talk to, someone to coun-
    sel with.
All men need understanding.
And all men have some claims upon us: the
    claim of having a common Father, the claim
    of being fellow occupants on the same earth.

RICHARD L. EVANS

NO BARRIER

From a playground we watch the children play. Some are light, others dark — but they are all beautiful. All of them have a live force animating their little bodies. All of them run, play, laugh, and cry, and yet if outwardly they look different, they have within the same emotions of life. Each enjoys living; all will later be in the arms of the mothers who love them, live for them, and raise them to be good and kind. If we can only understand this force that makes them live—the same love between mother and child, the same desire that you and I have to live; the love-aspirations-dreams like your mother with you, my mother with me—then no dogmas, no prejudices, no fears can stand barriers between man and man.

LEO POLITI

It is for this that we love democracy: for the emphasis it puts on character; for its tendency to exalt the purposes of the average man to some high level of endeavor; for its just principle of common assent in matters in which all are concerned; for its ideals of duty and its sense of brotherhood.

WOODROW WILSON

THE NEW TRINITY

Three things must a man possess if his soul
    would live,
    And know life's perfect good —
Three things would the all-supplying Father
    give —
    Bread, Beauty, and Brotherhood.

EDWIN MARKHAM

13

GOD SEES FACES

When God looks upon this world, He sees in the foreground of the human picture, not ideas, not things, but faces. And to His all-seeing eye these billions of faces do not resolve themselves into a nebulous blur. They are not represented by statistics on a page. In each face a loving heavenly Father sees mirrored life's dreams and disappointments, life's pains and pleasures, life's work and worship. The more like God we become, the greater will be our concern about people.

NORVAL F. PEASE

———

I met a hundred men on the road to Delhi, and they were all my brothers.

INDIAN PROVERB

EQUATION

No one can be perfectly free till all are free;
No one can be perfectly moral till all are moral;
No one can be perfectly happy till all are happy.

HERBERT SPENCER

———

ORTHODOX

They questioned my theology,
And talked of modern thought;
Bade me recite a dozen creeds —
I could not as I ought.

"I've but one creed," I answer made,
"And do not want another;
I know I've passed from death to life
Because I love my brother."

MARK GUY PEARSE

IF A MAN

If a man be gracious and courteous to strangers, it shows he is a citizen of the world, and that his heart is no island cut off from other lands, but a continent that joins to them.

If he be compassionate toward the afflictions of others, it shows that his heart is like the noble tree that wounds itself when it gives the balm.

If he easily pardons and remits offences, it shows that his mind is planted above injuries, so that he cannot be pained.

If he be thankful for small benefits, it shows that he weighs men's minds, and not their idle talk.

FRANCIS BACON

———

From THE STAR-SPLITTER

If one by one we counted people out
For the least sin, it wouldn't take us long
To get so we had no one left to live with.
For to be social is to be forgiving.

ROBERT FROST

———

GUILTY

I never cut my neighbor's throat;
  My neighbor's gold I never stole;
I never spoiled his house and land;
  But God have mercy on my soul!

For I am haunted night and day
  By all the deeds I have not done;
O unattempted loveliness!
  O costly valor never won!

MARGUERITE WILKINSON

Cheerfulness

Thou wilt shew me the path of life: in thy presence is fulness of joy; at thy right hand there are pleasures for evermore. PSALM 16:11

Be of good cheer; I have overcome the world. JOHN 16:33

I am not bound to make the world go right,
But only to discover and to do,
With cheerful heart, the work that God
  appoints.

JEAN INGELOW

————

PRAYER

O God, animate us to cheerfulness. May we
have a joyful sense of our blessings, learn to
look on the bright circumstances of our lot,
and maintain a perpetual contentedness under
Thy allotments. Fortify our minds against dis-
appointment and calamity. Preserve us from
despondency, from yielding to dejection.
Teach us that no evil is intolerable but a
guilty conscience; and that nothing can hurt
us, if, with true loyalty of affection, we keep
Thy commandments, and take refuge in Thee.

WILLIAM ELLERY CHANNING

————

CONTRIBUTION

The world would be better and brighter if our
teachers would dwell on the duty of happiness
as well as on the happiness of duty. We
ought to be as cheerful as we can, if only because to be happy ourselves is a most effectual
contribution to the happiness of others.

JOHN LUBBOCK

————

Judge not the Lord by feeble sense,
  But trust Him for His grace;
Behind a frowning providence
  He hides a smiling face.

WILLIAM COWPER

SYMBOL

Laughter is a beautiful symbol of humanity.
No creature but man can laugh. Beauty there
is and power and survival in the vegetable and
the animal and the mineral kingdoms, but
laughter can be heard in the forest only if
children play there or lovers stroll beneath its
high colonnades. Upon the ability to laugh,
to perceive the humorous, to sense perspec-
tives, to catch proportions, to see oneself as ri-
diculous on occasion, depends the achievement
of much of one's relationship to God. For to
be able to laugh presupposes personality and
humanity, moral nature and outlook.

WINNIFRED WYGAL

————

From YOUR HOUSE OF HAPPINESS
Take what God gives, O heart of mine,
  And build your house of happiness.
Perchance some have been given more;
  But many have been given less.
The treasure lying at your feet,
  Whose value you but faintly guess,
Another builder, looking on,
  Would barter heaven to possess.

B. Y. WILLIAMS

————

It is not fitting, when one is in God's service,
to have a gloomy face or a chilling look.

ST. FRANCIS OF ASSISI

————

Laugh, for the time is brief, a thread the length
  of a span,
Laugh, and be proud to belong to the old proud
  pageant of man.

JOHN MASEFIELD

17

GOD'S MEDICINE

Mirth is God's medicine. Everybody ought to bathe in it. Grim care, moroseness, anxiety—all this rust of life ought to be scoured off by the oil of mirth. It is better than emery. Every man ought to rub himself with it. A man without mirth is like a wagon without springs, in which everyone is caused disagreeably to jolt by every pebble over which it runs.

HENRY WARD BEECHER

PRAYER

O Holy Spirit, descend plentifully into my heart. Enlighten the dark corners of this neglected dwelling and scatter there Thy cheerful beams.

ST. AUGUSTINE

LITTLE PRIVILEGES

Happiness is the art of finding joy and satisfaction in the little privileges of life:

a quiet hour in the sun instead of a far-away journey,

a little outing in the nearby woods instead of long trips away,

an hour with a friend instead of an extended visit with relatives,

a few pages of a book instead of hours of reading at a time,

a flash of sunset, a single beautiful flower, a passing smile, a kindly word, a little gift bestowed anonymously, a little thoughtfulness here and there as the days slip by.

Lord God, how full our cup of happiness!
We drink and drink—and yet it grows not
    less;
But every morn the newly risen sun
Finds it replenished, sparkling, over-run!
Hast Thou not given us raiment, warmth, and
    meat,
And in due season all earth's fruits to eat?
Work for our hands and rainbows for our
    eyes,
And for our souls the wings of butterflies?
A father's smile, a mother's fond embrace,
The tender light upon a lover's face?
The talk of friends, the twinkling eye of mirth,
The whispering silence of the good green
    earth?
Hope for our youth, and memories for age,
And psalms upon the heavens' moving page?

GILBERT THOMAS

SMILE

Nobody ever added up
    The value of a smile;
We know how much a dollar's worth,
    And how much is a mile;
We know the distance to the sun,
    The size and weight of earth—
But no one's ever told us yet
    How much a smile is worth.

There are three green eggs in a small brown
    pocket,
And the breeze will swing and the gale will
    rock it,
Till three little birds on the thin edge teeter,
And our God be glad and our world be sweeter!

EDWIN MARKHAM

HAPPINESS

Happiness is like a crystal,
    Fair and exquisite and clear,
Broken in a million pieces,
    Shattered, scattered far and near.

Now and then along life's pathway,
    Lo! some shining fragments fall;
But there are so many pieces,
    No one ever finds them all.

PRISCILLA LEONARD

———

Delicate humor is the crowning virtue of the saints.

EVELYN UNDERHILL

———

GOD'S HEROES

To live well in the quiet routine of life,
to fill a little space because God wills it,
to go on cheerfully with a petty round of little
    duties, little avocations, and
to smile for the joy of others when the heart is
    aching—
who does this, his works will follow him.
He may not be a hero to the world,
but he is one of God's heroes.

———

A happy family is but an earlier heaven.

JOHN BOWRING

A LITTLE SONG OF LIFE

Glad that I live am I;
That the sky is blue;
Glad for the country lanes,
And the fall of dew.

After the sun the rain,
After the rain the sun;
This is the way of life,
Till the work be done.

All that we need to do,
Be we low or high,
Is to see that we grow
Nearer the sky.

LIZETTE WOODWORTH REESE

———

GOD'S DESIRE

There is an evident effort in nature to be happy. Everything blossoms to express beauty, as well as lead to fruitage. Even the inorganic fashions itself into crystals that absorb and flash back the sunlight. If one examines nature with the microscope or considers the heavens at night, he finds three things: truth as inherent, beauty beyond that which can be spoken, and goodness everywhere. God speaks through all things with an eternal desire to create happiness.

THE OUTLOOK

———

People are always good
company when they are
doing what they really
enjoy.

SAMUEL BUTLER

AT HEART AN OPTIMIST

This is a good world. We need not approve of all the items, nor of all the individuals in it; but the world itself is a friendly world. It has borne us; it has carried us onward; it has humanized us and guided our faltering footsteps throughout the long, slow advance; it has endowed us with strength and courage. It is full of tangle, of ups and downs. There is always enough to bite on, to sharpen wits on, to test our courage and manhood. It is indeed a world built for heroism, but also for beauty, tenderness, and mercy. I remain at heart an optimist.

JAN CHRISTIAN SMUTS

THE BRIGHT SIDE

There is no danger of developing eyestrain from looking on the bright side of things.

THE HAPPIEST MAN

Happy is he who by love's sweet song
Is cheered today as he goes along.
Happier is he who believes that tomorrow
Will ease all pain and take away all sorrow.
Happiest he who on earthly sod
Has faith in himself, his friends, and God.

The happiest people seem to be those who have no particular cause for being happy except the fact that they are so—a good reason, no doubt.

WILLIAM RALPH INGE

FRACTIONS

The happiness of life is made up of minute fractions—the little, soon forgotten charities of a kiss or a smile, a kind look, a heartfelt compliment, and the countless infinitesimals of pleasurable and genial feeling.

SAMUEL T. COLERIDGE

CHEERFULNESS OF WISDOM

The best part of health is fine disposition. It is more essential than talent, even in the works of talent. Nothing will supply the want of sunshine to peaches, and to make knowledge valuable, you must have the cheerfulness of wisdom.

RALPH WALDO EMERSON

WHAT MAKES MEN HAPPY?

To watch the corn grow, or the blossoms set; to draw hard breath over the ploughshare or spade; to read, to think, to love, to pray, are the things that make men happy.

JOHN RUSKIN

FESTIVE COMPANIONS

The highest wisdom and the highest genius have been invariably accompanied with cheerfulness. We have sufficient proofs on record that Shakespeare and Socrates were the most festive companions.

THOMAS LOVE PEACOCK

Christ

In the beginning was the Word, and the Word was with God, and the Word was God.

The same was in the beginning with God.

All things were made by him; and without him was not any thing made that was made.

In him was life; and the life was the light of men.

And the Word was made flesh, and dwelt among us, (and we beheld his glory, the glory as of the only begotten of the Father,) full of grace and truth.   John 1:1-4, 14

JUDEAN HILLS ARE HOLY

Judean hills are holy,
    Judean fields are fair,
For one can find the footprints
    Of Jesus everywhere.

One finds them in the twilight
    Beneath the singing sky,
Where shepherds watch in wonder
    White planets wheeling by.

His trails are on the hillsides
    And down the dales and deeps;
He walks the high horizons
    Where vesper silence sleeps.

He haunts the lowly highways
    Where human hopes have trod
The Via Dolorosa
    Up to the heart of God.

He looms, a lonely figure,
    Along the fringe of night,
As lonely as a cedar
    Against the lonely light.

Judean hills are holy,
    Judean fields are fair,
For one can find the footprints
    Of Jesus everywhere.

WILLIAM L. STIDGER

FOOTPRINTS

I have loved to hear my Lord spoken of, and wherever I have seen the print of His shoe in the earth, there have I coveted to put mine also.

JOHN BUNYAN

Christ be with me, Christ within me,
    Christ behind me, Christ before me,
Christ beside me, Christ to win me,
    Christ to comfort and restore me,
Christ beneath me, Christ above me,
    Christ in quiet, Christ in danger,
Christ in hearts of all that love me,
    Christ in mouth of friend and stranger.

WALTER RUSSELL BOWIE

A SEVENTEENTH-CENTURY TESTIMONY

He is a path, if any be misled,
He is a robe, if any naked be,
If any chance to hunger, He is bread,
If any be a bondman, He is free,
If any be but weak, how strong is He,
To dead men life He is, to sick men health,
To blind men sight, and to the needy wealth,
A pleasure without loss, a treasure without
    stealth.

GILES FLETCHER

INSCRIPTION

When Jesus comes, the shadows depart.

God speaks to me not through the thunder and the earthquake, nor through the ocean and the stars, but through the Son of Man, and speaks in a language adapted to my imperfect sight and hearing.

WILLIAM LYON PHELPS

HYMN FOR A HOUSEHOLD

Shepherd of mortals, here behold
A little flock, a wayside fold
That wait Thy presence to be blest —
O Man of Nazareth, be our guest.

DANIEL HENDERSON

LIGHT-GIVER

In darkness there is no choice. It is light that enables us to see the difference between things; and it is Christ that gives us light.

JULIUS CHARLES HARE

THE CHRIST

The good intent of God became the Christ,
And lived on earth — the Living Love of God,
That men might draw to closer touch with heaven,
Since Christ in all the ways of man hath trod.

JOHN OXENHAM

It is not difficult to see one vital significance of Jesus Christ: He has given us the most glorious interpretation of life's meaning that the sons of men have ever had. The fatherhood of God, the friendship of the Spirit, the sovereignty of righteousness, the law of love, the glory of service, the coming of the kingdom, the eternal hope—there never was an interpretation of life to compare with that.

HARRY EMERSON FOSDICK

WHAT JESUS DOES FOR ME

He gives me a clearer moral vision and the courage to try to live by that vision.

He gives me the desire to work in the world as intensely as He worked.

He gives me confidence in the truth and so helps me to rest, no matter what happens in the world, because I know that God and the truth must prevail.

He counterbalances, as I cannot, the variable circumstances and unequal conditions of life and takes care of the excesses that are beyond me.

He gives me grace and strength to try, at least, things that I know are impossible and to attempt the things that are hardest to be done.

He helps me refuse to do good when I know that something better can be done.

He helps me to keep on when I have to, even though I know I cannot.

He saves me from the fret and killing of pride and vanity, and helps me to cease to care for the things that make people spiritually sick.

He gives me a new and inward living principle. I believe that He is this principle and that there is another personality inside my personality that would not be there if it had not been for Him and if it were not for Him today.

ROBERT E. SPEER

The men who followed Him were unique in their generation. They turned the world upside down because their hearts had been turned right side up. The world has never been the same.

BILLY GRAHAM

OUR CHRIST

I know not how that Bethlehem's Babe
　　Could in the Godhead be;
I only know the Manger Child
　　Has brought God's life to me.

I know not how that Calvary's cross
　　A world from sin could free:
I only know its matchless love
　　Has brought God's love to me.

I know not how that Joseph's tomb
　　Could solve death's mystery:
I only know a living Christ,
　　Our immortality.

HARRY WEBB FARRINGTON

JESUS SAID "I AM"

"I am the bread of life" (John 6:35).
"I am the light of the world" (John 8:12).
"I am the door" (John 10:9).
"I am the good shepherd" (John 10:11).
"I am the way, and the truth, and the life"
　　(John 14:6).

Whatever may be the unexpected phenomena of the future, Jesus will not be surpassed. His worship will constantly renew its youth, the tale of His life will cause ceaseless tears, His sufferings will soften the best hearts. All the ages will proclaim that, among the sons of men, there is none born who is greater than Jesus.

ERNEST RENAN

TESTIMONY

If I knew a better person than Jesus Christ, I would give him my full, perfect, and lifelong allegiance. Not knowing any better person, I give my love, my obedience, my faith to Him.

If in all the domain of biography, if in all the wide range of human history, there were a better person, or if any had appeared that seemed worthier to follow, I would follow him.

If I knew a better ideal of personal life and a better means of reaching that ideal than the ideal of Jesus, I would make that ideal my own.

If I knew a better program for the world than that of Jesus, I would give my life to it.

I cannot get my heart's consent to follow any second-rate person. I can only satisfy my own sense of what is best and highest and most ideal by following the best person there is.

WILLIAM F. MC DOWELL

But Thee, but Thee, O sovereign Seer of time,
But Thee, O poets' Poet, Wisdom's Tongue,
But Thee, O man's best Man, O love's best
　　Love,
O perfect life in perfect labor writ,
O all men's Comrade, Servant, King, or
　　Priest —
What *if* or *yet*, what mole, what flaw, what
　　lapse,
What least effect or shadow of defect,
What rumor, tattled by an enemy,
Of inference loose, what lack of grace
Even in torture's grasp, or sleep's, or death's—
Oh, what amiss may I forgive in Thee,
Jesus, good Paragon, thou Crystal Christ?

SIDNEY LANIER

A SENSE OF HIM

For me 'twas not the truth you taught,
    To you so clear, to me so dim,
But when you came to me, you brought
    A sense of Him.

And from your eyes He beckons me
    And from your heart His love is shed,
Till I lose sight of you and see
    The Christ instead.

DISCIPLESHIP

Jesus promised His disciples three things: that they would be entirely fearless, absurdly happy, and that they would get into trouble.

W. RUSSELL MALTBY

HIS CAPACITY FOR FRIENDSHIP

The most striking characteristic and the most moving quality in the life of Jesus was His capacity for friendship. His abiding good will ran across every racial, social, economic, and political frontier. He held in the embrace of His love all mankind: the rich and the poor, the old and the young, the moron and the savant. It is true that He had intimate friends. There were those who lived in the inner circle of His comradeship. He loved some more than others. But beyond these intimate friendships Jesus lived with a sense of good will toward all mankind.

JOSEPH R. SIZOO

PASSION FOR HUMANITY

He set the first and greatest example of a life wholly governed and guided by the passion of humanity.

JOHN ROBERT SEELEY

WHAT HE WANTED

Christ wanted men to see, to see far and to see truly. To get that kind of vision, He pointed out, requires avoidance of hypocrisies and group prejudices, which distort the vision and make men imagine they see what is not really there.

Christ wanted men to have hearts that comprehend the human significance of what is seen. That kind of heart requires, He pointed out, avoidance of material self-seeking, which makes men hard and indifferent to all that cannot serve their selfish ends.

Christ wanted men to reason clearly and serenely. That requires, He pointed out, avoidance of evil emotions, such as hatred and vengefulness, which enflame men's minds and distract them from the real problems that confront them.

Christ wanted men to act.

JOHN FOSTER DULLES

From THE CHRIST OF THE ANDES

O Christ of Olivet, You hushed the wars
Under the far Andean stars:
Lift now Your strong nail-wounded hands
Over all peoples, over all lands:
Stretch out those comrade hands to be
A shelter over land and sea!

EDWIN MARKHAM

A rare jewel, but men know not His value;
A sun which ever shines, but men perceive
   not His brightness nor walk in His light;
A garden full of sweets;
A hive full of honey;
A sun without a spot;
A star ever bright;
A fountain ever full;
A brook which ever flows;
A rose which ever blooms;
A fountain which never yields;
A guide who never errs;
A friend who never forsakes —
No mind can fully grasp His glory, His
   beauty, His worth.
His importance no tongue can fully declare.

ARTHUR JAMES BALFOUR

ENCOUNTER

The greatest thing about any civilization is the
human person, and the greatest thing about
this person is the possibility of his encounter
with the person of Jesus Christ.

CHARLES MALIK

CRAFTSMAN

If Jesus built a ship, she would travel trim;
If Jesus roofed a barn, no leaks would be left
   by Him;
If Jesus made a garden, it would look like
   Paradise;
If Jesus did my day's work, it would delight
   His Father's eyes.

IN TOUCH

Christianity consists not in abstaining from
doing things no gentleman would think of
doing, but in doing things that are unlikely to
occur to anyone who is not in touch with the
spirit of Christ.

DICK SHEPPARD

———

Association with the Lord can bring
To any life a dignity and grace,
And ever looking up to Him will give
The high, white look of Christ to any face.

GRACE NOLL CROWELL

———

THE CHRIST OF THE WORLD'S HIGHWAY

He treads no more the paths of Galilee;
But where the sullen Ganges bares its breast
To burning skies, His sandaled feet are pressed
Into the dust, and seeking souls today
Have met a turbaned Comrade on the way.

He sits no more beside Samaria's wells;
Yet where a thousand far-off fountains spring
From jungle silence, wondering mothers bring
The children of a dark, bewildered race
Unto a Friend with kindly, dusky face.

He walks no more along the Syrian road;
Yet where a dim pagoda's haunting spire
Hides crumbling gods and dying altar fire,
A people old in burdens, race, and pride
Have found a Brother walking by their side.

DOROTHY CLARKE WILSON

DEVOUTLY LOVED

No one else holds or has held the place in the heart of the world which Jesus holds. Other gods have been as devoutly worshiped; no other man has been so devoutly loved.

JOHN KNOX

QUATRAIN

Here is the Truth in a little creed,
Enough for all the roads we go:
In Love is all the law we need,
In Christ is all the God we know.

EDWIN MARKHAM

WHAT JESUS DOES FOR ME

He comes to me as a Living Spirit today as well as a historic person who lived 1900 years ago.

He gives me assurance that if I accept Him as Savior and Guide and follow Him, I shall be saved from sin and wrong and helped to live as God would have me live.

He gives me an ideal to live by — a pattern for life — and helps me as I try to live up to that ideal.

He assures me of forgiveness when I fail and helps me to try again and do better.

His teachings give me guidance and counsel, truth and ideals, in a world of doubt and fear, and in the midst of changing standards and ways of life.

He is a living presence in my daily life. There is a spirit and purpose in me that would not be there but for Him.

He helps me in the choices of life to know right from wrong and to choose the best of the many good things life offers.

He gives me courage and hope in the testing hours of life and in the face of the problems of my generation.

He gives me the joy of introducing others to Him and to the happiness of the Christian life.

He calls me to work with Him in His Kingdom and makes me dissatisfied with anything in the life about me that is not in accord with His principles and spirit.

He introduces me to a fellowship that transcends all human barriers of race and creed, of space and time.

He gives me in His church a place of worship and training, of fellowship and service.

He shows me that, with all my shortcomings, I can be of use to Him and to the world mission in which He calls His followers to serve.

He helps me day by day to live in love and confidence and inner peace.

He assures me of life eternal beyond the grave and calls me to live for eternity now.

THEODORE F. ADAMS

From IN MEMORIAM

And so the Word had breath, and wrought
With human hands the creed of creeds
In loveliness of perfect deeds,
More strong than all poetic thought.

ALFRED TENNYSON

Jesus always speaks of eternity in terms of the little events of time.

SAMUEL H. MILLER

THE FELLOWSHIP OF PRAYER

O Son of Man, who walked each day
  A humble road, serene and strong,
Go with me now upon life's way,
  My Comrade all the journey long.

So shall I walk in happiness,
  So shall my task with love be fraught—
If Thou art near to mark and bless
  The labor done, the beauty wrought.

O Son of God, who came and shed
  A light for all the ages long,
Thy company shall make me glad,
  Thy fellowship shall keep me strong.

NANCY BYRD TURNER

Our Lord did what the best scientific minds do. He saw the universal behind the local, the infinite that hides behind the finite, the eternal meaning that lies just beyond the passing incident.

HAROLD E. KOHN

FOLLOWER

Christianity is a personal religion. Leave dogma to those who enjoy it; the true Christian is simply one of Christ's followers. I cannot understand the nature of Infinite Energy; but I can follow Jesus Christ because we have the story of His life, action, and words. I have more faith in the practical wisdom and knowledge of Jesus than I have in that of any statesman, soldier, or philosopher. He was the most independent and courageous individual of whom we have any record.

WILLIAM LYON PHELPS

PROFOUND DOCTRINE

The permanent place of power which Jesus occupies is by virtue of the new and simple and profound doctrine which He brought — the universal, loving Fatherhood of God and the coming of the Kingdom of Heaven, one of the most revolutionary doctrines that has ever stirred and changed human thought. The world began to be a different world from the day that doctrine was preached. Every step toward wider understanding and tolerance and good will is a step in the direction of universal brotherhood, which He proclaimed.

H. G. WELLS

THE TRIMMED LAMP

I dare not slight the stranger at my gate—
Threadbare of garb, and sorrowful of lot —
Lest it be Christ that stands, and goes His way
Because I, all unworthy, knew Him not.

I dare not miss one flash of loving cheer
From alien souls, in challenge fine and high:
Ah—what if God be moving very near—
And I, so blind, so deaf—had passed Him by?

LAURA SIMMONS

IN LOVE WITH JESUS

No other one thing has ever been such a power for the moral transformation of life as the experience of falling in love with Jesus.

JAMES BISSETT PRATT

The world sits at the feet of Christ,
Unknowing, blind, and unconsoled;
It yet shall touch His garment's fold,
And feel the heavenly Alchemist
Transform its very dust to gold.

JOHN GREENLEAF WHITTIER

Nature does reveal the wisdom and the power
of God, but love can be revealed only through
a person. Hence the necessity for the Incarnation.

D. H. GILLIATT

THE CENTER

We believe that the history of the world is but
the history of His influence and that the center
of the whole universe is the cross of Calvary.

ALEXANDER MACLAREN

To become Christlike is the only thing in the
whole world worth caring for, the thing before
which every ambition of man is folly and all
lower achievement vain.

HENRY DRUMMOND

By a Carpenter mankind was made, and only
by that Carpenter can mankind be remade.

DESIDERIUS ERASMUS

TEARS OF GRATITUDE

No other fame can be compared with that of
Jesus. He has a place in the human heart that
no one who ever lived has in any measure ri-
valed. No name is pronounced with a tone of
such love and veneration. All other laurels
wither before His. His are ever kept fresh with
tears of gratitude.

WILLIAM ELLERY CHANNING

Two thousand years ago there was One here
on this earth who lived the grandest life that
ever has been lived yet — a life that every
thinking man, with deeper or shallower meaning, has agreed to call divine.

FREDERICK W. ROBERTSON

THE STARLIT HILL

There was a night, there was a hill,
    There was a starlit sky;
An upturned face that hardly sensed
    The night wind blowing by.

There was a Voice—no human voice—
    I heard it clear and still;
And since that night, and since that Voice,
    I've loved each starlit hill.

RALPH S. CUSHMAN

HIS DWELLINGPLACE

All His glory and beauty come from within,
    and there He delights to dwell.
His visits there are frequent,
His conversation sweet,
His comforts refreshing,
    and His peace passing all understanding.

THOMAS A KEMPIS

Christmas

Therefore the Lord himself shall give you a sign; Behold, a virgin shall conceive, and bear a son, and shall call his name Immanuel.

For unto us a child is born, unto us a son is given: and the government shall be upon his shoulder: and his name shall be called Wonderful, Counsellor, The mighty God, The everlasting Father, The Prince of Peace.

ISAIAH 7:14; 9:6

Christmas is not a day or a season, but a condition of heart and mind.
If we love our neighbors as ourselves;
   if in our riches we are poor in spirit and in our poverty we are rich in grace;
   if our charity vaunteth not itself, but suffereth long and is kind;
   if when our brother asks for a loaf, we give ourselves instead;
   if each day dawns in opportunity and sets in achievement, however small—
   then every day is Christ's day and Christmas is always near.

JAMES WALLINGFORD

From THE CHRISTMAS STAR
Stars rise and set, that star shines on:
Songs fail, but still that music beats
Through all the ages come and gone,
In lane and field and city streets.
And we who catch the Christmas gleam,
Watching with children on the hill,
We know, we know it is no dream—
He stands among us still!

NANCY BYRD TURNER

The most amazing thing about the Christmas story is its relevance. It is at home in every age and fits into every mood of life. It is not simply a lovely tale once told, but eternally contemporary. It is the voice crying out in every wilderness. It is as meaningful in our time as in that long-ago night when shepherds followed the light of the star to the manger of Bethlehem.

JOSEPH R. SIZOO

PRAYER
We thank Thee, O God, for the return of the wondrous spell of this Christmas season that brings its own sweet joy into our jaded and troubled hearts.

Forbid it, Lord, that we should celebrate without understanding what we celebrate, or, like our counterparts so long ago, fail to see the star or to hear the song of glorious promise.

As our hearts yield to the spirit of Christmas, may we discover that it is Thy Holy Spirit who comes—not a sentiment, but a power—to remind us of the only way by which there may be peace on the earth and good will among men.

May we not spend Christmas, but keep it, that we may be kept in its hope, through Him who emptied Himself in coming to us that we might be filled with peace and joy in returning to God.

PETER MARSHALL

AND THE WORD WAS MADE FLESH
Light looked down and beheld Darkness.
   "Thither will I go," said Light.
Peace looked down and beheld War.
   "Thither will I go," said Peace.
Love looked down and beheld Hatred.
   "Thither will I go," said Love.
So came Light and shone.
So came Peace and gave rest.
So came Love and brought Life.

LAURENCE HOUSMAN

O Father, may that holy star
   Grow every year more bright,
And send its glorious beams afar
   To fill the world with light.

WILLIAM CULLEN BRYANT

KEEPING CHRISTMAS

There is a better thing than the observance of Christmas day and that is keeping Christmas.

Are you willing

to forget what you have done for other people, and to remember what other people have done for you;

to ignore what the world owes you, and to think what you owe the world;

to put your rights in the background, and your duties in the middle distance, and your chances to do a little more than your duty in the foreground;

to see that your fellow men are just as real as you are, and try to look behind their faces to their hearts, hungry for joy;

to own that probably the only good reason for your existence is not what you are going to get out of life, but what you are going to give;

to close your book of complaints against the management of the universe, and look around you for a place where you can sow a few seeds of happiness—

are you willing to do these things even for a day?

Then you can keep Christmas.

Are you willing to stoop down and consider the needs and the desires of little children;

to remember the weakness and loneliness of people who are growing old;

to stop asking how much your friends love you, and ask yourself whether you love them enough;

to bear in mind the things that other people have to bear in their hearts;

to try to understand what those who live in the same home with you really want,

without waiting for them to tell you;

to trim your lamp so that it will give more light and less smoke, and to carry it in front so that your shadow will fall behind you;

to make a grave for your ugly thoughts, and a garden for your good thoughts, with the gate open—

are you willing to do these things even for a day?

Then you can keep Christmas.

Are you willing to believe that love is the strongest thing in the world—stronger than hate, stronger than evil, stronger than death—and that the blessed life which began in Bethlehem nineteen hundred years ago is the image and brightness of the Eternal Love?

Then you can keep Christmas.

And if you keep it for a day, why not always?

But you can never keep it alone.

HENRY VAN DYKE

PROPHETIC DAY

Christmas is a prophetic day, looking not so much backward as forward. It belongs to an order of life not yet attained, to a religion not yet realized; to a coming, but distant, time which all prophets have foreseen, when men will be ruled by "the angels of our higher nature," and justice will reign, and pity and joy will walk the common ways of life.

JOSEPH FORT NEWTON

The purpose and cause of the incarnation was that He might illuminate the world by His wisdom and excite it to the love of Himself.

PETER ABÉLARD

HIS MONOGRAM

The very ordinariness of that first Christmas pleads knowingly and persuasively to common people. Christmas came to little Bethlehem that we might know that no place is unknown to God; at the stroke of twelve to remind us that there is no moment of the day or night when He is absent from us; to young Mary to convince us that all life is dear to Him; and in a Child that we may sense that all of life is in His hands. Christmas is His monogram, stenciled on our hearts, recalling to us year by year that "no more is God a Stranger."

WHEN CHRISTMAS CAME TO BETHLEHEM

THE MANGER MOUSE

He opened a window in the straw
And poked out his nose, two ears, and a paw,
And all of midnight filled the skies
Except where two dots were his eyes.

He saw the glow around the manger,
And knew that something so much stranger
Than he had ever seen before
Had come in at the stable door.

The Light spread out to darker places,
And fired the garnets in the faces
Of goats and sheep . . . and all the cows
Wore amber jewels at their brows.

He stared at eyes that watched from under
Horns and fleece, and gazed with wonder;
Unaware the Light had thrown
Starry diamonds into his own.

RALPH W. SEAGER

UNIVERSAL

Christ was born in the first century, yet He belongs to all centuries. He was born a Jew, yet He belongs to all races. He was born in Bethlehem, yet He belongs to all countries.

GEORGE W. TRUETT

CHRISTMAS CHEER RECIPE

Take a bushel of tinsel, sprinkle well throughout the house.
Add two dozen stars and one graceful Christmas tree.
Take a generous spray of mistletoe, an armload of holly, and a full measure of snow laid in curved hills along the window sills.
Toss in a Christmas carol, and season well with good will and friendly laughter.
Light the candles, "one for adoration, two for celebration."
Let the first burn brightly, and may those you love be near.
The yield: *one happy Christmas.*

CLEMENTINE PADDLEFORD

JOURNEYS

The world widens by starlight,
The mind reaches,
Stars beget journeys.

JOHN ERSKINE

ALCHEMY

The whole, wide world turned selfless for a day,
Lays down its gift beneath the Christmas fir,
And, strangely, touched by memory of a star,
Each gift is gold and frankincense and myrrh.

ADELAIDE LOVE

JOURNEY OF THE MAGI

'A cold coming we had of it,
Just the worst time of the year
For a journey, and such a long journey:
The ways deep and the weather sharp,
The very dead of winter.'
And the camels galled, sore-footed, refractory,
Lying down in the melting snow.
There were times we regretted
The summer palaces on slopes, the terraces,
And the silken girls bringing sherbet.
Then the camel men cursing and grumbling
And running away, and wanting their liquor
    and women,
And the night-fires going out, and the lack of
    shelters,
And the cities hostile and the towns unfriendly
And the villages dirty and charging high
    prices:
A hard time we had of it.
At the end we preferred to travel all night,
Sleeping in snatches,
With the voices singing in our ears, saying
That this was all folly.
Then at dawn we came down into a temperate
    valley,
Wet, below the snow line, smelling of vegeta-
    tion;
With a running stream and a water-mill beat-
    ing the darkness,
And three trees on the low sky,
And an old white horse galloped away in the
    meadow.
Then we came to a tavern with vine-leaves
    over the lintel,
Six hands at an open door dicing for pieces of
    silver,
And feet kicking the empty wine-skins.
But there was no information, and so we con-
    tinued

And arrived at evening, not a moment too soon
Finding the place; it was (you may say) satis-
    factory.

All this was a long time ago, I remember,
And I would do it again, but set down
This set down
This: were we led all that way for
Birth or Death? There was a Birth, certainly,
We had evidence and no doubt. I had seen
    birth and death,
But had thought they were different; this
    Birth was
Hard and bitter agony for us, like Death, our
    death.
We returned to our palaces, these Kingdoms,
But no longer at ease here, in the old dispensa-
    tion,
With an alien people clutching their gods.
I should be glad of another death.

                                        T. S. ELIOT

IF EVERY DAY WERE CHRISTMAS

If the spirit of Christmas were with us every
    day, some revolutionary events would
    occur:
Selfishness would die a death of starvation.
Avarice would be hung higher than Haman.
Foolish pride would go down in crushing
    defeat.
Senseless strife and silly bickerings would
    shame each other to death.
The prayer of Jesus for the unity of His fol-
    lowers would be answered.
Racial animosities would be drowned in a sea
    of brotherhood.
"Peace on earth" would become a glorious
    reality.

                            EDGAR DE WITT JONES

DAY OF HOPE

Christmas is the one day of the year that carries real hope and promise for all mankind.

It carries the torch of brotherhood.

It is the one day in the year when most of us grow big of heart and broad of mind.

It is the single day when most of us are as kind and as thoughtful of others as we know how to be;

when most of us are as gracious and generous as we would like always to be;

when the joy of the home is more important than the profits of the office;

when peoples of all races speak cheerfully to each other when they meet;

when high and low wish each other well;

and the one day when even enemies forgive and forget.

EDGAR A. GUEST

STORY OF LOVE

Bethlehem surely means many things to many people, and no genuine meaning is without significance. But towering over all, Christmas is a story of divine and human love. Christmas is a festival of love which has a magnetlike tug on our hearts. A compelling, compassionate, and all-encompassing love explains the attractiveness of this day. Without love, there could never have been a first Christmas. Apart from the love we bring and the love we offer and receive, Christmas would be as dreary as an all-day drizzle.

WHEN CHRISTMAS CAME TO BETHLEHEM

From LET US KEEP CHRISTMAS

Whatever else be lost among the years,
Let us keep Christmas still a shining thing:
Whatever doubts assail us, or what fears,
Let us hold close one day, remembering
Its poignant meaning for the hearts of men.
Let us get back our childlike faith again.

GRACE NOLL CROWELL

Happy, happy Christmas, that can win us back to the delusions of our childish days, recall to the old man the pleasures of his youth, and transport the traveler back to his own fireside and quiet home!

CHARLES DICKENS

THE CARPENTER OF GALILEE

The Carpenter of Galilee
Comes down the street again,
In every land, in every age,
He still is building men.
On Christmas Eve we hear Him knock;
He goes from door to door:
"Are any workmen out of work?
The Carpenter needs more."

HILDA W. SMITH

Christmas waves a magic wand over this world, and behold, everything is softer and more beautiful.

NORMAN VINCENT PEALE

CONTINUING ADVENTURE

As we leave Bethlehem, we ought to leave behind old grudges, old fears, old sorrows. We ought to continue our adventure of life by praising God and by walking on new and better roads. Sometime during the winter we shall need the friendly spirit of Christmas. Sometime in the spring we shall want the hope of Christmas. Let us not pack up the true spirit of Christmas when we put away the decorations.

CHRISTMAS IN OUR HEARTS

THE WISEST OF THE WISE

I'll stand beside the keeper of the inn,
Challenging those who charge him with the sin
That let the Child be born within his stable.
I say he did the best that he was able,
Under the circumstance. Where else would
  there
Be privacy and summer-scented air?
The beasts, benign in their nobility,
Stood watch; and this, at least it seems to me,
Gave courtesy unto the act of birth.
The hostel must have reeled with raucous
  mirth,
Jangling the laden night with feast and dance
As Roman taxes found the dice of chance.
Only a wise man would have seen the manger
As a cradle beyond the pry of stranger.
When pompous fingers shame his guiltless
  deed,
I'm on his side, disciple of the need
To say he was the wisest one of all,
Providing the sanctuary of the stall.

RALPH W. SEAGER

GIFTS THAT ARE MINE

Place these gifts on my altar this Christmas;
Gifts that are mine, as the years are mine:
The quiet hopes that flood the earnest cargo of
  my dreams:
The best of all good things for those I love,
A fresh new trust for all whose faith is dim.
The love of life, God's precious gift in reach of
  all:
Seeing in each day the seeds of the morrow,
Finding in each struggle the strength of
  renewal,
Seeking in each person the face of my brother.
I place these gifts on my altar this Christmas;
Gifts that are mine, as the years are mine.

HOWARD THURMAN

The door is on the latch tonight,
  The hearth-fire is aglow,
I seem to hear soft passing feet—
  The Christ child in the snow.

My heart is open wide tonight
  For stranger, kith or kin.
I would not bar a single door
  Where Love might enter in.

KATE DOUGLAS WIGGIN

From FAR TRUMPETS BLOWING
  But he who gets to Bethlehem
  Shall hear the oxen lowing;
  And, if he humbly kneel with them,
  May catch far trumpets blowing.

LOUIS F. BENSON

Church

How amiable are thy tabernacles, O Lord of hosts!

My soul longeth, yea, even fainteth for the courts of the Lord: my heart and my flesh crieth out for the living God.

Blessed are they that dwell in thy house: they will be still praising thee. A day in thy courts is better than a thousand. I had rather be a doorkeeper in the house of my God, than to dwell in the tents of wickedness.

PSALM 84:1-2, 4, 10

PRAYER

O Thou, who hast set Thy church in the valleys of our beloved land to be a bulwark and a sanctuary, and upon the hills to be a belfry and declarer of Thy truth: make strong her walls, wide her gates, fearless her witness. May her chief effort be to discern Thy will and faithfully to proclaim it.

BOYNTON MERRILL

———

From COUNTRY CHURCHES

Symbols of faith, they lift their reaching spires
Above green groves down many a country way,
And on the wide plains there are altar fires
That light the forms of those who kneel to pray.
And I have seen them stand knee-deep in wheat:
White country churches, rising from the sod,
Where men, in gratitude for bread to eat,
Have paused, and reared their altars to their God.

GRACE NOLL CROWELL

———

SOCIETY OF SINNERS

The Christian church is a society of sinners. It is the only society in the world, membership in which is based upon the single qualification that the candidate shall be unworthy of membership.

CHARLES CLAYTON MORRISON

LITTLE BOYS IN CHURCH

Small boys in the church pews grow
Very fast, the first you know
Ones only halfway up are older
And at their father's cheek or shoulder.

One day they are only bright
Heads that in the high church light
Look as if they were washed in dew,
Their ears and hair are all so new.

This Sunday only heads that dance,
Next Sunday heads and coats and pants,
All the boys have sprung uphill,
Heads are erect, and ears stand still.

One week they are boys, and then
Next week they are slim young men
Standing very still and lean,
Perilously scrubbed and clean.

Enjoy each small boy while you can,
Tomorrow there will be a man
Standing taller than belief,
Little boys in church are brief.

ROBERT P. TRISTRAM COFFIN

———

All the love of God, the great Architect,
All the sacrifice of Christ, the great Builder,
All the dreams of dauntless prophets,
All the faith of courageous pioneers,
All the hope of countless multitudes,
All the joy of conquering Christians—
Are enclosed within the walls of the Church.

BEULAH HUGHES

MY CHURCH

Before I was born my church gave to my parents ideals of life and love that made my home a place of strength and beauty.

In helpless infancy my church joined my parents in consecrating me to Christ.

My church enriched my childhood with the romance of religion and the lessons of life that have been woven into the texture of my soul. Sometimes I seem to have forgotten and then, when else I might surrender to foolish and futile ideals of life, the truths my church taught become radiant, insistent, and inescapable.

In the stress and storm of adolescence my church heard the surge of my soul and she guided my footsteps by lifting my eyes toward the stars.

When first my heart knew the strange awakenings of love, my church taught me to chasten and spiritualize my affections. She sanctified my marriage and blessed my home.

When my heart was seamed with sorrow and I thought the sun could never shine again, my church drew me to the Friend of all the weary and whispered to me the hope of another morning, eternal and tearless.

When my steps have slipped and I have known the bitterness of sin, my church has believed in me and willingly she has called me back to live within the heights of myself.

Now have come the children dearer to me than life itself, and my church is helping me to train them for all joyous and clean and Christly living.

My church calls me to her heart. She asks my service and my loyalty. She has a right to ask it. I will help her to do for others what she has done for me. In this place in which I live, I will help her keep aflame and aloft the torch of a living faith.

WILLIAM H. BODDY

YOUNG MINISTER

A ray of sun—from sparkling window high
  Above the pulpit—lit his golden hair,
    As though God's radiant fingers rested
      there.
It touched his face, as if to sanctify
The soul-deep joy, a tithe of God's supply,
  Already lighting it. His voice in prayer,
  Keen echo of our souls, made us aware
The omnipresent Son had knelt near by.

His sermon measured wit with graceful tongue,
  Bestirred our minds to quick, creative
    thought,
    And poured into our spirit's waiting cup
Such Godly love that we no longer clung
  To self, but gave the lives our Lord had
    wrought,
    In one resurgent chorus offered up.

RUTH M. PARKS

Let God be thanked there is on earth an institution that has a high opinion of man, declaring that he is in some sense a son of God, who has within himself divine possibilities; an institution that transcends race, nation, and class; an institution which is loyally undertaking to embody the spirit of Christ, and in His name to relieve human suffering, promote human welfare, and carry on a ministry of reconciliation among men.

ERNEST FREMONT TITTLE

WHY I GO TO CHURCH

I go because I would rather lie in bed late on Sunday mornings, the only chance for a good sleep I have during the week.

I go because I would rather read the Sunday papers.

I go because I know it will please my old father, when he learns of it, and my parents-in-law whom I shall undoubtedly see there.

I go because I shall meet and have to shake hands with people, many of whom do not interest me in the least;

because if I don't go, my children consider that they have a good reason for not going to Sunday School;

because I might be asked to do something I don't want to do;

because I may disagree with what the minister has to say.

I go because some of my best friends, who know the details of my life, consider me a hypocrite.

I go because I do not believe in all the doctrines of this church, or any other church.

I go, in short, because I hate to go and because I know that it will do me good.

HENRY C. LINK

MY CHURCH

My church to me means *life*;
A more abundant life, enlarged, full-grown;
Unchanging in a swiftly moving age
When hope has flown.

My church to me means *love*;
An all-embracing love, secure, serene,
With hands outstretched to help the passing throng;
With self unseen.

My church to me means *rest*;
A quiet, peaceful rest, calm and complete;
Unbroken by the din of worldly strife;
The soul's retreat.

My church to me means *home*;
A happy, cheerful home, within whose walls
An undivided circle kneels in prayer,
As evening falls.

My church to me means *hope*;
A never-failing hope when light descends,
For in that hour it lights the evening lamp
And comfort sends.

My church to me means *faith*;
Triumphant faith, clearing the cluttered way
Toward that City where for us awaits
Eternal day.

My church to me means *service*;
A place to serve with others day to day,
Remembering always how the Master toiled to win
Men to the Way.

INVITATION

To all who are weary and seek rest,
To all who mourn and long for comfort,
To all who struggle and desire victory,
To all who sin and need a Savior,
To all who are idle and look for service,
To all who are strangers and want fellowship,
To all who hunger and thirst after righteousness,
And to whosoever will come—
The church opens wide her doors and offers her welcome in the name of Jesus Christ her Lord.

SUNDAY SERVICE

He ruffles through his hymnbook,
He fumbles with his tie,
He laces up his oxfords,
He overworks a sigh,
He goes through all his pockets,
Engrossed in deep research—
There's no one quite so busy as
A little boy in church.

THELMA IRELAND

BUILDER OF CHURCHES

God builds no churches! By His plan
That labor has been left to man;
No spires miraculously arise,
No little mission from the skies
Falls on a bleak and barren place
To be a source of strength and grace;
The church demands its price
In human toil and sacrifice.

The humblest spire in mortal ken,
Where God abides, was built by men;
And if the church is still to grow,
Is still the light of hope to throw
Across the valleys of despair,
Man still must build God's house of prayer.
God sends no churches from the skies;
Out of our hearts they must arise.

BUILDING AND BUILT UPON

When you enter the church you hear a sound
—a sound as of some mighty poem chanted.
Listen long enough, and you will learn that it
is made up of the beating of human hearts, of
the nameless music of men's souls—that is, if
you have ears.

If you have eyes, you will presently see the
church itself—a looming mystery of many
shapes and shadows, leaping sheer from the
floor to the dome. The work of no ordinary
builder!

The pillars of it go up like the brawny
trunks of heroes. The sweet human flesh of
men and women is moulded about its bul-
warks, strong, impregnable. The faces of little
children laugh out from every corner. The
terrible spans and arches of it are the joined
hands of comrades.

It is yet building—building and built upon.
Sometimes the work goes forward in deep
darkness; sometimes in blinding light; now
beneath the burden of unutterable anguish;
now to the tune of a great laughter and heroic
shoutings like the cry of thunders.

Sometimes, in the silence of the nighttime,
one may hear the tiny hammerings of the comrades at work in the dome—the comrades that
climbed ahead.

CHARLES RANN KENNEDY

CANTICLE

There is in Man, as in all beings, something
more than the mere sum of the materials that
went to his making. A cathedral is a good deal
more than the sum of its stones. It is geometry
and architecture. The cathedral is not to be
defined by its stones, since those stones have
no meaning apart from the cathedral, receive
from it their sole significance. And how diverse
the stones that have entered into this unity!
The most grimacing of the gargoyles are easily
absorbed into the canticle of the cathedral.

ANTOINE DE SAINT-EXUPÉRY

44

GUESTS OF GOD

You enter this church not as a stranger but as a
guest of God. He is your heavenly Father.

Come, then, with joy in your heart and thanks
on your lips, offering Him your love and
service.

Be grateful to the strong and loyal men and
women and children who in the name of
God builded this place of worship, and to
all who have beautified it and hallowed it
with their prayers and praises.

May all who love this house of faith find the
inspiration of their labor and rejoice in the
power and love of God, that His blessing
may rest on you both on your going out and
on your coming in.

TWELFTH-CENTURY ENGLISH CHURCH

———

HOUSE OF LIFE

In the House of Life, I saw an altar, with
candles aglow and a cross thereon.

And as I bowed in reverence and closed my
eyes, I beheld the living church.

The walls were not of brick and stone, but
of dedicated wills held together with the mortar
of mutual dependence and common commit-
ment to the Best yet revealed.

The windows were not of stained glass, but
of multicolored dreams, hopes, and aspirations, through which there came the vision of
infinite beauty that shone with the broken
brilliance of a thousand suns.

The towering pillars and the vaulted arches
were not of stone and steel, but of far-reaching
arms lifted in prayers innumerable and inter-
mingling.

The long aisles were not carpeted with vel-
vet runners, but with temptations trampled
under foot and good resolutions kept.

The doors were never shut. They were wide
open with welcome to all humanity: saints and
sinners, rich and poor, black, brown, yellow,
and white—whomsoever.

The altar was not of carved wood, but of
penitent hearts, ashamed of their sins, made
strong with the sense of forgiveness.

The pulpit was not a dais for the declaration
of dogma, but a place of light and fire whence
came forth flashes of truth and the impact of
power.

The music was not compounded of organ
and voices, but of consecrated leadership and
well-developed diversities all harmonized into
the matchless melody of creative co-operation.

All the warmth of the living church, wherein
all glowed with radiant vitality, came not from
furnace and fuel, but from obedience to Him
who saith: "Thou shalt love the Lord thy God
with all thy heart, soul, mind, and strength;
and thy neighbor as thyself."

HENRY HITT CRANE

———

ON A CHURCH PLAQUE

Enter this door
As if the floor
Within were gold;
And every wall
Of jewels all
Of wealth untold;
As if a choir
In robes of fire
Were singing here;
Nor shout nor rush
But hush . . .
For God is here.

45

WHO BUILDS THE CHURCH?

Who builds the church—the engineer?
The architect, the workmen grave?
The draftsmen of the crew who rear
Steel girders to sustain the nave?
The unseen men who pour the steel
That belches from blast furnace door?
The gang who loads of mortar wheel?
The men who concrete pillars pour?

Who builds the church? That spirit fine
Whose preaching makes its folks divine,
The thrilling, surging plan of God
To guard the ways their fathers trod,
And makes them all empowered feel
To do the things His signs reveal.
Who builds the church? Those saintly souls
Whose gifts are brimming incense-bowls,
Who nothing have but daily bread,
Yet give of this, His feast to spread.

Who builds the church? Each child and man
Who lends some talent to the whole—
All blended to achieve His plan,
All fruiting in a Gothic soul.
God builds the church from all the skills
Of human minds and human wills;
From stalwart brawn and brilliant brain;
From artist-dream and muscle strain;
From childhood's mites, from gifts of age,
He builds His church, our heritage!

MADELEINE SWEENEY MILLER

———

DENOMINATIONS

We come to God by devious ways,
And who am I to say
That the road I take is the only road,
My way, the better way?

The earnest seeker after God
Can find Him like a flame,
Down any road, no matter what
His creed, or what his name.

So whether we may pause to pray
Where great cathedrals shine,
Or in some little weathered church,
Or at a wayside shrine,

The sincere traveler will arrive
Where the welcoming home lights shine,
Although the countless thousands take
A different road from mine.

GRACE NOLL CROWELL

———

All is holy where devotion kneels.

OLIVER WENDELL HOLMES

———

This is our House of Prayer, but more,
It is a door
Leading beyond our trivialities
To precious mysteries,
Beyond the bonds and bounds of sense
To the eternal confidence.

This is the place where we have heard God's
    Word;
With power
His will has gripped our hearts, and many an
    hour
Spent here in search sincere
Has opened windows to a surer view
Of what our God would have us do.

THOMAS JOHN CARLISLE

Contentment

The Lord is the portion of mine inheritance and of my cup: thou maintainest my lot.

The lines are fallen unto me in pleasant places; yea, I have a goodly heritage.

Therefore my heart is glad, and my glory rejoiceth. PSALM 16:5-6, 9

RECIPE FOR CONTENTMENT

Health enough to make work a pleasure,
Wealth enough to support your needs,
Strength enough to battle with difficulties and
forsake them,
Grace enough to confess your sins and over-
come them,
Patience enough to toil until some good is
accomplished,
Charity enough to see some good in your
neighbor,
Love enough to move you to be useful and
helpful to others,
Faith enough to make real the things of God,
and
Hope enough to remove all anxious fears con-
cerning the future.

JOHANN WOLFGANG VON GOETHE

INSCRIPTION

If you would have a mind at peace,
A heart that cannot harden,
Go find a door that opens wide
Upon a lovely garden.

CYPRESS GARDENS

A wise religion is indispensable for peace of
mind because it blesses us with inner gifts
beyond the bestowal of any science: a sense of
our purpose in the world, a feeling of related-
ness to God, the shared warmth of group fellowship, and the subordination of our little
egos to great moral and spiritual ends.

JOSHUA LOTH LIEBMAN

GRACE BEFORE SLEEP

How can our minds and bodies be
Grateful enough that we have spent
Here in this generous room, we three,
This evening of content?
Each one of us has walked through storm
And fled the wolves along the road;
But here the hearth is wide and warm,
And for this shelter and this light
Accept, O Lord, our thanks tonight.

SARA TEASDALE

Contentment is a home where mutual con-
sideration and love dwell. From such a home
one can go out in the morning with strength
and return in the evening with happy anticipation.

Contentment is happy memories of things
past, enjoyment of things present, and hope
of good to come.

Contentment is a consciousness of the inexhaustible abundance of spiritual power
around us upon which our spirits may end-
lessly draw.

HAROLD E. KOHN

I'm nobody! Who are you?
Are you nobody, too?
Then there's a pair of us—don't tell!
They'd banish us, you know.

How dreary to be somebody!
How public, like a frog
To tell your name the livelong day
To an admiring bog!

EMILY DICKINSON

FOR QUIETUDE OF MIND

1. You shall learn to desire nothing in the world so much but that you can be happy without it.

2. You shall seek that which you desire only by such means as are fair and lawful, and this will leave you without bitterness toward men or shame before God.

3. You shall take pleasure in the time while you are seeking, even though you obtain not immediately that which you seek, for the purpose of a journey is not only to arrive at the goal, but also to find enjoyment by the way.

4. When you attain that which you have desired, you shall think more of the kindness of your fortune than of the greatness of your skill. This will make you grateful and ready to share with others that which Providence hath bestowed upon you.

HENRY VAN DYKE

Leisure is an affair of mood and atmosphere rather than simply of the clock. It is not a chronological occurrence but a spiritual state. It is unhurried pleasurable living among one's native enthusiasms. Leisure consists of those pauses in our lives when experience is a fusion of stimulation and repose. Genuine leisure yields at once a feeling of vividness and a sense of peace. It consists of moments so clear and pleasant in themselves that one might wish they were eternal.

IRWIN EDMAN

If peace be in the heart
The wildest winter storm is full of solemn
     beauty,
The midnight lightning flash but shows the
     path of duty,
Each living creature tells some new and joyous
     story,
The very trees and stones all catch a ray of
     glory,
If peace be in the heart.

CHARLES FRANCIS RICHARDSON

PEACEFUL LIVING

I know the secret of peaceful living. I am not waiting for peace and happiness to come to me in another world. I am enjoying it here day by day. Because of this growing, giving, learning experience, I believe that I shall have greater capacity for receiving when I shall see Him who is the foundation of my life.

MARY MC LEOD BETHUNE

POSTPONEMENT

How small a portion of our life it is that we really enjoy! In youth we are looking forward to things that are to come. In old age we are looking backward to things that have past. In manhood, although we appear to be more occupied in things that are present, yet even that is too often absorbed in vague determination to be vastly happy on some future day when we have time.

CHARLES CALEB COLTON

A man's moments of serenity are few, but a few will sustain him a lifetime.

RICHARD E. BYRD

TO THOSE WHO ARE CONTENT

To those who are content
I lift my song—
To those who are at peace
Where they belong—

Who rise and question not,
Who go their way
Happily from dawn
To close of day;

Who labor and who earn
The bread they eat,
Who find their rest at night
Is deep and sweet;

Who ask no more of life
Than they can give,
Oh, beautifully fine
I think they live;

Who are content to serve,
To love and pray,
Leading their simple lives
From day to day.

GRACE NOLL CROWELL

True contentment is the power of getting out of any situation all that there is in it.

GILBERT KEITH CHESTERTON

But all the pleasure that I find
Is to maintain a quiet mind.

EDWARD DYER

FULLNESS OF LIFE

Contentment, and indeed usefulness, comes as the infallible result of great acceptances, great humilities—of not trying to make ourselves this or that, but of surrendering ourselves to the fullness of life—of letting life flow through us. To be used—that is the sublimest thing we know.

DAVID GRAYSON

JOURNEYS

How restful are unhurried things!—
The spreading light of dawn's gray hour,
Slow, rhythmic motion of birds' wings,
The opening petals of a flower . . .

Dim shadows moving on a wall,
The moon's calm light above the bay,
Soft murmurings that rise and fall
Within the dusk that hushes day.

My journey, too, may bring content
To the still place of heart's desire;
There, tranquilly, to pitch my tent—
Watch flames scale heavenward from my fire.

IDA NORTON MUNSON

All the misfortunes of men spring from their not knowing how to live quietly at home in their own rooms.

BLAISE PASCAL

No one is happy unless he is reasonably well satisfied with himself, so that the quest for tranquillity must of necessity begin with self-examination.

WILLIAM S. OGDON

However much I have to do,
　　However hard I strive,
I always tell myself that I
　　Am glad to be alive.
My heart is grateful for the sun
　　That keeps my body warm;
And for the comforts of this earth
　　Against whatever storm.
I have my friends to cheer me up
　　And books to read at night
With boundless beauty to behold,
　　Whenever stars are bright.
I have enough to eat and drink,
　　And clothes enough to wear;
A normal mind and healthy lungs
　　To breathe the best of air.
So why should I object when I
　　Have this my job to do,
As long as I have everything
　　To help me see it through?

JAMES J. METCALFE

SMALL THINGS

Blessed is the man who can enjoy the small things, the common beauties, the little day-by-day events; sunshine on the fields, birds on the bough, breakfast, dinner, supper, the daily paper on the porch, a friend passing by. So many people who go afield for enjoyment leave it behind them at home.

DAVID GRAYSON

THINGS ENOUGH

That man can thank his lucky stars
　　Whose things to keep are few,
To which the rain and moth and rust
　　Find little harm to do.

A faith to make his handshake warm
　　And simple things most wise,
A wife to make each morning fine
　　With morning-glory eyes.

A love to make him foot the roads
　　That others motor on,
A garden small and kind enough
　　To let him watch the dawn.

Pity for the hungry ones,
　　The ragged, and ill-shod,
A tree that's tall and straight enough
　　To make him think of God.

ROBERT P. TRISTRAM COFFIN

I do not ask for wealth—the simple things are
　　best:
The blazing sun at noon; the crimson-painted
　　west;
The silver nights, the breeze, the birds, the
　　flowers;
The lazy summer days with golden hours;
The running brooks; the haze on autumn hills;
The painted forest leaves; the prancing rills;
The deepening twilight when the work is done;
The winding forest path with shade and sun;
The growing grain, the lowing herds, the
　　horse's neigh,
The old gray barn with mounds of scented
　　hay;
The garden path, the well, the orchard trees;
The sighing of the lilting southern breeze;
The tented corn, the fallow land, the hilltop's
　　crest—
I do not ask for wealth—these things are best.

BLAINE C. BIGLER

Cross

I, if I be lifted up from the earth, will draw all men unto me.

This he said, signifying what death he should die.   John 12:32-33

We preach Christ crucified, unto the Jews a stumblingblock, and unto the Greeks foolishness;

But unto them which are called, both Jews and Greeks, Christ the power of God, and the wisdom of God.   I Corinthians 1:23-24

TOWARD JERUSALEM

Opening our windows toward Jerusalem,
And looking thitherward, we see
First Bethlehem,
Then Nazareth and Galilee,
And afterwards Gethsemane,
And then the little hill called Calvary.

AMY CARMICHAEL

———

I saw God bare His soul one day
   Where all the earth might see
The stark and naked heart of Him
   On lonely Calvary.

There was a crimson sky of blood
   And overhead a storm;
When lightning slit the clouds
   And light engulfed His form.

Beyond the storm a rainbow lent
   A light to every clod,
And on that cross mine eyes beheld
   The naked soul of God.

WILLIAM L. STIDGER

———

Christ who, being the holiest among the
mighty, and the mightiest among the holy,
lifted with His pierced hands empires off their
hinges and turned the stream of centuries out
of its channel, and still governs the ages.

JEAN PAUL RICHTER

EVERYMAN'S JERUSALEM

Every true life has its Jerusalem to which it is
always going up. At first far off and dimly
seen, laying but light hold upon our purpose
and our will, then gradually taking us more
and more into its power, compelling our study,
directing the current of our thoughts, arrang-
ing our friendships for us, deciding for us what
powers we shall bring out into use, deciding
for us what we shall be. So every live man's
Jerusalem, his sacred city, calls to him from
the hilltop where it stands.

PHILLIPS BROOKS

———

SYMBOL

My faith is all a doubtful thing,
   Wove on a doubtful loom—
Until there comes each showery spring,
   A cherry-tree in bloom.

And Christ who died upon a tree
   That death had stricken bare
Comes beautifully back to me
   In blossoms, everywhere.

DAVID MORTON

———

The Cross is any place where a saving love
goes out to undergird this life of ours and
comes back with the hot stab of nails in its
hands.

PAUL SCHERER

I see His blood upon the rose
And in the stars the glory of His eyes,
His body gleams amid eternal snows,
His tears fall from the skies.

I see His face in every flower;
The thunder and the singing of the birds
Are but His voice—and carven by His power
Rocks are His written words.

All pathways by His feet are worn,
His strong heart stirs the ever-beating sea,
His crown of thorns is twined with every
    thorn,
His cross is every tree.

JOSEPH MARY PLUNKETT

———

God made a show of the powers of evil and
darkness and at Calvary He put them to rout.

JAMES S. STEWART

———

The Cross is the ladder to heaven.

THOMAS DRAXE

———

QUATRAIN
Christ bears a thousand crosses now
    Where once but one He bore;
Each cruel deed unto His brow
    Adds one thorn more.

CHARLES G. BLANDEN

Surely we would hardly wish even our religion
to be without its cross, when He who pur-
chased it for us bought it at so costly a sacrifice.

WILLIAM BRIGHT

———

No pain, no palm;
No thorns, no throne;
No gall, no glory;
No cross, no crown.

WILLIAM PENN

———

"Three things there are," said one,
"That miracles are—
Dawn, and the setting sun,
    And a falling star."

"Two things there be," he said,
"Beyond man's quest:
The white peace of the dead,
    And a heart at rest."

"One only thing," he cried,
"Draws all men still—
A stark cross standing wide
    On a windy hill."

E. P. DICKIE

———

Jesus never succeeded in public save once,
when He was crucified. He never failed in
private save once, with Pontius Pilate.

JOHN WATSON

BARABBAS SPEAKS

I heard a man explaining
(they said his name was Paul)
how Jesus, on that fateful day,
had died to save us all.

I found it hard to follow
his fine-spun theory,
but I am very, very sure
He died that day for me.

EDWIN MC NEILL POTEAT

———

How soon would faith freeze without a cross!

SAMUEL RUTHERFORD

———

THE PASSION FLOWER

Thou lowly, meek, and lovely flower,
But yesterday, at evening's hour,
As trudged I upward with my load,
I saw thee blooming by the road,
And stayed my steps to wonder there
That beauty so supremely fair
Should waste its loveliness on me—
Even as the Flower of Calvary!

CHARLES G. BLANDEN

———

THE WAY

So short the road from Bethlehem
That led to Calvary,
So thronged with halt and maimed and blind,
Beggar and Pharisee.

So dark the slope of that last hill,
Yet up that way He trod
Man follows over the centuries—
Home to the heart of God!

LESLIE SAVAGE CLARK

———

THE SIGN OF THE CROSS

To many it is but an ornament to be worn about the neck.

To the architect it is a symbol, adorning churches.

To the scholar it is a goad, driving him on in intellectual pursuits.

To the preacher it is a sermon, filling the need of the hour—and of eternity.

To the skeptic it is a superstition, clouding men's souls.

To the Roman it was an instrument of execution, obnoxious and hated.

To Constantine it was a sign in which to conquer, turning defeat into victory.

To Paul it was a symbol of glory, pointing the way to heaven.

To Mary it was a memory of agony, piercing her soul.

To the motley mob on Golgotha it was a holiday, carnal and cursed.

To one thief it was the door to perdition, horrible and eternal.

To the other it was the gate to Paradise, wondrous beyond work of men or angels.

To Christ it was a bier and a throne, paradox of time, predestined to eternity.

To multiplied millions of storm-tossed souls it is an anchor, offering a haven of rest.

HERSCHEL H. HOBBS

HEART OF GOD

The Cross is not only the symbol for the life of man; it is equally the symbol for the life of God, and it may indeed be said that the Cross is in the heart of God.

JOHN WATSON

PRAYER

O dear Christ, crucified for our sins, make us
  to realize that in the Cross is salvation,
  in the Cross is life,
  in the Cross is protection against our
      enemies,
  in the Cross is infusion of heavenly sweet-
      ness,
  in the Cross is height of virtue,
  in the Cross is perfecting of holiness,
that we may therefore take us our cross and
follow Thee into life everlasting.

THE CROSS AT THE CROSSWAYS

See there! God's signpost, standing at the ways
  Which every man of his free will must go—
Up the steep hill, or down the winding ways,
  One or the other, every man must go.

He forces no man, each must choose his way,
  And as he chooses, so the end will be;
One went in front to point the Perfect Way,
  Who follows fears not where the end will be.

JOHN OXENHAM

AND CHRIST IS CRUCIFIED ANEW

Not only once, and long ago,
  There on Golgotha's rugged side,
  Has Christ the Lord been crucified
Because He loved a lost world so.
But hourly souls, sin-satisfied,
  Mock His great love, flout His commands,
  And drive nails deep into His hands,
And thrust the spear within His side.

JOHN R. MORELAND

VICTORY

It was not the Cross of Jesus, but His victory over the Cross, that set the world singing and brought into the soul of man a new hope, a new joy, a new and haunting kind of goodness.

JOSEPH FORT NEWTON

KEY

The key to the world is in the form of a cross, but it cannot do anything until someone's hand lifts it and fits it into the keyhole.

HOWARD C. SCHARFE

Whatever else Thou sendest me, oh, send
    this—
Not ecstasy of love or lover's kiss,
But strength to know the joy of sacrifice,
To see life deeply as with opened eyes!
Oh, grant me this, dear God,
    Through tears or loss—
To know the joyous secret
    Of Thy Cross!

RALPH SPAULDING CUSHMAN

Devotion

Grace and peace be multiplied unto you through the knowledge of God, and of Jesus our Lord,

According as his divine power hath given unto us all things that pertain unto life and godliness, through the knowledge of him that hath called us to glory and virtue:

Whereby are given unto us exceeding great and precious promises.

And beside this, giving all diligence, add to your faith virtue; and to virtue knowledge;

And to knowledge temperance; and to temperance patience; and to patience godliness;

And to godliness brotherly kindness; and to brotherly kindness charity.

I Peter 1:2-4, 5-7

Devotion to an aim,
or an idea,
or a power transcending man
    such as God,
is an expression of the need
for completeness
in the process of living.

ERICH FROMM

———

From SANCTUARY
'Mid all the traffic of the ways,
Turmoils without, within,
Make in my heart a quiet place,
And come and dwell therein.

A little shrine of quietness,
All sacred to Thyself,
Where Thou shalt all my soul possess,
And I may find myself.

A little place of mystic grace,
Of self and sin swept bare,
Where I may look into Thy face,
And talk with Thee in prayer.

JOHN OXENHAM

———

QUIET REPOSE
When God intended to reveal any future events or high notions to His prophets, He then carried them either to the deserts or the seashore, that having so separated them from amidst the press of people and business, and the cares of the world, He might settle their mind in a quiet repose, and there make them fit for revelation.

IZAAK WALTON

WIDER VISION
To live simply, knowing that life's fullness is
    in its height and depth, not in its scattering
    or accumulating;
to put oneself at the disposal of humble needs,
    to be as humble as God and as self-effacing;
to take time, realizing with the Psalmist that
    "he that believeth will not wish to make
    haste";
to kneel before the burning bush, and to wait
    for the Voice;
to lay the world away and lure the soul from
    hiding—
all this and more will widen out the vision.

SAMUEL H. MILLER

———

INSCRIPTION
I come here to find myself.
It is so easy to get lost
    in the world.

THE SINGING TOWER

———

And so I find it well to come
    For deeper rest to this still room,
For here the habits of the soul
    Feel less the outer world's control;
And from the silence multiplied
    By these still forms on either side
The world that time and sense have known
Falls off and leaves us God alone.

JOHN GREENLEAF WHITTIER

A man's religion is his ultimate attempt to enlarge and complete his own personality by finding the supreme context in which he rightly belongs.

GORDON W. ALLPORT

AT DAYBREAK

Every morning lean thine arms awhile
Upon the window sill of heaven
And gaze upon thy Lord.
Then, with the vision in thy heart,
Turn strong to meet thy day.

MATINS

Flowers rejoice when night is done,
Lift their heads to greet the sun;
Sweetest looks and odours raise,
In a silent hymn of praise.

So my heart would turn away
From the darkness to the day;
Lying open in God's sight
Like a flower in the light.

HENRY VAN DYKE

THE AWAKENING

When the Light of Life falls upon the life of men, secret powers begin to unfold, sleeping perceptions begin to awake, and the whole being becomes alive unto God.

JOHN HENRY JOWETT

GOD'S LOVE

Could we with ink the ocean fill,
Were every blade of grass a quill,
Were the world of parchment made,
And every man a scribe by trade,
　　To write the love
　　Of God above
Would drain that ocean dry;
　　Nor would the scroll
　　Contain the whole,
Though stretched from sky to sky.

INSCRIPTION

Men go to their garden for pleasure;
　　Go, thou, to thy garden for prayer;
The Lord walks in the cool of the evening
　　With those who seek sanctuary there.

From THE SECRET

I met God in the morning
　　When my day was at its best,
And His presence came like sunrise,
　　Like a glory in my breast.

All day long the Presence lingered,
　　All day long He stayed with me,
And we sailed in perfect calmness
　　O'er a very troubled sea.

So I think I know the secret,
　　Learned from many a troubled way:
You must seek Him in the morning
　　If you want Him through the day!

RALPH SPAULDING CUSHMAN

Easter

In the end of the sabbath, as it began to dawn toward the first day of the week, came Mary Magdalene and the other Mary to see the sepulchre.

And, behold . . . the angel of the Lord descended from heaven, and came and rolled back the stone from the door.

And the angel . . . said unto the women, Fear not ye: for I know that ye seek Jesus, which was crucified.

He is not here: for he is risen, as he said. Come, see the place where the Lord lay.

And go quickly, and tell his disciples that he is risen from the dead; and, behold, he goeth before you into Galilee; there shall ye see him.

MATTHEW 28:1-2, 5-7

THE MESSAGE OF EASTER

Easter is the demonstration of God that life itself is essentially spiritual and timeless.

Easter tells us that life is to be interpreted not simply in terms of things but in terms of ideals.

Easter speaks of life not only by years but by yearnings also.

Easter identifies life not only with decay and destruction but with continuance and creation.

Easter is God's way of saying that man through Christ shares the life of God now and forever.

CHARLES M. CROWE

CALVARY AND EASTER

A song of sunshine through the rain,
  Of Spring across the snow;
A balm to heal the hurts of pain,
  A peace surpassing woe.
Lift up your heads, ye sorrowing ones,
  And be ye glad of heart,
For Calvary and Easter Day,
Earth's saddest day and gladdest day,
  Were just three days apart!

SUSAN COOLIDGE

God expects from men that their Easter devotions would in some measure come up to their Easter dress.

ROBERT SOUTH

EMPHASES

A great scholar, in treating of the resurrection, points out the different features emphasized in the accounts of the four evangelists. Matthew dwells chiefly on the majesty and glory of the resurrection. Mark insists upon it as a fact. Luke treats it as a spiritual necessity. John explains that it is a touchstone of character.

GEORGE H. MORRISON

PRAYER

With Thee, O Christ, we would arise to newness of life.

We beseech Thee to make all things new to us.

Let the old duties, the old work, the old burdens, the old friendships be transfigured as Thou dost touch them.

Let the resurrection joy lift us from loneliness and weakness and despair to strength and beauty and happiness.

We would fain live the risen life.

Help us by Thy call, by Thy message, by Thy beauty, by Thy goodness, to be Thy true children, looking to Thee and serving Thee, until at last we see Thee face to face.

FLOYD W. TOMKINS

The joyful news that He is risen does not change the contemporary world. Still before us lie work, discipline, sacrifice. But the fact of Easter gives us the spiritual power to do the work, accept the discipline, and make the sacrifice.

HENRY KNOX SHERRILL

AN EASTER CAROL

Tomb, thou shalt not hold Him longer;
Death is strong, but Life is stronger;
Stronger than the dark, the light;
Stronger than the wrong, the right;
Faith and Hope triumphant say,
Christ will rise on Easter Day.

PHILLIPS BROOKS

BEATITUDES OF THE RISEN LIFE

Blessed is the man whose heart today burns as he walks with Jesus by the way.

Blessed is the man who having not seen yet believes.

Blessed is the man who hears the voice of the Risen Lord saying, "Peace be unto you."

Blessed is the man who accepts the glorious Master, Jesus Christ, as his Lord and his God and worships Him.

Blessed is the man who thus lives the power of the endless life through fellowship with the Risen Lord.

Blessed is the man whose words and deeds are day by day and every day a witness to the living and loving Lord.

Blessed is the man who obeys the Risen Lord's last great command and commission, "Go ye into all the world and preach my gospel," for unto him shall be fulfilled the Lord's promise, "Lo, I am with you always, even unto the end."

OLIVER HUCKEL

And He departed from our sight that we might return to our heart, and there find Him. For He departed, and behold, He is here.

ST. AUGUSTINE

ACQUAINTANCE

Jesus Christ is actually more alive today than He was before His death. He influences more people, He is better understood, He is more inspiring and comforting. It is pathetic to hear people repining that they did not live to know Him in His physical lifetime, for it only means that they do not know that they have better opportunities to be acquainted with His whole life, and His purposes, and their significance for the world, than the most intimate of His disciples could possibly have had.

EDWARD SCRIBNER AMES

The resurrection of Jesus is precisely what one would expect from a universe that is morally solvent.

HAROLD COOKE PHILLIPS

NO MANGER FOR EASTER

He stirs—He moves—in the lifting gloom
He wakes, and searching through the tomb
Finds no one waiting at night's end;
Only Himself—no other friend.

Where are the heralding angels now?
Where the donkey and the cow
That warmed Him when the night was deep?
Where are the shepherds, the kindly sheep?
Where that star of Christmas skies?
Where the kingly and the wise?
Where are the righteous, those in sin?
And where is the keeper of the inn?

He folds the linen cloths away,
Then facing the sunrise side of day,
Steps into Easter, a lonely stranger
Longing for old friends round His manger.

RALPH W. SEAGER

EASTER MORNING

The stone is lifted from the tomb,
And Christ is risen from the gloom
In bursting bud, in leafing tree,
In singing bird and winging bee,
In grass with gleaming dew-gems set,
In pansy and in violet,
In each fair fragrant lilac spray
That gives its sweetness to the day—
Christ is now risen and new birth
With singing fills the joyful earth!

EDGAR DANIEL KRAMER

Easter is no time for argument.
Lilies don't argue; they bloom.
Springtime doesn't argue; it comes.
Music doesn't argue; it sings.
Beauty doesn't argue; it beckons and points.
Love doesn't argue; it outlives our griefs.

FREDERICK B. SPEAKMAN

He takes men out of time and makes them feel
eternity.

RALPH WALDO EMERSON

EASTER LIGHT

Because upon the first
  glad Easter day,
The stone that sealed His tomb
  was rolled away,
So through the deepening shadows
  of death's night,
Men see an open door—
  beyond it, light.

IDA NORTON MUNSON

ONLY ONE

In the long succession of historical personalities who rise up majestically like pillars of smoke, and then disappear in a higher stratum of air, leaving behind only the lustre of memory, there is one sole exception. There is One who can say, "I am with you alway."

KARL HEIM

SEQUENCE

Look at the sequence: risen from the dead, therefore alive for ever; therefore our contemporary; therefore able to confront us face to face.

JAMES S. STEWART

EASTER TIDINGS

In the Easter tidings many notes mingle: notes which strike the deepest chords in our human make-up, and answer to our highest aspirations and direst needs.

There is ineffable tenderness in the greeting of the risen Lord to the weeping woman who loved Him devotedly.

There is manly forthrightness in His restoration of the conscience-stricken Peter.

There is stimulating reasoning with the disconsolate two on the road to Emmaus.

There is irrefutable evidence for the wondering group in the upper room.

There is kindly yet stern rebuke for the willful doubts of Thomas.

There is the stirring challenge for all His followers to proclaim the glad tidings unto the ends of the earth.

HERBERT F. STEVENSON

RESURRECTION

The whole history of the Christian life is a series of resurrections.

Every time a man bethinks himself that he is not walking in the light, that he has been forgetting himself, and must repent;

that he has been asleep and must awake;

that he has been letting his garments trail, and must gird up the loins of his mind;

every time this takes place there is a resurrection in the world.

Yes, every time a man finds his heart is troubled, that he is not rejoicing in God, a resurrection must follow;

a resurrection out of the night of troubled thought into the gladness of the truth.

For the truth is, and ever was, and ever must be, gladness, however much the souls on which it shines may be obscured by the clouds of sorrow, troubled by fears, or shot through with the lightnings of pain.

GEORGE MACDONALD

And He was only thirty-three . . .
The year had come to spring—
And He hung dead upon a tree,
Robbed of its blossoming.
Sorrow of sorrows that Youth should die
On a dead tree 'neath an April sky.
And He was only thirty-three . . .
Anthems of joy be sung—
For, always, the Risen Christ will be
A God divinely young.
Glory of glories, a Tree, stripped bare,
Shed now Faith's blossoms everywhere.

VIOLET ALLEYN STOREY

PRAYER

O Thou living God, our Father, who by Thy life-giving Spirit didst raise our Lord Jesus from the dead and who by that same Spirit dost give life to all who put their trust in Thee, grant us, we beseech Thee, a new vision of Thyself. May we see Thee as Thou art, in Thy majesty, in Thy holiness, in Thy compassionate and understanding love, that seeing Thee we may desire Thee, and desiring Thee may surrender to Thee, and surrendering to Thee, body, mind, and spirit without reserve, may find our lives transformed by Thy Spirit into the likeness of Jesus Christ, Thy Son, our Lord.

WILLIAM ADAMS BROWN

ETERNAL FACT

Easter not only happened; it happens. It is not only a past event to be celebrated with new hats and hallelujahs; it is an eternally present fact to be appropriated by faith and obedience.

LEONARD GRIFFITH

May the glad dawn
Of Easter morn
Bring joy to thee.

May the calm eve
Of Easter leave
A peace divine with thee.

May Easter night
On thine heart write,
O Christ, I live for Thee.

Faith

Jesus said unto her, I am the resurrection, and the life: he that believeth in me, though he were dead, yet shall he live:

And whosoever liveth and believeth in me shall never die. Believest thou this?

She saith unto him, Yea, Lord: I believe that thou art the Christ, the Son of God, which should come into the world.   JOHN 11:25-27

FAITH

Faith is not merely praying
    Upon our knees at night:
Faith is not merely straying
    Through darkness into light:
Faith is not merely waiting
    For glory that may be—
Faith is the brave endeavor,
    The splendid enterprise,
The strength to serve, whatever
    Conditions may arise.

S. E. KISER

———

To have faith is to have wings.

JAMES M. BARRIE

———

IF I HAD THREE WISHES

I would not ask for health because unbroken health might rob me of experiences that come through sharing illness and suffering. My first wish would be for sympathy and understanding of others. My second wish would be for a sense of humor; and my third wish, a very firm one indeed, for the gift of faith, the Christian faith, because men and women get from such a faith strength to live, and, indeed, strength to die.

MALCOLM SARGENT

———

THE CHAIN

Faith is the subtle chain
which binds us to the Infinite; the voice
of a deep life within, that will remain
until we crowd it thence.

ELIZABETH OAKES SMITH

FAITH AND DOUBT

Doubt sees the obstacles,
    Faith sees the way;
Doubt sees the blackest night,
    Faith sees the day;
Doubt dreads to take a step,
    Faith soars on high;
Doubt questions, "Who believes?"
    Faith answers, "I!"

———

From BISHOP BLOUGRAM'S APOLOGY

Just when we are safest, there's a sunset-touch,
A fancy from a flower-bell, some one's death,
A chorus-ending from Euripides—
And that's enough for fifty hopes and fears
As old and new at once as nature's self,
To rap and knock and enter in our soul.

ROBERT BROWNING

———

There is no great future for any people whose faith has burned out.

RUFUS M. JONES

———

Wherever man has been left to develop as he would, he has always reacted to his environment in these three ways. In science, he has sought to understand, to master, and to control his environment for the improvement of his own life. In art, he has sought to harmonize, to beautify, and to enrich his life. In religion, he has sought to unify, to integrate, and to relate his life to certain abiding sources of motive and stimulus.

SOME FAITH AT ANY COST

No vision and you perish;
   No ideal, and you're lost;
Your heart must ever cherish
   Some faith at any cost.

Some hope, some dream to cling to,
   Some rainbow in the sky,
Some melody to sing to,
   Some service that is high.

               HARRIET DU AUTERMONT

OVERCOMING OBSTACLES

Faith that obstacles could be surmounted made men and women venture upon the seas, dare the wilderness, cross the rivers, the plains, the Rockies, and the High Sierras to open up America.

               FLORENCE E. ALLEN

Faith is an assurance inwardly prompted, springing from the irrepressible impulse to do, to fight, to triumph.

               GEORGE SANTAYANA

VERBS

Faith *sees* the best that glimmers through the
   worst,
She *feels* the sun is hid but for the night,
She *spies* the summer through the winter bud,
She *tastes* the fruit before the blossom falls,
She *hears* the lark within the songless egg,
She *finds* the fountain where they wailed
   "Mirage."

I have closed the door on doubt.
I will go by what light I can find,
And hold up my hands and reach them out
To the glimmer of God in the dark, and call,
"I am Thine. Though I grope and stumble and
   fall,
I serve, and Thy service is kind."

               IRENE PETTIT MC KEEHAN

The steps of faith fall on the seeming void and find the rock beneath.

               WALT WHITMAN

The only limit to our realization of tomorrow will be our doubts of today. Let us move forward with strong and active faith.

               FRANKLIN D. ROOSEVELT

FAITH AND SIGHT

So I go on, not knowing,
   —I would not, if I might—
I would rather walk in the dark with God
   Than go alone in the light;
I would rather walk with Him by faith
   Than walk alone by sight.

               MARY GARDNER BRAINARD

The faith that saves is the total response of the whole self to the will of God. It is the response of the mind in belief, the heart in trust, the will in conduct. It is to accept the fact that God goes all out for us, and then to be willing to go all out for God.

               JOHN A. REDHEAD

Fellowship

Where two or three are gathered together in my name, there am I in the midst of them.   MATTHEW 18:20

Behold, I stand at the door, and knock: if any man hear my voice, and open the door, I will come in to him, and will sup with him, and he with me.   REVELATION 3:20

Human understanding is possible only so long as channels of communication are kept open. Unless we can communicate with our neighbor we stand no chance of understanding him, or he us. Sustained goodwill keeps the door open—at least on our side.

GORDON LYNN FOSTER

People need other people as a performer needs
    an audience.
People need to know that other people are
    depending upon them, waiting for them,
    pulling with them.
People need people who believe in them, trust
    them, and expect much of them.

RICHARD L. EVANS

"What is the real good?"
    I asked in musing mood.
"Order," said the law court;
    "Knowledge," said the school;
"Truth," said the wise man;
    "Pleasure," said the fool;
"Love," said the maiden;
    "Beauty," said the page;
"Freedom," said the dreamer;
    "Home," said the sage;
"Fame," said the soldier;
    "Equity," the seer.
Spake my heart full sadly,
    "The answer is not here."
Then within my bosom
    Softly this I heard:
"Each heart holds the secret,
    Kindness is the word."

JOHN BOYLE O'REILLY

Make all, within your society, members of the crew and permit no passengers.

ELTON TRUEBLOOD

One person alone
is simply
no person at all.

RUFUS M. JONES

THE PASTURE

I'm going out to clean the pasture spring;
I'll only stop to rake the leaves away
(And wait to watch the water clear, I may):
I sha'n't be gone long.—You come too.

I'm going out to fetch the little calf
That's standing by the mother. It's so young
It totters when she licks it with her tongue.
I sha'n't be gone long.—You come too.

ROBERT FROST

ANGELS UNAWARE

Open the door of the heart; let in
    Sympathy sweet for stranger and kin.
It will make the halls of the heart so fair,
    That angels will enter unaware.

PROJECTION

As I look around me, I seem to find that the one thing which deepens life, which gives it resonance, which brings it great joy, is the putting of one's self outside one's self into another self or personality.

HARRY A. OVERSTREET

ONE PERSON

I believe in people. I feel, love, need, and respect people above all else, including the arts, natural scenery, organized piety, or nationalistic superstructures. One human figure on the slope of a mountain can make the whole mountain disappear for me. One person fighting for the truth can disqualify for me the platitudes of centuries. And one human being who meets with injustice can render invalid the entire system which has dispensed it.

LEONARD BERNSTEIN

From THE KINDLY NEIGHBOR

I have a kindly neighbor, one who stands
Beside my gate and chats with me awhile,
Gives me the glory of his radiant smile
And comes at times to help with willing hands.
No station high or rank this man commands;
He, too, must trudge, as I, the long day's mile;
And yet, devoid of pomp or gaudy style,
He has a worth exceeding stocks or lands.

To him I go when sorrow's at my door;
On him I lean when burdens come my way;
Together oft we talk our trials o'er,
And there is warmth in each good-night we
     say.
A kindly neighbor! Wars and strife shall end
When man has made the man next door his
     friend.

EDGAR A. GUEST

The people with whom we travel are much more important than the place to which we travel.

RONALD SELBY WRIGHT

As long as there are postmen, life will have zest!

OLIVER WENDELL HOLMES

The story of the ascent of Everest is one of teamwork. If there is a deeper and more lasting message behind our venture than the mere ephemeral sensation of a physical feat, I believe this to be the value of comradeship and the many virtues which combine to create it. Comradeship, regardless of race or creed, is forged among high mountains, through the difficulties and dangers to which they expose those who aspire to climb them, the need to combine their efforts to attain their goal, the thrills of a great adventure shared together.

JOHN HUNT

Only in recent times has it been practicable for men to extend their fellowship to all humanity.

POPE JOHN XXIII

All real democracy is an attempt, like that of a jolly hostess, to bring the shy people out.

GILBERT KEITH CHESTERTON

I thank Thee for my quiet home,
     'Mid cold and storm,
And that, beyond my need, is room
     For friend forlorn:
I thank Thee much for place to rest,
But more for shelter for my guest.

ROBERT DAVIS

Who practices hospitality entertains God himself.

Friendship

And Ruth said, Entreat me not to leave thee, or to return from following after thee: for whither thou goest, I will go; and where thou lodgest, I will lodge: thy people shall be my people, and thy God my God:

Where thou diest, will I die, and there will I be buried: the Lord do so to me, and more also, if aught but death part thee and me.

Ruth 1:16-17

The soul of Jonathan was knit with the soul of David, and Jonathan loved him as his own soul. I Samuel 18:1

DISCOVERY

Today a man discovered gold and fame;
Another flew the stormy seas;
Another saw an unnamed world aflame;
One found the germ of a disease.
But what high fates my paths attend:
For I—today I found a friend.

HELEN BAKER PARKER

A friend is a present you give yourself.

ROBERT LOUIS STEVENSON

TRUE FRIENDSHIP

To have a friend is to have one of the sweetest
gifts that life can bring; to be a friend is to
have a solemn and tender education of soul
from day to day.
A friend gives us confidence for life.
A friend makes us outdo ourselves.
A friend remembers us when we have forgotten ourselves or neglected ourselves; he
takes loving heed of our health, our work,
our aims, our plans.
A friend may praise us, and we are not em-
barrassed; he may rebuke us, and we are
not angered. If he be silent, we understand.
It takes a great soul to be a true friend—a large,
catholic, steadfast, and loving spirit. One
must forgive much, forget much, forbear
much.
It costs to be a friend or to have a friend. There
is nothing else in life except motherhood
that costs so much. It not only costs time,
affection, patience, love, but sometimes a
man must even lay down his life for his
friends. There is no true friendship without self-abnegation, self-sacrifice.

ANNA R. BROWN LINDSAY

RECOGNITION

In the progress of personality, first comes a
declaration of independence, then a recognition of interdependence.

HENRY VAN DYKE

Friendship cannot be permanent unless it becomes spiritual. There must be fellowship in
the deepest things of the soul, community in
the highest thoughts, sympathy with the best
endeavors.

HUGH BLACK

There are unrecognized heroes among our ordinary neighbors.

HAROLD W. BERNARD

Friendship is the positive and unalterable
choice of a person whom we have singled out
for qualities that we most admire.

ABEL BONNARD

A FRIEND TO MAN

I see from my house by the side of the road,
    By the side of the highway of life,
The men who press with the ardor of hope,
    The men who are faint with the strife.
But I turn not away from their smiles nor their
    tears,
    Both parts of an infinite plan—
Let me live in a house by the side of the road
    And be a friend to man.

SAM WALTER FOSS

ON FRIENDSHIP

And a youth said, Speak to us of Friendship.

And he answered, saying:

Your friend is your needs answered.

He is your field which you sow with love and reap with thanksgiving.

And he is your board and your fireside.

For you come to him with your hunger, and you seek him for peace.

When your friend speaks his mind you fear not the "nay" in your own mind, nor do you withhold the "ay."

And when he is silent your heart ceases not to listen to his heart;

For without words, in friendship, all thoughts, all desires, all expectations are born and shared, with joy that is unacclaimed.

When you part from your friend, you grieve not;

For that which you love most in him may be clearer in his absence, as the mountain to the climber is clearer from the plain.

And let there be no purpose in friendship save the deepening of the spirit.

For love that seeks aught but the disclosure of its own mystery is not love but a net cast forth; and only the unprofitable is caught.

And let your best be for your friend.

If he must know the ebb of your tide, let him know its flood also.

For what is your friend that you should seek him with hours to kill?

Seek him always with hours to live.

For it is his to fill your need, but not your emptiness.

And in the sweetness of friendship let there be laughter, and sharing of pleasures.

For in the dew of little things the heart finds its morning and is refreshed.

KAHLIL GIBRAN

NEW FRIENDS

Constantly look for a new friend, a truly first-class person, one who has the courage to criticize, to demand your best self, a person who has different interests and different beliefs from yours, a friend for whom you can render a constructive service. Devote energy toward making such friends. Retain them, never let them go, and continue making new friends until you die.

WILLIAM TERHUNE

CHOICE OF FRIENDS

Friends should be chosen by a higher principle of selection than any worldly one. They should be chosen for character, for goodness, for truth and trustworthiness, because they have sympathy with us in our best thoughts and holiest aspirations, because they have community of mind in the things of the soul.

HUGH BLACK

We do not make friends as we make houses, but discover them as we do the arbutus, under the leaves of our lives, concealed in our experience.

WILLIAM RADER

DIVERSITY

It is possible for two people who have wide differences of preference and opinion, of habits, of teaching, of training, of background and belief to enjoy the company of each other in many ways. Indeed, a diversity of friendships is one of life's real enrichments. To learn of the goodness of those who are unlike—their worth, their sincerity, their good hearts, their good minds, their good company—is rich and rewarding. It is wonderful to have a wide range of choice friends who can be counted on, friends who can be enjoyed and loved and trusted. Such is the meaning of friendship.

RICHARD L. EVANS

The friend is the person whom one is in need of and by whom one is needed.

ARTHUR CHRISTOPHER BENSON

GENTLE HANDS

A friend is one to whom one may pour out all the contents of one's heart, chaff and grain together, knowing that the gentlest of hands will take and sift it, keep what is worth keeping, and with a breath of kindness, blow the rest away.

In the hour of distress and misery the eye of every mortal turns to friendship. In the hour of gladness and conviviality, what is our want? It is friendship. When the heart overflows with gratitude or with any other sweet and sacred sentiment, what is the word to which it would give utterance? A friend.

WALTER SAVAGE LANDOR

THE BEST TREASURE

There are veins in the hills where jewels hide,
　And gold lies buried deep;
　　There are harbor-towns where the great
　　　ships ride,
　And fame and fortune sleep;
But land and sea though we tireless rove,
And follow each trail to the end,
　Whatever the wealth of our treasure-trove,
The best we shall find is a friend.

JOHN J. MOMENT

It brings comfort to have companions in whatever happens.

ST. JOHN CHRYSOSTOM

THE STRANGER

When you go walking down a street
No matter whom you chance to meet,
No matter if he's tall or slim,
No matter if he's Joe or Jim,
No matter if he's rich or poor,
No matter if he thinks the cure
To certain problems of the day
Is not the cure that you would say,
No matter what his race may be,
Remember only this, that he
Who is to you a stranger yet,
Is just a friend you've never met.

THE CURTAIN

It is a noble and great thing to cover the blemishes and excuse the failings of a friend;
to draw a curtain before his weaknesses and to display his perfections;
to bury his shortcomings in silence but to proclaim his virtues on the housetop.

ROBERT SOUTH

MY FRIENDS

My friends are little lamps to me,
 Their radiance warms and cheers my ways,
And all the pathway dark and lone
 Is brightened by their rays.

I try to keep them bright by faith,
 And never let them dim with doubt;
For every time I lose a friend
 A little lamp goes out.

ELIZABETH WHITTEMORE

FRUIT OF FRIENDSHIP

The whole fruit of friendship is in the love itself, for it is not the advantage, procured
through a friend, but his love itself that gives
delight.

MARCUS TULLIUS CICERO

BECAUSE OF A FRIEND

Life is a sweeter, stronger, fuller, more gracious
thing for the friend's existence, whether he be
near or far. If the friend is close at hand, that
is best; but if he is far away he is still there to
think of, to wonder about, to hear from, to
write to, to share life and experience with, to
serve, to honor, to admire, to love.

ARTHUR CHRISTOPHER BENSON

Those who best knew Sir Walter Scott used to
say of him, "He spoke to every man he met as
if he were a blood relative."

CREED OF A GOOD NEIGHBOR

I believe that good will is the divinest activity
of the spirit of man, the wisest method, the
secret of co-operative living, the most
powerful force in the realm of human affairs.

I believe in the sacred sovereignty of my neighbor over his life. Therefore, I will not trespass on his domain or seek domination over
his ideas or conduct in any way.

I believe in the good will of my neighbor. I
believe that he is trying, according to his
lights, as I am trying according to mine, to
do what is right and good, even when we do
not agree.

I believe that I see some truth which my neighbor may not see, and to which I must be
true. I believe equally that my neighbor sees
some truth which I may not see. So I must
be open-minded but sympathetic, because
I want to know his truth too.

I believe that I have more defects in manner,
speech, disposition, and temperament than
I can detect or am willing to admit. Therefore, it ill becomes me to be too sharp a
critic of my fellows.

I believe that humor is one of the major gifts of
God. I hope for my sake that my neighbor
possesses it. I pray for his sake that I may
have enough of it to laugh at myself.

I believe that the happiness and success of my
neighbor are as important as my own.
Therefore, I will seek in behalf of others the
same things that I seek and ask for myself.

I believe in the Eternal Good Will; that there
is a Spirit in this universe which prompts,
inspires, and sustains men who make life
an adventure in brotherhood; and I trust
that Spirit.

JOSEPH FORT NEWTON

God

The heavens declare the glory of God; and the firmament sheweth his handiwork.

Day unto day uttereth speech, and night unto night sheweth knowledge. There is no speech nor language, where their voice is not heard.

Their line is gone out through all the earth, and their words to the end of the world. In them hath he set a tabernacle for the sun,

Which is as a bridegroom coming out of his chamber, and rejoiceth as a strong man to run a race.

His going forth is from the end of the heaven, and his circuit unto the ends of it: and there is nothing hid from the heat thereof.   PSALM 19:1-6

MIRACLE

We muse on miracles who look
    But lightly on a rose!
Who gives it fragrance or the glint
    Of glory that it shows?

Who holds it here between the sky
    And earth's rain-softened sod?
The miracle of one pale rose
    Is proof enough of God!

EDITH DALEY

VISIBLE

To us also, through every star, through every
blade of grass, is not God made visible if we
will open our minds and eyes?

THOMAS CARLYLE

GOD OUR FRIEND

In this vast universe
There is but one supreme truth—
That God is our friend!
By that truth meaning is given
To the remote stars, the numberless centuries,
The long and heroic struggle of mankind . . .
O my Soul, dare to trust this truth!
Dare to rest in God's kindly arms,
Dare to look confidently into His face,
Then launch thyself into life unafraid!
Knowing thou art within thy Father's house,
That thou art surrounded by His love,
Thou wilt become master of fear,
Lord of life, conqueror even of death!

JOSHUA LOTH LIEBMAN

GOD IS AT THE ANVIL

God is at the anvil, beating out the sun;
    Where the molten metal spills,
    At His forge among the hills
He has hammered out the glory of a day
        that's done.

God is at the anvil, welding golden bars;
    In the scarlet-streaming flame
    He is fashioning a frame
For the shimmering silver beauty of the even-
    ing stars.

LEW SARETT

I come in the little things,
    Saith the Lord:
My starry wings
I do forsake,
Love's highway of humility to take:
Meekly I fit My stature to your need.

EVELYN UNDERHILL

God keeps up a continual conversation with
every creature.

PAUL CLAUDEL

PRAYER

O Light of the world, who daily enterest our
conscious life on the wings of the dawn,
illumine our minds this day with wisdom and
our hearts with joy, that, being defended by
the brightness of Thy countenance from the
darkness of sin, we may radiate Thy gracious
influence among our fellow men to the puri-
fication of human life and the glory of Thy
great name.

CHARLES H. BRENT

MYSTERY

I have observed the power of the watermelon seed. It has the power of drawing from the ground and through itself 200,000 times its weight. When you can tell me how it takes this material and out of it colors an outside surface beyond the imitation of art, and then forms inside of it a white rind and within that again a red heart, thickly inlaid with black seeds, each one of which in turn is capable of drawing through itself 200,000 times its weight— when you can explain to me the mystery of a watermelon, you can ask me to explain the mystery of God.

WILLIAM JENNINGS BRYAN

Human things must be known in order to be loved, but divine things must be loved in order to be known.

BLAISE PASCAL

CROWDED KINDNESS

Seek to cultivate a buoyant, joyous sense of the crowded kindnesses of God in your daily life.

ALEXANDER MACLAREN

From EACH IN HIS OWN TONGUE

Like tides on a crescent sea-beach,
When the moon is new and thin,
Into our hearts high yearnings
Come welling and surging in;
Come from the mystic ocean
Whose rim no foot has trod—
Some of us call it Longing
And others call it God.

WILLIAM HERBERT CARRUTH

DIRECTION

Religion is the direction of the mind toward
what is conceived to be the highest truth,
of the will toward the highest duty, the chief
thing to be done,
and of the heart toward the highest beauty,
the most complete harmony and satisfaction.

DAWN

The immortal spirit hath no bars
To circumscribe its dwelling place;
My soul hath pastured with the stars
Upon the meadow lands of space.

My mind and ears at times have caught
From realms beyond our mortal reach,
The utterance of eternal thought
Of which all nature is the speech.

And high above the seas and lands
On peaks just tipped with morning light,
My dauntless spirit mutely stands
With eagle wings outspread for flight.

FREDERICK GEORGE SCOTT

From THE BREWING OF SOMA

Drop Thy still dews of quietness,
Till all our strivings cease;
Take from our souls the strain and stress,
And let our ordered lives confess
The beauty of Thy peace.

JOHN GREENLEAF WHITTIER

The best conception hitherto gained for the elevation of humanity is the idea of God.

FELIX ADLER

CIRCUMFERENCE

A person who wishes to begin a good life should be like a man who draws a circle. Let him get the center in the right place and keep it so and the circumference will be good. Let a man first learn to fix his heart on God and then his good deeds will have virtue, but if a man's heart is unsteady, even the great things he does will be of small advantage.

JOHANNES ECKHART

The most important thought that ever occupied my mind is that of my individual responsibility to God.

DANIEL WEBSTER

Man without God
is a seed
upon the wind.

PROOFS

I never hear the loud solitary whistle of the curlew in a summer noon, or the wild mixing cadence of a troop of gray plover in an autumnal morning, without feeling an elevation of soul. Do these workings argue something within us above the trodden clod? I own myself partial to such proofs of awful and important realities: a God that made all things, man's immaterial and immortal nature.

ROBERT BURNS

Be sure that on Life's common street
Are crossways, where God's chariots meet.

FRANK W. GUNSAULUS

PRAYER

Lord, the newness of this day
Calls me to an untried way:
Let me gladly take the road,
Give me strength to bear my load,
Thou my guide and helper be—
I will travel through with Thee.

HENRY VAN DYKE

It is too small and unsatisfactory,
whatsoever Thou bestowest on me,
apart from Thyself.

THOMAS A KEMPIS

I find the doing of the will of God leaves me no time for disputing about His plans.

GEORGE MACDONALD

God will not change. The restless years may
bring
Sunlight and shadow, the glories of the spring,
And silent gloom of sunless winter hours;
Joy mixed with grief, sharp thorns with fra-
grant flowers.
Earth lights may shine awhile, and then grow
dim,
But God is true—there is no change in Him.

THE WATCHMAN-EXAMINER

Perhaps history is a thing that would stop happening if God held His breath.

HERBERT BUTTERFIELD

That man is a saint for whom the attraction of God is supreme over all other attractions.

GOD'S WONDERS

If all the trees on earth were pens and if there were seven oceans full of ink, they could not suffice to describe the wonders of the Almighty.

THE KORAN

It is difficult to make a man miserable while he feels he is worthy of himself and claims kindred to the great God who made him.

ABRAHAM LINCOLN

HIGHEST DESTINY

We and God must have business one with the other and in opening our hearts to Him our highest destiny is fulfilled.

WILLIAM JAMES

BE STILL AND KNOW THAT I AM GOD

All beauty whispers to the listening heart:
   Love does not shout, and ecstasy is still;
The friendly silence of infinity
   Forever broods above a lifted hill.

A flower leaps to life—the quiet clod
   Has uttered music; noiselessly a tree
Flings forth green song; the snow breathes
   soundless prayers;
   And stars are vocal with tranquility!

MARY HALLET

God who gives the bird its anguish maketh
   nothing manifest,
But upon our lifted forehead pours the boon of
   endless quest.

WILLIAM VAUGHN MOODY

I have felt
A presence that disturbs me with the joy
Of elevated thoughts; a sense sublime
Of something far more deeply interfused,
Whose dwelling is the light of setting suns,
And the round ocean, and the living air,
And the blue sky, and in the mind of man:
A motion and a spirit, that impels
All thinking things, all objects of all thought,
And rolls through all things.

WILLIAM WORDSWORTH

From STRANGE HOLINESS

There is strange holiness around
Our common days on common ground.

I have heard it in the birds
Whose voices reach above all words

Going upward, bars on bars,
Until they sound as high as stars.

I have seen it in the snake,
A flowing jewel in the brake.

It has sparkled in my eyes
In luminous breath of fireflies.

I have come upon its track
Where trilliums curled their petals back.

ROBERT P. TRISTRAM COFFIN

Growth

Blessed is the man that walketh not in the counsel of the ungodly, nor standeth in the way of sinners, nor sitteth in the seat of the scornful.

But his delight is in the law of the Lord; and in his law doth he meditate day and night.

And he shall be like a tree planted by the rivers of water, that bringeth forth his fruit in his season; his leaf also shall not wither; and whatsoever he doeth shall prosper. PSALM 1:1-3

They returned into Galilee, to their own city Nazareth.

And the child grew, and waxed strong in spirit, filled with wisdom: and the grace of God was upon him. LUKE 2:39-40

How does the soul grow? Not all in a minute;
Now it may lose ground, and now it may win
    it;
Now it resolves, and again the will faileth;
Now it rejoiceth, and now it bewaileth;
Now its hopes fructify, and then they are
    blighted;
Now it walks sullenly, now gropes benighted;
Fed by discouragements, taught by disaster;
So it goes forward, now slower, now faster,
Till all the pain is past, and failure made whole,
It is full grown, and the Lord rules the soul.

                SUSAN COOLIDGE

The unexamined life is not worth living.

                SOCRATES

The urge of growth is the creative urge, the creative power in the universe. It lures and fires us in the people we love. It lights enthusiasm for an adventure, for a college, for a business, for a child, for a garden, for a home or a family, for the majesty of a forest after sunset. In such moments we feel more alive, more genuinely ourselves than usual. The fire within us is fed by the life around us and we get into the current of that life. In such moments we grow in sympathy, in self-mastery, in honesty, or in sensitiveness to beauty.

                RICHARD C. CABOT

INSCRIPTION
You yourself must set flame to the torches which you have brought.

The strongest principle of growth lies in human choice.

                GEORGE ELIOT

THE PRAYER OF THE QUEST
Take us on the Quest of Beauty,
    Poet Seer of Galilee,
Making all our dreams creative,
    Through their fellowship with Thee.

Take us on the Quest of Knowledge,
    Clearest Thinker man has known!
Make our minds sincere and patient,
    Satisfied by Truth alone.

Take us on the Quest of Service,
    Kingly Servant of man's needs,
Let us work with Thee for others,
    Anywhere Thy purpose leads.

All along our Quest's far pathway,
    Christ our Leader and our guide,
Make us conscious of Thy presence,
    Walking always at our side.

                ELEANOR B. STOCK

PURPOSE
I do not know what we are here for upon this wonderful and beautiful earth, this incalculably interesting earth, unless it is to crowd into a few short years every possible fine experience and adventure; unless it is to live our lives to the uttermost; unless it is to seize upon every fresh impression, develop every latent capacity; unless it is to grow as much as ever we have it in our power to grow.

                DAVID GRAYSON

Blessed are all bulbs and seeds, for they are
  promise of a spring to come,
for they are symbols of a world to be,
a promise of immortality,
of life out of death and hope within despair,
of whiter dawns on other days,
of harvests, beautiful and brown,
of plenty and of prophecy.

WILLIAM L. STIDGER

PER ASPERA

Thank God, a man can grow!
He is not bound
With earthward gaze to creep along the
  ground:
Though his beginnings be but poor and low,
Thank God, a man can grow!
The fire upon his altars may burn dim,
The torch he lighted may in darkness fail,
And nothing to rekindle it avail—
Yet high beyond his dull horizon's rim,
Arcturus and the Pleiades beckon him.

FLORENCE EARLE COATES

REQUIREMENT

Nature does not require that we be perfect; it
requires only that we grow, and we can do this
as well from a mistake as from a success.

ROLLO MAY

A child may be as new to the world as snow-
drops in January, and yet already have a good
and keen and deep understanding, a full mind
and a hospitable heart. He may be able to think
hard, imagine richly, face trouble, take good
care of himself and of others, keep well, and
live abundantly

WALTER DE LA MARE

LIVING TRUTH

I would rather plant a single acorn that will
make an oak of a century and a forest of a
thousand years than sow a thousand morning
glories that give joy for a day and are gone
tomorrow. For the same reason, I would rather
plant one living truth in the heart of a child
that will multiply through the ages than scatter
a thousand brilliant conceits before a great
audience that will flash like sparks for an instant and like sparks disappear forever.

EDWARD LEIGH PELL

From ANOTHER LINCOLN

When Spring comes and the evening robin
  calls,
Ten million little boys in overalls,
Ten million small Americans in blue
Run home with bare toes through the dust and
  dew
To split up wood and put their tangled heads
Into books before they mount their beds;
They lie upon their bellies, and they plan
The things that turn a boy into a man.
And there may be another Lincoln there
Under the freckles and the tousled hair.

ROBERT P. TRISTRAM COFFIN

PROVERB

A tree that it takes both arms to encircle grew
from a tiny rootlet. A many-storied pagoda is
built by placing one brick upon another brick.
A journey of three thousand miles is begun
by a single step.

LAO-TZU

QUESTIONING

Humble questioning is the recognition that one does not know it all;

sincere questioning is genuine hospitality to another's viewpoint;

brave questioning means a willingness to be disturbed mentally, morally, and spiritually;

intelligent questioning witnesses to a conviction that only in another's answers may lie salvation from absurdity.

ALBERT EDWARD DAY

———

I ask not for a larger garden, but for finer seeds.

RUSSELL H. CONWELL

———

The potential of a child is the most intriguing thing in all creation.

RAY LYMAN WILBUR

———

From THE CHAMBERED NAUTILUS

Built thee more stately mansions, O my soul,
　As the swift seasons roll!
　Leave thy low-vaulted past!
Let each new temple, nobler than the last,
Shut thee from heaven with a dome more vast,
　Till thou at length art free,
Leaving thine outgrown shell by life's unrest-
　　ing sea!

OLIVER WENDELL HOLMES

———

The only new thing that ever enters into this world is a human personality.

ERNEST F. SCOTT

THEIR BOYHOOD WAS MADE IN AMERICA

A man called Mark Twain put them in a book, but they wouldn't stay there. You can't keep boys like Tom Sawyer and Huck Finn cooped up in a book.

They came busting out of the pages, barefooted and dirty, and they lit out for the free and open spaces, and they've been romping around there ever since.

One day you met them, and Tom let you whitewash his fence, and Huck let you touch his dead cat. And suddenly you knew you were home.

You threw away your shoes. You cut yourself a fishing pole. You lay on your belly in the soft moss at the river bank. You played hookey, you smoked cornsilk, you got sick and you learned better. You were trying out freedom, getting the taste and heft of it, learning to handle it. You were an American growing up.

You learned a lot from Tom and Huck. They showed you how to make lost marbles come back, and how to cure warts with rainwater from a hollow stump. You learned what a hoot owl is saying, and what the wind wants to tell you when it hollers in the trees at night.

Some of these you forgot later, but they taught you one thing you'll never forget, and it's this:

There is a special quality to being young in America. There is a special air of freedom, a special kind of hopefulness, a deep-down faith that life will turn out good. Every man who remembers how it felt will do all he can to keep that faith alive for those who are young today.

LOUIS REDMOND

NEVER TOO OLD

The larger and the richer triumphs begin with
   graying hair.
Handel wrote *The Messiah* when fifty-six, and
   Bach *The Saint Matthew Passion* at forty-
   four.
Haydn's best works came after fifty, and his
   Creation was done at sixty-seven.
Beethoven improved with every passing year;
   his most wonderful melodies came between
   forty-five and fifty-seven.
Wagner's *Tristan and Isolde* came at forty-six
   and *Parsifal* at sixty-nine.
In painting, Leonardo did Mona Lisa at fifty-
   four, while Rembrandt's five or six greatest
   canvases were conjured after fifty.
Frans Hals did some of his loveliest things after
   seventy, while Michelangelo's most tremendous conceptions were projected into paint
   between his fifty-ninth and eighty-ninth
   years.

WALTER B. PITKIN

What is the present, after all, but a growth out
of the past?

WALT WHITMAN

TO MY LITTLE SON

In your face I sometimes see
Shadowings of the man to be,
And eager, dream of what my son
Will be in twenty years and one.

But when you are to manhood grown,
And all your manhood ways are known,
Then shall I, wistful, try to trace
The child you once were in your face?

JULIA JOHNSON DAVIS

TO A CHILD

The greatest poem ever known
Is one all poets have outgrown:
The poetry, innate, untold,
Of being only four years old.

CHRISTOPHER MORLEY

GUARANTEE

A generation of children who have been well
   loved,
who are wholesomely self-confident,
who have disciplined their instinctive drives
   and harmonized self-interest with enjoy-
   able give-and-take with others,
who can think critically and objectively,
who have become accustomed to making decisions while adapting to change, and whose
   personalities are well integrated and mature,
are the best guarantee that problems of human
   relationships can and will be worked out.

THOMAS A. C. RENNIE *and* **LUTHER E. WOODWARD**

FORECAST

Unless a tree has borne blossoms
in spring you will vainly look
for fruit on it in autumn.

AUGUST W. HARE

THE CROSS ROADS

Oft as we jog along life's winding way,
Occasion comes for every man to say—
"This road?—or That?" and as he chooses
   then,
So shall his journey end in Night or Day.

JOHN OXENHAM

Heaven

In my Father's house are many mansions: if it were not so, I would have told you. I go to prepare a place for you.

And if I go and prepare a place for you, I will come again, and receive you unto myself; that where I am, there ye may be also.

And whither I go ye know, and the way ye know.   JOHN 14:2-4

HEAVEN

Heaven is
The place where
Happiness is
Everywhere.

Animals
And birds sing
As does
Everything.

To every stone,
"How-do-you-do?"
Stone answers back,
"Well! And you?"

LANGSTON HUGHES

ANTICIPATION

Always I have stood in the bow looking forward with hopeful anticipation to the life before me. When the time comes for my embarkation, and the ropes are cast off and I put out to sea, I think I shall still be standing in the bow, and still looking forward with eager curiosity and glad hopefulness to the new world to which the unknown voyage will bring me.

LYMAN ABBOTT

From THE ETERNAL GOODNESS

I know not where His islands lift
  Their fronded palms in air;
I only know I cannot drift
  Beyond His love and care.

JOHN GREENLEAF WHITTIER

THE MYSTERY

He came and took me by the hand
  Up to a red rose-tree;
He kept His meaning to Himself,
  But gave a rose to me.

I did not pray Him to lay bare
  The mystery to me;
Enough the rose was Heaven to smell,
  And His own face to see.

RALPH HODGSON

TWO WORLDS

That we should survive death is not to me incredible. The thing that is incredible is life itself.

Why should there be any life at all? Why should this world of stars have ever come into existence? Why should you be here and why I here? Why should we be here in this sun-illumined universe? Why should there be green earth under our feet? How did all this happen?

This wonder that we know, this is the incredible thing. What power projected it all into existence? This challenges my faith, excites my astonishment, lifts me to the ineffable.

Some Power has called us here out of the unknown. We did not come here of our own wills. Some Higher Power has evolved it all. And the Power that has caused this revelation of wonder and mystery can easily have prepared for us another surprise beyond the shadows of death. I believe that this stupendous Power we call God has created a world beyond this world, a world of spirit for the spirit of man.

EDWIN MARKHAM

It is only from the light which streams constantly from heaven that a tree can derive the energy to strike its roots deep into the soil. The tree is in fact rooted in the sky.

SIMONE WEIL

From THE KEY

The Cross of Calvary
Was verily the Key
By which our Brother Christ
Unlocked the Door
Of Immortality
To you and me;
And, passing through Himself before,
He set it wide
For evermore,
That we, by His grace justified,
And by His great love fortified,
Might enter in all fearlessly,
And dwell for ever by His side.

JOHN OXENHAM

You never enjoy the world aright till the sea itself floweth in your veins, till you are clothed with heaven and crowned with stars.

THOMAS TRAHERNE

RADIANCE

The Christian faith sheds revealing light upon the mystery of the hereafter. It catches the overtones in the heart's cry of love, throws into high relief the glorious outlines dimly perceived by intuition and reason, and fills the canvas of human life with the radiance of Easter glory.

CARL A. GLOVER

CROSSING THE BAR

Sunset and evening star,
    And one clear call for me!
And may there be no moaning of the bar,
    When I put out to sea,

But such a tide as moving seems asleep,
    Too full for sound and foam,
When that which drew from out the boundless
        deep
    Turns again home.

Twilight and evening bell,
    And after that the dark!
And may there be no sadness of farewell,
    When I embark;

For tho' from out our bourne of Time and
        Place
    The flood may bear me far,
I hope to see my Pilot face to face
    When I have crost the bar.

ALFRED TENNYSON

As much of heaven is visible as we have eyes to see.

WILLIAM WINTER

UNDERSTANDING

I did not know, till 'neath the rod
I passed, how sore I needed God;
In sorrow's night, lo! like a star
I saw His love shine from afar.

I did not know, until above
God called the idol of my love
Beyond the reach of yearning eyes,
How beautiful is Paradise.

SUSIE M. BEST

IN THE TIME OF TROUBLE

How hard for unaccustomed feet
Which only knew the meadow
Is this bleak road they now must tread
Through valleys dark with shadow.
Until they learn how sure Thy love
That girds each day, each morrow,
O Father, gently lead all hearts
That newly come to sorrow!

LESLIE SAVAGE CLARK

Christ's grave was the birthplace of an inde-
structible belief that death is vanquished and
there is life eternal.

ADOLPH HARNACK

From HARBOUR LIGHTS

Pilot, how far from home?—
    Not far, not far tonight,
    A flight of spray, a sea-bird's flight,
A flight of tossing foam,
    And then the lights of home!

Pilot, how far from home?—
    The great stars pass away
    Before Him as a flight of spray,
Moons as a flight of foam!
    I see the lights of home.

ALFRED NOYES

For resurrection living
    There is resurrection power,
And the praise and prayer of trusting
    May glorify each hour.
For common days are holy
    And year's an Easter-tide
To those who with the living Lord
    In living faith abide.

TEARS

When I consider Life and its few years—
A wisp of fog betwixt us and the sun;
A call to battle, and the battle done
Ere the last echo dies within our ears;
A rose choked in the grass; an hour of fears;
The gusts that past a darkening shore do beat,
The burst of music down an unlistening
    street,—
I wonder at the idleness of tears.

Ye old, old dead, and ye of yesternight.
Chieftains, and bards, and keepers of the
    sheep,
By every cup of sorrow that you had,
Loose me from tears, and make me see aright
How each hath back what once he stayed to
    weep:
Homer his sight, David his little lad!

LIZETTE WOODWORTH REESE

SLEEP

If Christ had done nothing more for humanity
than give it the word *sleep* in place of *death*,
He would have been the greatest of bene-
factors.

He taught new truth about death, explaining that it is not what it seems.

It is to life what sleep is to the day.

Sleep rests and restores the body to a fuller
and fresher life.

Christ would not have called death sleep
merely because of its external likeness.

His thought struck deeper than that.

He meant that death does for us what sleep
does for the body: repairs, invigorates, and
repeats for us the morning of life.

T. T. MUNGER

ENCOUNTER WITH ETERNITY

Who keeps a rendezvous with stars,
Who sees across the night
The Pole Star's ageless constancy
Need dread no more the flight
Of time. Who marks the destined course
Orion nightly swings,
Undaunted, braves the darkening years—
Certain of deathless things.

LESLIE SAVAGE CLARK

THE RESURRECTION AND THE LIFE

Here on this earth we are gathered together in families. Our loved ones become inexpressibly precious to us. We live in intimate associations. One gets so close to mother and father, wife or husband, sons and daughters, that they literally become a part of one's life. Then comes a day when a strange change comes over one we love.

He is transformed before our very eyes. The light of life goes out of him. He cannot speak to us nor we to him. He is gone and we are left stunned and heartbroken. An emptiness and loneliness comes into our hearts. We broken-heartedly say, "That one whom I loved is dead." It is such a cold, hopeless thing to realize.

Then, out of the very depths of our despair, like the melody of music coming from a mighty organ, like the refreshing sound of rippling waters, comes that marvelous declaration of our Lord. "I am the resurrection, and the life: he that believeth in me, though he were dead, yet shall he live: and whosoever liveth and believeth in me shall never die."

Then we know! We *know* we have not lost our loved ones who have died. We have been separated, and so long as we live there will be an empty place left in our hearts. To some extent, the loneliness will always be there. But when we really know that one is not forever lost, it does take away the sorrow. There is a vast difference between precious memories, loneliness, the pain of separation, on the one hand, and a sorrow that ruins and blights our lives, on the other hand.

CHARLES L. ALLEN

INSCRIPTION

To live in hearts
We leave behind
Is not to die.

Some seek a heaven for rest,
And some an ample shore
For doing work they cannot do
While they are prisoned here.

Some seek a heaven of song,
And others fain would rise
From an articulate utterance
To silent ecstasies.

Some seek a home in heaven,
And some would pray to be
Alone with God, beyond the reach
Of other company.

But in God's perfect heaven
All aspirations meet,
Each separate longing is fulfilled,
Each separate soul complete.

EDWIN HATCH

REQUIEM

Under the wide and starry sky,
Dig the grave and let me lie.
Glad did I live and gladly die,
 And I laid me down with a will.

This be the verse you grave for me:
Here he lies where he longed to be;
Home is the sailor, home from the sea,
 And the hunter home from the hill.

ROBERT LOUIS STEVENSON

RECOGNITION

You shall know Him when He comes
Not by any din of drums,
Nor by vantage of His airs,
Nor by His crown,
Nor by His gown,
Nor by anything He wears;
He shall only well known be
By the holy harmony
That His coming makes in thee.

HOME

Think of stepping on shore and finding it
 Heaven!
Of taking hold of a hand and finding it God's!
Of breathing a new air and finding it celestial
 air!
Of feeling invigorated and finding it im-
 mortality!
Of passing from storm and stress to a perfect
 calm!
Of waking and finding it Home!

The secret is that you and I come equipped
with a built-in inclination to expect life to
have some kind of sequel beyond death.

FREDERICK B. SPEAKMAN

FOR SLEEP, OF DEATH

Cure me with quietness,
Bless me with peace;
Comfort my heaviness,
Stay me with ease.
Stillness in solitude
Send down like dew;
Mine armour of fortitude
Pierce and make new:
That when I rise again
I may shine bright
As the sky after rain,
Day after night.

RUTH PITTER

Eternal life is much more than eternal existence. It implies happiness, vigor, peace, and
all that makes life worth living. It is the divine
life which is implanted in us when we are
born of the Spirit and become children of
God. It begins in this life, but, being divine
and natural, it endures forever. It is life that
belongs to heaven, which inspires all heavenly
beings and makes heaven what it is.

FRANCIS N. PELOUBET

We are so foolish about death. We will not
 learn
How it is wages paid to those who earn,
How it is gift for which on earth we yearn
To be set free from bondage to the flesh;
How it is winning Heaven's eternal gain,
How it means freedom evermore from pain,
How it untangles every mortal mesh . . .
We forget that it means only life—
Life with all joy, peace, rest, and glory rife,
The victory won and ended all the strife.

W. C. DOANE

FROM DARKNESS TO LIGHT

Death is not death if it kills no part of us, save
that which hindered us from perfect life.

Death is not death if it raises us in a moment
from darkness into light, from weakness into strength, from sinfulness into holiness.

Death is not death if it brings us nearer to
Christ, who is the fount of life.

Death is not death if it perfects our faith by
sight and lets us behold Him in whom we
have believed.

Death is not death if it gives us to those whom
we have loved and lost, for whom we have
lived, for whom we long to live again.

Death is not death if it rids us of doubt and
fear, of chance and change, of space and
time, and all which space and time bring
forth and then destroy.

Death is not death, for Christ has conquered
Death for Himself and for those who trust
in Him.

CHARLES KINGSLEY

BEYOND THE HORIZON

When men go down to the sea in ships,
'Tis not to the sea they go;
Some isle or pole the mariners' goal,
And thither they sail through calm and gale,
When down to the sea they go.

When souls go down to the sea by ship,
And the dark ship's name is death,
Why mourn and wail at the vanishing sail?
Though outward bound, God's world is round,
And only a ship is Death.

When I go down to the sea by ship,
And Death unfurls her sail,
Weep not for me, for there will be
A living host on another coast
To beckon and cry, "All hail!"

ROBERT FREEMAN

Those are dead even for this life who hope for
no other.

JOHANN WOLFGANG VON GOETHE

CELESTIAL PATHS

Oh! Thou who taught my infant eye
To pierce the air and view the sky,
To see my God in earth and seas,
To hear Him in the vernal breeze,
To know Him midnight thoughts among,
O guide my soul and aid my song.
Spirit of Light, do Thou impart
Majestic truths and teach my heart:
How vain my powers, how weak my frame;
Teach me celestial paths untrod—
The ways of glory and of God.

GEORGE CRABBE

With silence only as their benediction,
    God's angels come
Where, in the shadow of a great affliction,
    The soul sits dumb.
Yet would I say what thy own heart approveth:
    Our Father's will,
Calling to Him the dear one whom He loveth,
    Is mercy still.
Not upon thee or thine the solemn angel
    Hath evil wrought;
Her funeral anthem is a glad evangel—
    The good die not.

JOHN GREENLEAF WHITTIER

Heritage

Thou visitest the earth, and waterest it: thou greatly enrichest it with the river of God.

Thou waterest the ridges thereof abundantly: thou settlest the furrows thereof: thou makest it soft with showers: thou blessest the springing thereof.

Thou crownest the year with thy goodness.

The pastures are clothed with flocks; the valleys also are covered over with corn; they shout for joy, they also sing.   PSALM 65:9-11, 13

AN OLD CHURCH

The walls which now
Are crumbling lime
Could not withstand
The urge of time.

The wood has rotted
On the doors;
Rain has ravished
Roof and floors. . . .

And yet because
Men worshipped here,
Something holy
And austere

Lingers on
And fills the air,
Like echoes
Of a quiet prayer.

HANNAH KAHN

From THE PSALM OF LIFE

Lives of great men all remind us
   We can make our lives sublime,
And, departing, leave behind us
   Footprints on the sands of time.

Footprints, that perhaps another,
   Sailing o'er life's solemn main,
A forlorn and shipwrecked brother,
   Seeing, shall take heart again.

HENRY WADSWORTH LONGFELLOW

CONTEMPORARIES

The great artists are all contemporaries.

LIONEL JOHNSON

THEIR MAPS

Each of us is in charge of an individual life
and must steer it by his own senses and by his
own ideas. But you and I are not the first
travelers over the road. Job, Plato, Jesus,
Paul, Augustine, Spinoza, Kant, Montaigne,
Mill, and Emerson have explored the ethical
difficulties that we must pass through. The
main features of the land, its mountains, deserts, canyons, rivers, and swamps are still on
the map. We shall do our own bit of explor-
ing, but we still can use their maps.

RICHARD C. CABOT

I desire no future
that will break
the ties of the past.

GEORGE ELIOT

What from your fathers' heritage is lent,
Earn it anew to really possess it.

JOHANN WOLFGANG VON GOETHE

CARGOES FROM THE PAST

The future is never quite a thing apart from
all that has gone before. We bring into the
present ingredients and cargoes from the past,
and these are with us as we take the unknown
road. All that we have learned, felt, and
thought, all our experience from birth to now;
all the love that nourished us at other times,
all the yearnings rooted in our spirits—all
these are with us as we move into the unknown
way.

HOWARD THURMAN

THE FAITH OF ADVENTURERS

The power which has moved adventurers is faith.

They have believed in something unseen, something that other men have not believed in, and they have set forth to seek it.

A new continent across the ocean, a new passage from sea to sea, a new land among the forests, a goal beyond sight and beyond knowledge, apprehended and realized by a heroic faith, has drawn them over stormy seas and inhospitable deserts.

They have believed and therefore adventured.

Nor has their faith been lacking, for the most part, in a spiritual element.

There is hardly one of them—not one, I think, among the very greatest of the world's explorers—who has not believed in God, and in his overruling Providence, and in his call to them to undertake their adventures.

It is beautiful to see how this religious element has entered into the exploration of the earth, and how faith has asserted itself in the most famous and glorious journeys of men.

We see Columbus planting the standard of the cross on the lonely beach of San Salvador; Balboa kneeling silent on the cliff from which he first caught sight of the Pacific; Livingstone praying in his tent in the heart of Africa.

From all the best and the bravest adventurers we hear the confession that they are the servants of a Divine Being, summoned and sent by Him to work for which they would give Him the glory.

HENRY VAN DYKE

The young, whether they know it or not, live on borrowed property.

RICHARD W. LIVINGSTONE

TREASURE ISLAND

If you'd move to a bygone measure,
  Or shape your heart to an ancient mould,
Maroons and schooners and buried treasure
  Wrought on a page of gold—

Then take the book in the dingy binding,
  Still the magic comes, bearded, great,
And swaggering files of sea-thieves winding
  Back, with their ruffling cut-throat gait,
Reclaim an hour when we first went finding
  Pieces of Eight—of Eight.

PATRICK REGINALD CHALMERS

Wisdom is to be gained only as we stand upon the shoulders of those who have gone before.

LEARNED HAND

In the inner loyalties of the spirit the modern reader treads on common ground with the thinkers of the past.

ELEANOR SHIPLEY DUCKETT

My father transmitted to me a sound heredity on his own side, and he gave me a good mother.

ALICE STONE BLACKWELL

There has been a calculated risk in every stage of American development. The nation was built by men who took risks: pioneers who were not afraid of the wilderness, brave men who were not afraid of failure, scientists who were not afraid of truth, thinkers who were not afraid of progress, dreamers who were not afraid of action.

BROOKS ATKINSON

Home

For this cause shall a man leave his father and mother, and cleave to his wife;

And they twain shall be one flesh: so then they are no more twain, but one flesh.

What therefore God hath joined together, let not man put asunder.

MARK 10:7-9

BEATITUDES FOR THE HOME

Blessed is the home where God is at home and where the spirit of Christ rules.

Blessed is the home where children are welcomed and given their rightful place.

Blessed is the home having a church home where father, mother, and children worship regularly together.

Blessed is the home where each puts the other's happiness first.

Blessed is the home where all show their love in ways that mean the most to those they love.

Blessed is the home where each seeks to bring out the best in the other and to show his own best self at all times.

Blessed is the home where all have learned to face their daily problems in a Christian spirit and to disagree without being disagreeable.

Blessed is the home where children grow up and grown-ups do not act like children.

Blessed is the home having the assurance of a heavenly home.

THEODORE F. ADAMS

My mother, who boasted of no degree,
   Was tutored in philosophy:
Five butter beans within a pod
   Were generosity from God;
A broom could sweep the shadows out;
   Churning put many a fear to rout;
A young pear tree in bridal veil
   Was beauty's triumph over the gale;
And every star that blinked on high
   Was proof that, body and breath put by,
No darkness was so vast, so deep,
   But that the Shepherd would find His sheep.

JOHN ROBERT QUINN

A HAPPY HOME

Among the most important privileges of parents is the making of a happy home—
a home where children want to be,
to which they will want to return:
not a place of perfection,
not a place of spotlessness,
but a place of pleasantness,
of helpfulness and hospitality,
of some reasonable order and of understanding,
of love and loyalty,
not marred by the tension of expecting the impossible,
nor strained by constant quarreling and contention;
a place where mealtime is not for scolding or for finding fault,
but for good memories of getting together.

RICHARD L. EVANS

The family is the only institution in our world where the Kingdom of God can actually begin.

ELTON TRUEBLOOD

The little child digs his well in the seashore sand, and the great Atlantic, miles deep, miles wide, is stirred all through and through to fill it for him.

PHILLIPS BROOKS

The cornerstone in Truth is laid,
The guardian walls of Honor made,
The roof of Faith is built above,
The fire upon the hearth is Love,
Though rains descend and loud winds call,
This happy home shall never fall.

JOHN OXENHAM

CONFESSION

I like to spread clean sheets on beds,
  I like to wield a broom,
I like to bring tranquility
  Of order to a room.

I like to straighten linen shelves,
  Set dresser drawers aright,
To hang crisp ruffled curtains and
  To keep the silver bright.

I like to set a batch of bread,
  Then watch it as it rises,
I like to plan and cook a meal
  Of savory surprises.

Let other women have careers—
  None of them arouse
One twinge of envy in my heart—
  I like keeping house.

ETHEL ROMIG FULLER

HOME VIRTUES

The first essential for a man's being a good citizen is his possession of the home virtues, based on recognition of the great underlying laws of religion and morality. No piled up wealth, no splendor of material growth, no brilliance of artistic development, will permanently avail any people unless its home life is healthy.

THEODORE ROOSEVELT

Happy homes
are built
of blocks
of patience.

HAROLD E. KOHN

CHARACTER OF A HAPPY HOME

  Economically sound
  Physically healthful
  Morally wholesome
  Mentally stimulating
  Spiritually inspiring
  Artistically satisfying
  Socially responsible
  Center of unselfish love.

TRUE PATHOS

To make a happy fireside clime
  For weans and wife,
That's the true pathos and sublime
  Of human life.

ROBERT BURNS

FATHERS

Fathers are for giving a name and a heritage to their children—clean and honorable.
Fathers are for long, hard work, mostly their own kind of work;
for not being home so much as mothers;
for seeming to be pretty busy—and for trying to give their children things that fathers never had.
Fathers are for talking with, for encouraging, for putting arms around;
for understanding mistakes, but not condoning them;
for disciplining when needed, then loving all the more;
for being strong and forceful, and for being tender and gentle.

RICHARD L. EVANS

FAMILY PLAY

Happy are the families that learn to play. The family needs to play together. In play people are brought to one attention and to one level. There can be indoor games and outdoor sports according to age and circumstance: hikes, picnics, bicycle trips, all kinds of travel. There can be informal conversation, listening to programs together, going to worthwhile movies, plays, or musical entertainments; for smaller children, imaginative games unlimited. The son who now beats me at chess still remembers the fascinating boat races we had with twigs on the Neponset River when he was three. Playing together, whether it be actual games or reading together for fun or going to entertainment together, gives real cohesiveness to family life. Anyone too busy for such play is too busy to be married. Too busy to live, one cannot hope to find or make religion real.

NELS F. S. FERRÉ

PRAYER

Our families in Thine arms enfold
As Thou didst keep Thy folk of old.

OLIVER WENDELL HOLMES

The family is a storehouse in which the world's finest treasures are kept. Yet the only gold you'll find is golden laughter. The only silver is in the hair of Dad and Mom. The family's only real diamond is on Mother's left hand. Yet can it sparkle like children's eyes at Christmas or shine half as bright as the candles on a birthday cake?

ALAN BECK

PRAYER OF A HOMEMAKER

I thank You Father for a home to keep
Where I, in simple unadorned attire,
May satisfy the heart's age-old desire
To daily bake and cleanse and dust and sweep.

I thank You Father for the love I reap
In fields of duty where I often tire,
But where, relaxed before contentment's fire,
I yield at night to gentle arms of sleep.

I thank You Father for Your presence here
In this, my home, my citadel on earth.

LYDIA O. JACKSON

From THE DEATH OF THE HIRED MAN
"Home is the place where, when you have to go there,
They have to take you in."
　　　　　"I should have called it
Something you somehow haven't to deserve."

ROBERT FROST

Perhaps, for most people, the best results of travel are that they return with a sense of grateful security to the familiar scene:
the monotonous current of life has been enlivened,
the old relationships have gained a new value,
the old talk is taken up with a comfortable zest;
the old rooms are the best, after all,
the homely language is better than the strange tongue;
it is a comfort to have done with cramming the trunk:
it is good to be at home.

ARTHUR CHRISTOPHER BENSON

111

A MOTHER'S PRAYER

Father in Heaven, make me wise,
So that my gaze may never meet
A question in my children's eyes;
God keep me always kind and sweet,

And patient, too, before their need;
Let each vexation know its place,
Let gentleness be all my creed,
Let laughter live upon my face!

A mother's day is very long,
There are so many things to do!
But never let me lose my song
Before the hardest day is through.

MARGARET E. SANGSTER

WHAT IS A HOME?

I pity him whose soul does not leap at the mere
utterance of the word home.
It is not the house, though that may have its
charms;
nor the fields streaked with your own foot-
paths;
nor the trees, though their shadow be to
you like that of a great rock in a weary
land;
nor yet is it the fireside;
nor the pictures which tell of loved ones;
nor the cherished books—
but more far than all these, it is the Presence.
The lares of your worship are there;
the altar of your confidence there;
the end of your worldly faith is there;
and adorning it all is the ecstasy of the conviction that there at least you are beloved;

that there you are understood;
that there your errors will meet ever with
gentlest forgiveness;
that there you may unburden your soul,
fearless of harsh, unsympathizing ears;
and that there you may be entirely and joy-
fully yourself.

DONALD GRANT MITCHELL

GOD'S CHILDREN

Although God loves the whole wide world
And blesses every part,
I think He has a special place
For children in His heart.

I think He cherishes their smiles,
Their eagerness and mirth,
And their appreciation of
The wonders of His earth.

I think He listens closely to
Whatever words they say;
I think He follows them to school
And watches them at play.

And when they go to bed at night,
He probably is there,
To see that they have happy dreams
Beneath their tousled hair.

All children in a special way
Belong to God above,
And I am sure He favors them
With everlasting love.

JAMES J. METCALFE

112

PRAYER

O God, who art our Father, take my human fatherhood and bless it with thy Spirit. Let me not fail this little son of mine. Help me to know what thou wouldst make of him, and use me to help and bless him. Make me loving and understanding, cheerful and patient and sensitive to all his needs, so that he may trust me enough to come close to me and let me come very close to him. Make me ashamed to demand of him what I do not demand of myself; but help me more and more to try to be the kind of man that he might pattern after. And this I ask in the name and by the grace of Christ.

WALTER RUSSELL BOWIE

The home should be to the children the most attractive place in the world, and the mother's presence should be the greatest attraction.

ELLEN G. WHITE

EVERYDAY MADONNA

When Father carved our Christmas bird
And asked us each what we preferred,
As sure as summer follows spring
Came Mother's, "Please, I'll take the wing."

We children never wondered why
She did not sometimes take a thigh,
Or choose a drumstick or a breast.
We thought she liked a wing the best.

She said it with such easy voice,
It seemed so certainly her choice . . .
I was a man before I knew
Why mothers do the things they do.

RICHARD ARMOUR

EN ROUTE

We have sailed seas of vastness and of wonder;
We have known ports of beauty, fame, and
    song;
We have seen distance cut the world asunder;
We have crossed deserts wide, traced highways
    long;
We have seen capitals of pride and glory,
Visited crowded street and lordly dome,
Looked upon scenes of oft-repeated story
With eager eyes. And now, let us go home.

Let us go home where kindly friends await us,
Home to good neighbors and to busy days,
Home to the common people who will rate us
By honest worth, in simple, human ways;
Let us go home where dooryard flowers are
    growing,
And song and laughter speak the heart's
    release,
Where days are like a sunny river's flowing,
And nights come down in quietness and peace.

CLARENCE EDWIN FLYNN

CHILDREN

They are the idols of hearts and households;
They are the angels of God in disguise.
His sunlight still sleeps in their tresses;
His glory still gleams in their eyes.
Those truants from home and heaven—
They have made me more manly and mild,
And I know how Jesus could liken
The Kingdom of God to a child.

THESE TIMES

113

WHAT IS HOME?

Home's not merely four square walls,
    Though with pictures hung and gilded;
Home is where Affection calls,
    Filled with shrines the Heart hath builded!
Home!—go watch the faithful dove,
    Sailing 'neath the heaven above us;
Home is where there's one to love!
    Home is where there's one to love us!

CHARLES SWAIN

MOTTO

Christ is the Head of this house,
The unseen Guest at every meal,
The silent Listener to every conversation.

Home that our feet may leave, but not our hearts.

THE MAIN AIMS

Happy is the family
    Whose members know what a home is for,
And keep the main aims in view;

Who give more thought to affection
    Than to the shelter that houses it;
And more attention to persons
    Than to the things amid which they live.

For a home is a shelter for love
    And a setting for joy and growth,
Rather than a place to be kept up.

It is a hallowed place,
    To which its members shall turn
With a lifting of the heart.

LELAND FOSTER WOOD

HEAVENLY ECONOMY

It is one thing to feel chained to the dishpan, and another to feel that we have an important part in making a house a home. We can't hoax ourselves into feeling jolly about dishwater, but when a morning comes that we feel ourselves singing over the sink and stacking the dishes with genuine indifference—or even with a kind of tenderness—then we know that we have stumbled upon the meaning of small tasks in the heavenly economy.

MARGUERITTE HARMON BRO

Home should be a place of mutual responsibility and respect, of encouragement and co-operation and counsel, of integrity, of willingness to work, of discipline when necessary, with the tempering quality of love added to it, with a sense of belonging, and with someone to talk to.

RICHARD L. EVANS

THE MOTHER IN THE HOUSE

For such as you, I do believe,
Spirits their softest carpets weave,
And spread them out with gracious hand
Wherever you walk, wherever you stand.

For such as you, of scent and dew
Spirits their rarest nectar brew,
And where you sit and where you sup
Pour beauty's elixir in your cup.

For all day long, like other folk,
You bear the burden, wear the yoke,
And yet when I look in your eyes at eve
You are lovelier than ever, I do believe.

HERMANN HAGEDORN

Hope

Now faith is the substance of things hoped for, the evidence of things not seen.

By faith Abraham, when he was called to go out into a place which he should after receive for an inheritance, obeyed; and he went out, not knowing whither he went.

For he looked for a city which hath foundations, whose builder and maker is God.   HEBREWS 11:1, 8, 10

HINT FROM GOD

A possibility is a hint from God. One must follow it. In every man there is latent the highest possibility.

SØREN KIERKEGAARD

THE LAST DEFILE

Make us Thy mountaineers:
We would not linger on the lower slope,
Fill us afresh with hope, O God of Hope,
That undefeated we may climb the hill
As seeing Him who is invisible.

AMY CARMICHAEL

One furnace melts all hearts—love;
One balm soothes all pain—patience;
One medicine cures all ills—time;
One light illumines all darkness—hope.

IVAN PANIN

From THE LAND OF BEYOND

Thank God! there is always a Land of Beyond
  For us who are true to the trail;
A vision to seek, a beckoning peak,
  A farness that never will fail;
A pride in our soul that mocks at a goal,
  A manhood that irks at a bond,
And try how we will, unattainable still,
  Behold it, our Land of Beyond!

ROBERT W. SERVICE

He who plants a tree plants a hope.

LUCY LARCOM

THE GOAL

Each life converges to some center
Expressed or still;
Exists in every human nature
A goal . . .

EMILY DICKINSON

TOMORROW

A way unknown, a book unread,
A tree with fruit unharvested,
A sea unsailed, a word unsaid,
A house with rooms untenanted,
A tale untold, a tear unshed,
A reel unrolled of colored thread,
A field untilled, a friend unfed,
A loaf unbaked of living bread,
A song unsung, a hill ahead,
A beauty spot unvisited,
A web unspun, a wing unspread,
A hope as yet unheralded,
A fight unfought, a fear unfled,
A conqueror with uncrowned head.

PRESENTIMENT

Presentiment of better things on earth
Sweeps in with every force that stirs our souls
To admiration, self-renouncing love,
Or thoughts, like light, that bind the world in
  one.

GEORGE ELIOT

Hope is wishing for a thing to come true; faith is believing that it will come true.

NORMAN VINCENT PEALE

WITNESS

From Novgorod to Cadiz, from Jerusalem to the Hebrides, steeples and spires raised themselves precariously into the sky because men cannot live without hope.

WILL DURANT

DREAM AND DREAMER

For man is a dreamer ever,
    He glimpses the hills afar,
And plans for the things out yonder
    Where all his tomorrows are;
And back of the sound of the hammer,
    And back of the hissing steam,
And back of the hand on the throttle
    Is ever a daring dream.

A WIFE'S TESTIMONY

I have never known a man who gave one a greater sense of security. That was because I never heard him say that there was a problem that he thought it was impossible for human beings to solve.

ELEANOR ROOSEVELT

From EXPOSTULATION AND REPLY

Think you mid all this mighty sum
    Of things forever speaking,
That nothing of itself will come,
    But we must still be seeking?

WILLIAM WORDSWORTH

HENRY HUDSON SPEAKS

The Northwest Passage?
Yes, I seek it still—
My great adventure and my guiding star!
For look ye, friends, our voyage is not done;
We hold by hope as long as life endures.
Somewhere among those floating fields of ice,
Somewhere along this westward widening
    bay,
Somewhere beneath this luminous northern
    night —
The channel opens to the Farthest East . . .
We'll keep the honor of a certain aim
Amid the peril of uncertain ways,
And sail ahead, and leave the rest to God.

HENRY VAN DYKE

What is to come in the future is not predictable from what has occurred in the past. The laws of nature are not immutable, in the sense that new laws shall not be exemplified as new conditions arise. There is nothing in legitimate science or scientific method that makes it unreasonable to hope for the appearance in the future of what has not been seen in the past. Nothing in science is incompatible with striving to realize ideals that have never yet been realized.

HERBERT SPENCER JENNINGS

Not for one single day
Can I discern my way,
    But this I surely know—
Who gives the day
Will show the way,
    So I securely go.

JOHN OXENHAM

Ideals

Whatsoever things are true, whatsoever things are honest, whatsoever things are just, whatsoever things are pure, whatsoever things are lovely, whatsoever things are of good report; if there be any virtue, and if there be any praise, think on these things. PHILIPPIANS 4:8

BEYOND THE HORIZON

Human nature loses its most precious quality when it is robbed of its sense of things beyond, unexplored and yet insistent.

ALFRED NORTH WHITEHEAD

A MIND ALIVE

Sometimes a person's mind is stretched by a new idea and never does go back to its old dimensions.

OLIVER WENDELL HOLMES

PRAYER

Dear heavenly Father,
Give me clean hands, clean words, and clean
    thoughts;
Help me to stand for the hard right
Against the easy wrong;
Save me from habits that harm;
Teach me to work as hard,
And play as fair in thy sight alone,
As if the whole world saw;
Forgive me when I am unkind,
And help me to forgive those who are unkind
    to me;
And keep me ready to help others.

WILLIAM DE WITT HYDE

SINGING HEART

Idealism never yet made a person unhappy, grave-faced, and portentously solemn. It inspires, exhilarates, and gives one a joyful countenance. The person who finds his life's work early, the true course to run, the right mark at which to aim, has a singing heart and a lighthearted step no matter what disasters may overtake him. And the worthier the goal to be won and the higher the purpose to be accomplished, the nobler the harmonies that pour through the soul.

HOLD FAST YOUR DREAMS

Hold fast your dreams!
Within your heart
Keep one, still, secret spot
Where dreams may go,
And sheltered so,
May thrive and grow—
Where doubt and fear are not.
O, keep a place apart,
Within your heart,
For little dreams to go!

LOUISE DRISCOLL

COME UP HIGHER

I saw the mountains stand
Silent, wonderful, and grand,
Looking across the land
When the golden light was falling
On distant dome and spire;
And I heard a low voice calling,
"Come up higher, come up higher,"
From the lowlands and the mire,
From the mists of earth's desire,
From the vain pursuit of pelf,
From the attitude of self:
"Come up higher, come up higher."

JAMES S. CLARK

PURPOSE

To have striven, to have made an effort, to have been true to certain ideals—this alone is worth the struggle. We are here to add what we can to, not to get what we can from, life.

WILLIAM OSLER

ASPIRATION

We aspire by setting up ideals and striving after them.

HARRY EMERSON FOSDICK

When speaks
a man of great thought,
he uses words
as a musician uses strings;
the greater his theme
the deeper he sighs
for an instrument
that is better.

OSWALD W. S. MCCALL

SOLITARY DREAMERS

The dreamers are the saviors of the world. As the visible world is sustained by the invisible, so men, through all their trials and sins and sordid vocations, are nourished by the beautiful visions of their solitary dreamers. Humanity cannot forget its dreamers; it cannot let their ideals fade and die; it lives in them; it knows them as the realities which it shall one day see and know.

JAMES ALLEN

WHAT THE HEART CHERISHES

No vision, and you perish;
No ideals, and you're lost;
The heart must ever cherish
Some faith at any cost—
Some dream, some hope to cling to,
Some rainbow in the sky;
Some melody to sing to,
Some service that is high.

AUDACIOUS YOUTH

Never tell a young person that something cannot be done. God may have been waiting for countless centuries for somebody ignorant enough of the impossibility to do that thing.

Conscience is the voice of our ideal self, our complete self, our real self, laying its call upon the will.

RUFUS M. JONES

AIM OF LIFE

Not perfection as a final goal, but the ever-enduring process of perfecting, maturing, refining, is the aim in living. The good man is the man who, no matter how morally unworthy he has been, is moving to become better. Such a conception makes one severe in judging himself and humane in judging others.

JOHN DEWEY

UNIVERSAL WISH

There is one great and universal wish of mankind expressed in all religions, in all art and philosophy, and in all human life: the wish to pass beyond himself as he now is.

BEATRICE HINKLE

ROYALTY

The king lays a sword on a man's shoulder and calls him a knight; but he was a knight before he was knighted or he would not have received the title. It was the heroic endurance, the death-defying courage, the skill and coolness with which he achieved his notable deeds that made him a knight. He was in himself royal and noble and the king said to all men, I see it, when he laid his sword on his shoulder.

PHILLIPS BROOKS

POWER OF IDEALS

The power of ideals is incalulable. We see no power in a drop of water. But let it get into a crack in the rock and be turned to ice, and it splits the rock; turned into steam, it drives the pistons of the most powerful engines. Something has happened to it which makes active and effective the power that is latent in it.

ALBERT SCHWEITZER

LIVING CENTER

To accomplish anything you need an interest, a motive, a center of your thought. You need a star to steer by, a cause, a creed, an idea, a passionate attachment.

M. MACNEILE NIXON

Our ideals are our better selves.

BRONSON ALCOTT

BEING THERE

I feel that the best thing in man or woman is being "there." Physical bravery, which is always inspiring, is surprisingly common; but the sure and steady quality of being "there" belongs to comparatively few. This is why we hear on every hand, "If you want a thing well done, do it yourself"; not because the man who wants it done is best able to do it, but because to many persons it seems a hopeless quest to look for anyone who cares enough for them, who can put himself vigorously enough into their places, to give them his best, to give them intelligent, unremitting, loyal service until the job is done—not half-done, or nine-tenths done, or ninety-nine hundredths done, but done with intelligence and devotion in every nail he drives or every comma he writes. Being "there" is the result of three things—intelligence, constant practice, and something hard to define but not too fancifully called an ideal.

LE BARON RUSSELL BRIGGS

MAN

Heir of the Kingdom 'neath the skies,
Often he falls, yet falls to rise;
Stunned, bleeding, beaten back,
Holding still to the upward track,
Playing his part in Creation's plan—
God-like in image, this is man.

ENDEAVOR

I know of no more encouraging fact than the unquestionable ability of man to elevate his life by a conscious endeavor.

HENRY DAVID THOREAU

MEASUREMENT

The degree of vision
that dwells in a man
is the correct measure
of the man.

THOMAS CARLYLE

MEN OF VISION

He who cherishes a beautiful ideal in his heart,
will one day realize it. Columbus cherished a
vision of another world, and he discovered it;
Copernicus fostered the vision of a multiplicity
of worlds and a wider universe, and he revealed it; Buddha beheld the vision of a spiritual world of stainless beauty and perfect
peace, and he entered into it. Cherish your
visions; cherish your ideals; cherish the music
that stirs in your heart, the beauty that forms
in your mind, the loveliness that drapes your
purest thoughts, for out of them will grow all
delightful conditions, all heavenly environment; of these, if you but remain true to them,
your world will at last be built.

JAMES ALLEN

Character is singularly contagious.

SAMUEL A. ELIOT

INEXHAUSTIBLE

A man who thinks that he is all that he ought
to be is obviously not what he ought to be.
Anyone who has reached his ideal has not an
ideal, and a man without an ideal is not a man,
for the world of moral action is as inexhaustible as the world of knowledge.

C. DELISLE BURNS

IDEAL LIFE

It was reserved for Christianity to present to
the world an Ideal Character, which through
the changes of nineteen centuries has inspired
the hearts of men with an impassioned love;
has shown itself capable of acting on all ages,
nations, temperaments, and conditions; has
been not only the highest pattern of virtue
but the strongest incentive to its practice; and
has exercised so deep an influence that it may
be truly said that the simple record of three
short years of active life has done more to
regenerate and to soften mankind than all the
disquisitions of philosophers and all the ex-
hortations of moralists. This has indeed been
the well-spring of whatever is best and purest
in the Christian life, which has preserved, in
the character and example of its Founder, an
enduring principle of regeneration.

WILLIAM H. LECKY

Live every day of your life as though you ex-
pected to live forever.

DOUGLAS MAC ARTHUR

Every one of us has in him a continent of undiscovered character. Blessed is he who acts
the Columbus to his own soul.

OUT OF THE HEART

It is in the heart a man carries his life, it is
through the heart come his finest ideals, from
the heart his truest words and deeds.

RALPH CONNOR

Influence

Ye are the light of the world. A city that is set on an hill cannot be hid.

Neither do men light a candle, and put it under a bushel, but on a candle-stick; and it giveth light unto all that are in the house.

Let your light so shine before men, that they may see your good works, and glorify your Father which is in heaven. MATTHEW 5:14-16

ONE CANDLE

A candle is a small thing.

But one candle can light another.

And as it gives its flames to the other, see how its own light increases!

Light is the power to dispel darkness.

You have this power to move back the darkness in yourself and in others with the birth of light created when one mind illuminates another, when one heart kindles another, when one man strengthens another.

And its flame also enlarges within you as you pass it on.

THE ETERNAL LIGHT

Whenever you hear of a man doing a great thing, you may be sure that behind it somewhere is a great background. It may be a mother's training, a father's example, a teacher's influence, or an intense experience of his own, but it has to be there or else the great achievement does not come, no matter how favorable the opportunity.

CATHERINE MILES

LAMPLIGHTER

He has taken his bright candle and is gone
Into another room I cannot find,
But anyone can tell where he has been
By all the little lights he leaves behind.

No picture however beautiful can be so great as a congregation of people influencing each other.

ALFRED NORTH WHITEHEAD

AS I GO ON MY WAY

My life shall touch a dozen lives before this day is done,

Leave countless marks for good or ill ere sets the evening sun;

So this the wish I always wish, the prayer I ever pray,

Let my life help the other lives it touches by the way.

STRICKLAND GILLILAN

The personal influence of the Master still bears upon us in this latest age. A divine discontent invades our souls, and, even in the midst of all the satisfactions which this earth can give, makes mere enjoyment base. Everywhere we see Him, where the manifold music of this world is most clearly heard. He fills our vision — Victor, Master, Judge, Eternal King. Still men will rise at His call to dare and suffer and die for Him. He remains the one magnet of magnanimous service which does not lose its virtue with the passing ages and the change of conditions. This twentieth century will witness many changes and departures. Institutions which seem now to stand firmly will crumble and fall; incalculable changes will re-order society. It would be an excessive expectation to hope that the creeds and churches of Christendom will hold their own without alterations and transformations unimaginably great. There will be one exception to this general rule. The personal influence of Jesus Christ will continue to shape character and to inspire conduct.

HENSLEY HENSON

When a child goes away from home, he carries his mother's hand with him.

TWELVE BASKETS FULL

127

THE SIGNIFICANT HOURS

I always think that we live, spiritually, by what others have given us in the significant hours of our life. These significant hours do not announce themselves as coming, but arrive unexpected. Nor do they make a great show of themselves; they pass almost unperceived. Often, indeed, their significance comes home to us first as we look back, just as the beauty of a piece of music or of a landscape often strikes us first in our recollection of it. Much that has become our own in gentleness, modesty, kindness, willingness to forgive, in veracity, loyalty, resignation under suffering, we owe to people in whom we have seen or experienced these virtues at work, sometimes in a great matter, sometimes in a small. A thought which had become an act sprang into us like a spark, and lighted a new flame within us.

ALBERT SCHWEITZER

INSCRIPTION

As one lamp lights another, nor grows less,
So nobleness enkindleth nobleness.

LIBRARY OF CONGRESS

From SERMONS WE SEE

I'd rather see a sermon than hear one any day;
I'd rather one should walk with me than merely tell the way.
The eye's a better pupil and more willing than the ear,
Fine counsel is confusing, but example's always clear;
And the best of all the preachers are the men who live their creeds,
For to see good put in action is what everybody needs.

EDGAR A. GUEST

Now and then we meet a man who seems to live high above the little things that vex our lives, and who makes us forget them. He may speak or he may be silent; it is enough that he lives and that we are with him. When we face him, we feel somewhat as we feel when we first see the ocean, or Niagara, or the Alps, or Athens, or when we first read the greatest poetry. Nothing is more like great poetry than the soul of a great man; and when the great man is good, when he loves everything that is beautiful and true and makes his life like what he loves, his face becomes transfigured, for the soul within him is the light of the world.

LE BARON RUSSELL BRIGGS

THE CENTRAL DEEP

It is they
Who utter wisdom from the central deep,
And, listening to the inner flow of things,
Speak to the age out of eternity.

JAMES RUSSELL LOWELL

The good person
increases the value
of every other person
whom he influences
in any way.

When we read the lives of the saints, we are struck by a certain large leisure which went hand in hand with a remarkable effectiveness. They were never hurried; they did comparatively few things, and these not necessarily striking or important; and they troubled very little about their influence.

EMILY HERMAN

Inspiration

Not by might, nor by power, but by my spirit, saith the Lord of hosts.

Zechariah 4:6

Behold, the Lord passed by, and a great and strong wind rent the mountains, and brake in pieces the rocks before the Lord; but the Lord was not in the wind: and after the wind an earthquake; but the Lord was not in the earthquake:

And after the earthquake a fire; but the Lord was not in the fire; and after the fire a still small voice.   I Kings 19:11-12

INFINITE OCEAN

If you could take the human heart and listen to it, it would be like listening to a seashell. You would hear in it the hollow murmur of the infinite ocean to which it belongs, from which it draws its profoundest inspiration, and for which it yearns.

EDWIN HUBBELL CHAPIN

———

At some time in our life we feel a trembling, fearful longing to do some good thing. Life finds its noblest spring of excellence in this hidden impulse to do our best.

ROBERT COLLYER

———

And not by eastern windows only,
   When daylight comes, comes in the light;
In front the sun climbs slow, how slowly,
   But westward, look, the land is bright.

ARTHUR HUGH CLOUGH

———

There is beauty in homely things which many
   people have never seen:
Sunlight through a jar of beach-plum jelly;
A rainbow in soapsuds in dishwater;
An egg yolk in a blue bowl;
White ruffled curtains sifting moonlight;
The color of cranberry glass;
A little cottage with blue shutters;
Crimson roses in an old stone crock;
The smell of newly baked bread;
Candlelight on old brass;
The soft brown of a cocker's eyes.

PETER MARSHALL

INVASIONS OF BEAUTY

Experiences of beauty steal up swiftly on us
   and take us over for the moment.
A clump of wild pink lady's-slippers deep in
   the wood;
the song of the hermit thrush at dusk;
a marshy bank of a brook ablaze with cardinal
   flowers;
an opening in the veil of "thundering smoke"
   and the flash of the mighty Zambezi majestically hurling itself into its chasm at
   Victoria Falls;
the sight of a lone column of a Greek temple
   standing sentinel on the deserted Sicilian
   plain at Segesta;
a sonnet of Shakespeare's;
a line of Gerard Manley Hopkins such as
   "Glory be to God for dappled things";
a fugue of Bach's;
a Van Gogh sunflower—
and the curtain to the inner stage has lifted.
These invasions of beauty may be rung down
   at once, or the lights to the stage may fade
   gradually, but after such openings, a man is
   not the same and the memory may shed its
   fragrance over all that follows.

DOUGLAS V. STEERE

———

In every house should be
a window toward the sky.

———

DISTANT STARS

The vision of the better-yet-to-be is the stuff of inspiration. Given vision, our lives are lived under the light of distant stars, fore-seeing upon our present workmanship the judgment of future generations.

T. V. SMITH

From ULYSSES

Death closes all; but something ere the end,
Some work of noble note, may yet be done,
Not unbecoming men that strove with Gods.
The long day wanes; the slow moon climbs;
  the deep
Moans round with many voices. Come, my
  friends,
'Tis not too late to seek a newer world.
Push off, and sitting well in order smite
The sounding furrows; for my purpose holds
To sail beyond the sunset, and the baths
Of all the western stars, until I die.
It may be that the gulfs will wash us down;
It may be we shall touch the Happy Isles,
And see the great Achilles, whom we knew.
Tho' much is taken, much abides.

                                ALFRED TENNYSON

If you follow poetry, you will grow up; you
will take on spiritual stature; you will be better
able to bear the things we all have to bear; you
will have a continuing and permanent "ram-
part to the mind."

                            WILLIAM ROSE BENÉT

POETRY

What is poetry? Who knows?
Not the rose, but the scent of the rose;
Not the sky, but the light of the sky;
Not the fly, but the gleam of the fly;
Not the sea, but the sound of the sea;
Not myself, but something that makes me
See, hear, and feel something that prose
Cannot. What is it? Who knows?

                                ELEANOR FARJEON

From THE SEEKERS

Not for us are content, and quiet, and peace of
  mind,
For we go seeking a city that we shall never
  find.

Only the road and the dawn, the sun, the
  wind, and the rain,
And the watch fire under the stars, and sleep,
  and the road again.

We travel the dusty road till the light of the
  day is dim,
And sunset shows us spires away on the wide
  world's rim.

We travel from dawn to dusk, till the day is
  past and by,
Seeking the Holy City beyond the rim of the
  sky.

                                JOHN MASEFIELD

Good men in all ages have interpreted their
moral decisions, not in terms of something
they have made, but in terms of something to
which they have become sensitive.

                                ELTON TRUEBLOOD

Nobody can inspire who does not have deep
convictions. They are the results, but also the
feeders of the spirit.

                                ROBERT ULICH

Religion is man's response as a whole to what
he considers most important and most real.

                                NELS F. S. FERRÉ

Joy

As the rain cometh down, and the snow from heaven, and returneth not thither, but watereth the earth, and maketh it bring forth and bud, that it may give seed to the sower, and bread to the eater:

So shall my word be that goeth forth out of my mouth: it shall not return unto me void, but it shall accomplish that which I please, and it shall prosper in the thing whereto I sent it.

For ye shall go out with joy, and be led forth with peace: the mountains and the hills shall break forth before you into singing, and all the trees of the field shall clap their hands.

Instead of the thorn shall come up the fir tree, and instead of the brier shall come up the myrtle tree: and it shall be to the Lord for a name, for an everlasting sign that shall not be cut off.　　　Isaiah 55:10-13

PRAYER

Grant to us, O Lord, the royalty of inward happiness, and the serenity which comes from living close to Thee. Daily renew in us the sense of joy, and let the eternal spirit of the Father dwell in our souls and bodies, filling us with light and grace, so that, bearing about with us the infection of a good courage, we may be diffusers of life, and may meet all ills and accidents with gallant and highhearted happiness, giving Thee thanks always for all things.

L. H. SOULE

From I HAVE FOUND SUCH JOY

I have found such joy in simple things;
A plain clean room, a nut-brown loaf of bread,
A cup of milk, a kettle as it sings,
The shelter of a roof above my head,
And in a leaf-laced square along a floor,
Where yellow sunlight glimmers through a
   door.

I have found such joy in things that fill
My quiet days: a curtain's blowing grace,
A potted plant upon my window sill,
A rose fresh-cut and placed within a vase,
A table cleared, a lamp beside a chair,
And books I long have loved beside me there.

GRACE NOLL CROWELL

Any man can again have the joy of his first meeting with God if he will go back over the same road.

ROY L. SMITH

Joy is the gigantic secret of the Christian.

GILBERT KEITH CHESTERTON

Peace does not mean the end of all our striving,
   Joy does not mean the drying of our tears;
Peace is the power that comes to souls arriving
   Up to the light where God Himself appears.
Joy is the wine that God is ever pouring
   Into the hearts of those who strive with
    Him,
Light'ning their eyes to vision and adoring,
   Strength'ning their arms to warfare glad
   and grim.

G. A. STUDDERT-KENNEDY

From SHEER JOY

Oh the sheer joy of it!
   Walking with Thee,
Out on the hilltop,
   Down by the sea,
Life is so wonderful,
   Life is so free.

Oh the sheer joy of it!
   Working with God,
Running His errands,
   Waiting His nod,
Building His heaven,
   On common sod.

RALPH SPAULDING CUSHMAN

ALCHEMY

When life seems just a dreary grind,
And things seem fated to annoy,
Say something nice to someone else—
And watch the world light up with joy.

Uncertainty and expectation are the joys of life.

RICHARD CONGREVE

PRAYER

Oh, not for more or longer days, dear Lord,
  My prayer shall be—
But rather teach me how to use the days
  Now given me.

I ask not more of pleasure or of joy
  For this brief while—
But rather let me for the joys I have
  Be glad and smile.

                    B. Y. WILLIAMS

LIFE

A little sunshine,
A little rain,
A little loss,
A little gain;
A little happiness,
A little pain,
Not all sweet,
Not all sour;
Now a weed,
Now a flower;
A goodly average
Of sunshine and shower.

                FRANK R. JENNINGS

A JOY FOREVER

You take a few words, you put them together, and in a way not explicable they flash into life and you have not a sentence, but a song, a revelation, a new creation, a joy forever.

                GEORGE SAMPSON

PRIVILEGE

What a privilege to be alive in this particular day and age!

              FRANKLIN D. ROOSEVELT

A CHRISTIAN'S JOY

The fundamental joy of being a Christian consists not in being good. I get tired of that. But in standing with God against some darkness or some void and watching the light come. The joy of religion is in having your fling, by the mercies of God, at shaping where you are, as a potter shapes a vase, one corner of His eternal Kingdom.

              PAUL SCHERER

JOY AND WOE

Joy and woe are woven fine,
A clothing for the soul divine;
Under every grief and pine
Runs a joy with silken twine;
It is right it should be so;
Man was made for joy and woe;
And when this we rightly know
Safely through the world we go.

              WILLIAM BLAKE

ANGEL'S HAND

The gloom of the world is but a shadow. Behind it, and yet within our reach, is joy. There is radiance and glory in darkness could we but see; and to see we have only to look. Life is so generous a giver, but we, judging its gifts by their covering, cast them away as ugly, or heavy, or hard. Remove the covering and you will find beneath it a living splendor woven of love, by wisdom, with power. Welcome it, grasp it, and you touch the angel's hand that brings it to you. Everything that we call a trial, a sorrow, or a duty—believe me, that angel's hand is there; the gift is there, and the wonder of an overshadowing Presence.

           ERNEST TEMPLE HARGROVE

WHAT IS THE SOURCE OF YOUR JOY?
There are some who are dependent upon the mood of others for their happiness. They seem bound in mood one to another like Siamese twins. If the other person is happy, the happiness is immediately contagious. If the other person is sad, there is no insulation against his mood.

There are some whose joy is dependent upon circumstances. When things do not go well, a deep gloom settles upon them, and all who touch their lives are caught in the fog of their despair.

There are some whose joy is a matter of disposition and temperament. They cannot be sad because their glands will not let them. Their joy is not a matter for congratulations or praise; it is a gift of life, a talent, a gratuitous offering placed in their organism.

There are some who must win their joy against high odds, squeeze it out of the arid ground of their living or wrest it from the stubborn sadness of circumstance. It is a determined joy, sharpened by the zest of triumph.

There are still others who find their joy deep in the heart of their religious experience. It is not related to, dependent upon, or derived from, any circumstances or conditions in the midst of which they must live. It is a joy independent of all vicissitudes. There is a strange quality of awe in their joy, that is but a reflection of the deep calm water of the spirit out of which it comes. It is primarily a discovery of the soul, when God makes known his presence, where there are no words, no outward song, only the Divine Movement. This is the joy that the world cannot give. This is the joy that keeps watch against all the emissaries of sadness of mind and weariness of soul. This is the joy that comforts and is the companion, as we walk even through the valley of the shadow of death.

HOWARD THURMAN

From EARTH'S COMMON THINGS
Go not abroad for happiness. For see,
  It is a flower that blooms at thy door.
  Bring love and justice home, and then no
    more
Thou'lt wonder in what dwelling joy may be.

MINOT J. SAVAGE

Oh, the wild joys of living! the leaping from
  rock up to rock.
The strong rending of boughs from the fir-
  tree, the cool silver shock
Of the plunge in a pool's living water, the
  hunt of the bear,
And the sultriness showing the lion is couched
  in his lair.
How good is man's life, the mere living! How
  fit to employ
All the heart and the soul and the senses for
  ever in joy!

ROBERT BROWNING

Cheerfulness and content are great beautifiers and are famous preservers of youthful looks.

CHARLES DICKENS

JOY OF LIVING
The ideals which have always shone before me and filled me with the joy of living are goodness, beauty, and truth.

ALBERT EINSTEIN

THE BEST WIND
Whichever way the wind doth blow,
Some heart is glad that it is so;
So blow it east or blow it west,
The wind that blows—that wind is best.

Love, in the divine alchemy of life, transmutes all duties into privileges, all responsibilities into joys.

WILLIAM GEORGE JORDAN

THE DEEPEST JOY
Wherever joy is, creation has been, and the richer the creation the deeper the joy. The mother looking upon her child is joyous because she has the consciousness of having created it, physically and morally. A man who succeeds in his enterprise—for example, a captain of industry whose business is prospering —is joyous in having established an enterprise which marches on, something that goes ahead. There is no greater joy than that of feeling oneself a creator. The triumph of life is expressed by creation.

HENRI BERGSON

He who bends to himself a Joy
Doth the winged life destroy.
But he who kisses a Joy as it flies
Lives in Eternity's sunrise.

WILLIAM BLAKE

INGREDIENT
Nothing great was ever achieved without enthusiasm.

RALPH WALDO EMERSON

ODD MOMENTS
The happiest life, seen in perspective, can hardly be better than a stringing together of odd little moments.

NORMAN DOUGLAS

The soul's joy lies in doing.

PERCY BYSSHE SHELLEY

ON HIS NINETY-FIFTH BIRTHDAY
I am still at work, with my hand to the plow, and my face to the future. The shadows of evening lengthen about me, but morning is in my heart. I have had varied fields of labor, and full contact with men and things, and have warmed both hands before the fire of life.

The testimony I bear is this: that the Castle of Enchantment is not yet behind me. It is before me still, and daily I catch glimpses of its battlements and towers. The rich spoils of memory are mine. Mine, too, are the precious things of today—books, flowers, pictures, nature, and sport. The first of May is still an enchanted day to me. The best thing of all is friends. The best of life is always further on. Its real lure is hidden from our eyes, somewhere behind the hills of time.

WILLIAM MULOCK

The happiest person
is the person who
thinks the most
interesting thoughts.

TIMOTHY DWIGHT

Joy is the sign of spiritual maturity.

THE PURE IN HEART

Learning

Teach me, O Lord, the way of thy statutes; and I shall keep it unto the end.

Give me understanding, and I shall keep thy law; yea, I shall observe it with my whole heart.

Make me to go in the path of thy commandments; for therein do I delight.

Incline my heart unto thy testimonies, and not to covetousness.

Turn away mine eyes from beholding vanity; and quicken thou me in thy way.

Stablish thy word unto thy servant, who is devoted to thy fear.

Turn away my reproach which I fear: for thy judgments are good.

Behold, I have longed after thy precepts: quicken me in thy righteousness.

PSALM 119:33-40

THE TEACHER

He sent men out to preach the living Word,
  Aflame with all the ardor of His fire;
They spoke the Truth, wherever truth was
    heard
  But back to Him they brought their hearts'
    desire;
They turned to Him through all the lengthen-
    ing days
  With each perplexity of life or creed.
His deep reward, not that they spoke His
    praise,
  But that they brought to Him their human
    need.

HILDEGARDE HOYT SWIFT

THE TEACHER'S CREED

I believe in boys and girls, the men and women
  of a great tomorrow.
I believe in the efficacy of schools, in the dignity of teaching, and in the joy of serving
  others.
I believe in wisdom as revealed in human lives
  as well as in the pages of a printed book, in
  lessons taught not so much by precept as by
  example, in ability to work with the hands
  as well as to think with the head, in everything that makes life large and lovely.
I believe in beauty in the schoolroom, in the
  home, in daily life, and in the out-of-doors.
I believe in laughter, in love, in faith, in all
  ideals and distant hopes that lure us on.
I believe in the present and its opportunities,
  in the future and its promises, and in the
  divine joy of living.

EDWIN OSGOOD GROVER

HORIZONS

What we need, in education, is some sense of
far horizons and beautiful prospects, some
consciousness of the largeness and mystery
and wonder of life.

ARTHUR CHRISTOPHER BENSON

PRAYER

Almighty God, the Giver of Wisdom, without
whose help resolutions are vain, without
whose blessing study is ineffectual, enable me,
if it be Thy will, to attain such knowledge as
may qualify me to direct the doubtful and instruct the ignorant, to prevent wrongs, and
terminate contentions; and grant that I may
use that knowledge which I shall attain, to Thy
glory and my own salvation.

SAMUEL JOHNSON

Our safety does not lie in the present perfection of our knowledge of the will of God, but
in our sincerity in obeying the light we have,
and in seeking for more.

EDWARD WORSDELL

THE FOUR P'S

Education fails unless the three R's at one end
of the school spectrum lead ultimately to the
four P's at the other end:
  Preparation for Earning,
  Preparation for Living,
  Preparation for Understanding, and
  Preparation for Participation in the prob-
lems involved in the making of a better world.

NORMAN COUSINS

THINKING

As you think, you travel; as you love, you attract. You are today where your thoughts have brought you; you will be tomorrow where your thoughts take you. You cannot escape the result of your thoughts, but you can endure and learn, can accept and be glad. You will realize the vision of your heart, be it base or beautiful, or a mixture of both, for you will always gravitate toward that which you secretly most love. Into your hands will be placed the exact result of your thoughts; you will receive that which you earn; no more, no less. Whatever your present environment may be, you will fall, remain, or rise with your thoughts, your vision, your ideal. You will become as small as your controlling desire; as great as your dominant aspiration.

JAMES ALLEN

THE MASTER TEACHER

In all the arts of the teacher Jesus is incomparable. He roused very wide attention, but He did better than that. To keep attention the teacher has to awaken affection, and it is plain that the warmest affection bound his disciples to Jesus and opened their minds to Him.

He had the gift of saying things that people could not forget. He told a story amazingly well, cutting away all but the essential and giving that much absolutely alive.

The methods of such a teacher show his mind. Style is thought; a man's style is an index to his thinking. It was so that Jesus thought and we do not. We forget God— Jesus did not; and for Him God is alive, always near with a question or a blessing or both. The story lives because Jesus had His eyes on the living God, an actor in every man's drama.

Jesus was a young man when He was crucified; and His Gospel is new and young, fresh and freshening, full of ardour and energy. "I am come that they might have vitality and overflow with it." "Because I live, you shall live also." We lose sight of the immense life and vitality that made Jesus. His freshness and some of His charm are lost for us in old acquaintance; we take Him for granted. Jesus fired His followers with His own originality, and inspired them with so independent a spirit, with so moving a sense of a living God beside them and before them, that they accepted the hint of Jesus to re-think God.

In Christ a new life came to the world; and, as that life stirred within it, the world turned to God, as it found Him in Christ.

T. R. GLOVER

THE CHARIOT

There is no frigate like a book
To take us lands away,
Nor any coursers like a page
Of prancing poetry.
This traverse may the poorest take
Without oppress of toll;
How frugal is the chariot
That bears a human soul!

EMILY DICKINSON

DISCOVERY

The greatest discovery of my generation is that human beings can alter their lives by altering their attitudes of mind.

WILLIAM JAMES

WHERE BEAUTY DWELLS

A well-kept garden filled with flowers
Has no room left for weeds to share;
The mind keeps out unworthy thoughts
When loveliness is dwelling there.

LEONA BOLT MARTIN

When you sell a man a book you don't sell him just twelve ounces of paper and ink and glue —you sell him a whole new life.

CHRISTOPHER MORLEY

TEN AXIOMS FOR A CHRISTIAN TEACHER

1. A personal God is the creative and ultimately controlling force in nature and human destiny. This becomes the teacher's point of reference.
2. Man is capable of growth and development. In each member of the student group, there is capacity for desirable change.
3. Truth is at least partially discoverable, and man's partial comprehension can be accepted as real, but incomplete.
4. Truth is apprehensible by other means than "the scientific method." The Christian teacher will never yield to science and science's method the exclusive right to uncover new truth.
5. Human life and human personality call for the attitude of reverence.
6. Integrity is a basic element in all human relations.
7. Mutual respect and friendship constitute the highest form of relationship between student and teacher.
8. The Christian teacher is tolerant, patient, and understanding.
9. The goal of education is the full development of the whole man, according to his potentialities in harmony with the will of God.
10. A Christian teacher is a disciple of Jesus Christ. Disciple means learner; so that the Christian teacher never loses his position as seeker after truth, endeavoring in his seeking to embody the spirit of Christ.

NOT MINDS ALONE

Reality — Dreams = Animal Being
Reality + Dreams = A Heart-Ache (usually called Idealism)
Reality + Humor = Realism (also called Conservatism)
Dreams — Humor = Fanaticism
Dreams + Humor = Fantasy
Reality + Dreams + Humor = Wisdom

LIN YUTANG

Lucky the lad whose teachers know
That it takes time for a boy to grow;
That Rome was not achieved in a day,
Nor a boy perfected the easy way;
Teachers view his falls from grace,
His strident voice, his reckless pace,
His scorn for dentifrice and soap
With an inexhaustible fund of hope.
Lucky the lad whose teachers know
That it takes time for a boy to grow.

MAY RICHSTONE

CURIOSITY

God spare me sclerosis of the curiosity, for the curiosity which craves to keep us informed about the small things no less than the large is the mainspring, the dynamo, the jet propulsion of all complete living. Our curiosities are what feed our consciousness, and our consciousness is the proof that our minds are still functioning. Nothing that happens to us, nothing we do, no walk we take, nothing we see or read, no one we meet or listen to, means anything to us unless we have the mind to use our minds, and keep them refreshed.

JOHN MASON BROWN

WHAT A TEACHER NEEDS

The education of a college president,
The executive ability of a financier,
The humility of a deacon,
The adaptability of a chameleon,
The hope of an optimist,
The courage of a hero,
The wisdom of a serpent,
The gentleness of a dove,
The patience of Job,
The grace of God, and
The persistence of the Devil.

PHENOMENA

The manner in which one single ray of light, one single precious hint, will clarify and energize the whole mental life of him who receives it is among the most wonderful and heavenly of intellectual phenomena.

ARNOLD BENNETT

HIGH-SCHOOL DIPLOMA

It doesn't look heavy, a high-school diploma: only a bit of paper (it isn't really sheepskin), a few drops of ink, a bit of colored ribbon from Woolworth's. It doesn't weigh much; nevertheless, a high-school diploma is heavy. It is heavy with expectations.

There is the expectation of teachers that the diploma bearer will be willing to use the dictionary and the encyclopedia, the expectation that he will think clean and clear and straight and frequently.

There is the expectation of both teachers and parents that he will be teachable, and being teachable is essentially wanting to grow in wisdom and understanding.

There are the citizens who expect him to be a good citizen, informed about the world with its variety of governments but loyal to America.

There are the neighbors who expect him to be dependable, able to carry routine for a succession of days.

And there are those friends who expect him to have a special ability of understanding and caring for people, any people, all people.

The high-school diploma is a heavy bit of luggage when the proud graduate sets out for college.

KENNETH IRVING BROWN

Teaching that would lay any claim at all to distinction, if not to actual greatness, is the influence of personality upon personality, rather than the mere imparting of a set of facts.

FRANK E. GAEBELEIN

PREFERENCE

Did the Almighty, holding in his right hand Truth, and in his left Search after Truth, deign to tender me the one I might prefer, in all humility, but without hesitation, I should request Search after Truth.

GOTTHOLD LESSING

THE UNIVERSITY

There are few earthly things more beautiful than a University. It is a place where those who hate ignorance may strive to know, where those who perceive truth may strive to make others see; where seekers and learners alike, banded together in the search for knowledge, will honour thought in all its finer ways, will welcome thinkers in distress or in exile, will uphold ever the dignity of thought and learning and will exact standards in these things. They give to the young in their impressionable years the bond of a lofty purpose shared, of a great corporate life whose links will not be loosed until they die. They give young people that close companionship for which youth longs, and that chance of the endless discussion of the themes which are endless, without which youth would seem a waste of time.

JOHN MASEFIELD

Genius is many-tongued. A Jesus speaks, a Gandhi lives, a Tagore writes, and the message each has to give is clear to every thinking mind.

EVELYN WELLS

GRACE OF WONDER

There must be surprise in the books that I keep in the worn case at my elbow, the surprise of a new personality perceiving for the first time the beauty, the wonder, the humor, the tragedy, the greatness of truth. It doesn't matter at all whether the writer is a poet, a scientist, a traveller, an essayist, or a mere daily space-maker, if he have the God-given grace of wonder.

DAVID GRAYSON

The world of books
Is the most remarkable creation of man.
Nothing else he builds lasts.
Monuments fall,
Nations perish,
Civilizations grow old and die out
And after an era of darkness
New races build others,
But in the world of books are volumes
That have seen this happen again and again
And yet live on,
Still young,
Still as fresh as the day they were written,
Still telling men's hearts
Of the hearts of men centuries dead.

CLARENCE DAY

Education, in the deepest sense, is continuous and lifelong and in essence unfinishable. What we think we already know is often less helpful than the desire to learn.

JAMES HILTON

SEEKING

Whoever seeks truth with an earnest mind, no matter when or how, belongs to the school of intellectual men.

WILLIAM ELLERY CHANNING

RECIPE FOR EDUCATION

1 cup of thinking
2 cups of dreams
2 to 4 years of youth
3½ cups of persistence
3 teaspoons of ability
1 cup of co-operation
1 teaspoon of borrowing
1 cup of good books, lectures, and
    teachers
1 cup of health
1 cup of plans made and followed through

Cream the thinking and the dreams.

Add the years and beat until creamy.

Sift persistence and ability together and add alternately, with co-operation, to the first mixture.

Add borrowing, books, lectures, teachers, health, and plans.

Fold in the years of youth, beaten stiff.

Bake in any moderately good college or university.

Time in college: 4 or more years, depending on how you like your finished product.

Temperature: plenty hot.

Servings will last for life.

TEACHER'S TREASURY OF STORIES

As we acquire more knowledge, things do not become more comprehensible but more mysterious.

ALBERT SCHWEITZER

GOOD BOOKS

A good book is a wonder-thing
That sets the spirit traveling
Down strange exciting ways, and through
New doors undreamed of hitherto.
It opens vistas to the eyes
Where the happy, far-off distance lies;
It lifts the cares of every day
When one is off and on his way.
For oh, indeed, a heart can roam
Through a good book, yet stay at home.
A table, lamp, a chair, and he
Absorbed in rhyme or mystery,
Absorbed in words upon a page—
O questioning Youth, O seeking Age,
Read books, good books, and you will find
Adventure, and new worlds outlined.

GRACE NOLL CROWELL

There are no foolish questions and no man becomes a fool until he has stopped asking questions.

CHARLES P. STEINMETZ

PILGRIMAGE

I believe that the American teacher is the most solid supporter of democracy and that education ought to be teacher-centered as well as child-centered. Teaching can never be mediocre or it becomes self-defeating. Teaching must be great, yet greatness has many dimensions. It is not a possession, but a pilgrimage. It is measured by consequences—its influence on the lives of students and on culture.

FREDERICK MAYER

Life

Blessed are the poor in spirit: for theirs is the kingdom of heaven.

Blessed are they that mourn: for they shall be comforted.

Blessed are the meek: for they shall inherit the earth.

Blessed are they which do hunger and thirst after righteousness: for they shall be filled.

Blessed are the merciful: for they shall obtain mercy.

Blessed are the pure in heart: for they shall see God.

Blessed are the peacemakers: for they shall be called the children of God.

Matthew 5:3-9

PRAYER

I do not ask, O Lord,
A life all free from pain;
I do not seek to be
In this vast world of need
Without my load of care.
For this I know, the cross
Is my eternal gain,
And he who struggles on
At last shall enter in,
And be victorious there.

So, Lord, just keep me fit within,
And give me strength to fight,
And I will follow through the din,
From darkness up to light.

DANIEL A. POLING

Life is occupied both in perpetuating itself and
in surpassing itself.

SIMONE DE BEAUVOIR

MYSELF

I have to live with myself, and so
I want to be fit for myself to know.
I want to be able as days go by
Always to look myself in the eye.

I don't want to stand with the setting sun
And hate myself for the thing I've done.
I never can hide myself from me,
I see what others may never see.

I know what others may never know,
I never can fool myself, and so
Whatever happens I want to be
Self-respecting and conscience-free.

EDGAR A. GUEST

BLESSINGS IN A MINOR KEY

The ability to get tired and to be renewed by
  rest and relaxation;
the whole range of tastes from sweet to bitter
  with the subtleties in between;
the peculiar quality that cool water has for
  quenching the thirst;
the color of sky and sea and the vast complex
  of hues that blend with objects, making the
  eye the inlet from rivers of movement and
  form;
the sheer wonder of sound that gives to the inward parts feeling tones of the heights and
  the depths;
the tender remembrance of moments that were
  good and whole, of places that reached out
  and claimed one as their very own, of persons who shared at depths beyond all meas-
  uring;
the coming of day and the sureness of the
  return of the night, and all the dimensions
  of meaning that each of us finds in this cycle
  of movement which sustains and holds fast
  in the security of its rhythms.

HOWARD THURMAN

WHY WAS I BORN?

To be happy, says the Greek philosopher.
To do unto others, says the humanitarian.
To find onself, says the psychologist.
To glorify God and enjoy him forever, says the
  Calvinist.
To be morally responsible, says the prophet
  of Israel.
To be united with the Father, says Jesus, which
  means establishing the kinship, the unity
  of spirit—responding to Reality, as if one
  belonged.

WINNIFRED WYGAL

THE TRUE GENTLEMAN

The true gentleman is the man whose conduct proceeds from good will, whose self-control is equal to all emergencies;

who does not make the poor man conscious of his poverty, the obscure man of his obscurity, or any man of his inferiority or deformity;

who is himself humbled if necessity compel him to humble another;

who does not flatter wealth, cringe before power, or boast of his own possessions or achievements;

who speaks with frankness, but always with sincerity and sympathy, and whose deed follows his word;

who thinks of the rights and feelings of others rather than of his own;

who appears well in any company, and who is at home when he seems to be abroad—a man with whom honor is sacred and virtue safe.

JOHN W. WAYLAND

WIDE WALLS

Give me wide walls to build my house of Life—
The North shall be of Love, against the winds of fate;
The South of Tolerance, that I may outreach hate;
The East of Faith, that rises clear and new each day;
The West of Hope, that e'en dies a glorious way.
The threshold 'neath my feet shall be Humility;
The roof—the very sky itself—Infinity.
Give me wide walls to build my house of Life.

ASPECTS

The greatest sin is fear.

The best day is today.

The greatest deceiver is the man who deceives himself.

The greatest mistake is giving up.

The most expensive indulgence is hate.

The most foolish thing to do is to find fault.

The worst bankrupt is the soul that has lost its enthusiasm.

The most clever man is he who always does what he thinks is right.

The best part of any religion is gentleness and cheerfulness.

The meanest feeling is jealousy.

The best gift is forgiveness.

FRANK CRANE

ABUNDANT LIVING

Think deeply,
Speak gently,
Laugh often,
Work hard,
Give freely,
Pay promptly,
Pray earnestly,
Be kind.

ROMANCE OF LIFE

This constitutes the romance of life. At every bend of the road there are new unfoldings and each new day reveals undiscovered grandeurs. Life holds many surprises.

JOSEPH R. SIZOO

SOUNDS

One does not live in vain to have heard
   the birds' songs in spring,
   the cicadas' songs in summer,
   the insects' chirps in autumn, and
   the sounds of crunching snow in winter,
and furthermore, to have heard
   the sound of chess in daytime,
   the sound of flute in moonlight,
   the sound of winds whistling through the
      pines, and
   the sound of rippling, lapping water.

CHANG CHAO

LIFE GOES ON

In three words I can sum up everything I've
learned about life: *It goes on.* The important
thing to remember is that there is a direction
and a continuity. Despite our fears and wor-
ries, life continues.

ROBERT FROST

IDENTITY

That I am a man,
this I share with other men.
That I see and hear and
that I eat and drink
is what all animals do likewise.
But that I am I is only mine
and belongs to me
and to nobody else;
to no other man,
not to an angel, nor to God—
except inasmuch
as I am one with Him.

JOHANNES ECKHART

SIX LIVES

It has always been a fancy of mine that I'd
   love to live at least six lives simultaneously.
One life for the necessary work of earning my
   living, hard concentrated work without
   petty interruptions and irrelevancies.
One life for reading and study and meditation
   on what I'd read and what I'd studied.
One life for doing things with my hands like
   sewing and gardening and polishing mirrors
   and cleaning silver and maybe a craft or so
   like woodcarving or weaving.
One life to see my friends and acquaintances,
   for travel and hospitality.
One life for political and public interest proj-
   ects where I could be certain that I was
   doing something, be it ever so small, of
   value to my country and my times.
And among these I would tuck in the pleasure
   and pain of shopping, the pleasure and
   pain of housekeeping, and the complete
   pleasure of aimless, frivolous loafing.

SOPHIE KERR

To give life a meaning one must have a purpose larger than one's self.

WILL DURANT

CHARM OF HOMER

Once, after puzzling long over the charm of
Homer, I applied to a learned friend and said
to him, "Can you tell me why Homer is so
interesting?" "Well," said my friend, "Homer
looked long at a thing. Do you know that if
you should hold up your thumb and look at it
long enough, you would find it immensely
interesting?"

GEORGE HERBERT PALMER

ADVENTURE OF LIVING

Life's supreme adventure is the adventure of living. Life's greatest achievement is the continual remaking of yourself so that at last you do know how to live.

The man who is set for the building up of a self he can live with in some kind of comfort and with the hope of continued improvement chooses deliberately what he will let himself think and feel, thoughts of admiration and high desire, emotions that are courageous and inspiring. It is by these that we grow into more abundant and truer life, a more harmonious inner state and a more stalwart personality.

WINFRED RHOADES

FIRST THINGS

The mind that understands and creates,
the spirit that suffers and sacrifices and loves
    and is at peace with itself,
the fellowship of the pure and free and trans-
    parent,
the joy of conversation and reason and sharing,
the soul that rejoices in beauty and grace and
    being,
the good will that is full of light and positive
    intent,
God, the absolute mind, the absolute spirit,
    absolute reason, absolute love, absolute
    grace, absolute goodness, absolute Being—
these things come first, and everything else
    second.

CHARLES MALIK

OTHERWISE

There must be magic,
    Otherwise
How could the day turn to night?
And how could sailboats
    Otherwise
Go sailing out of sight?
And how could peanuts otherwise
Be covered up so tight?

AILEEN FISHER

RENDEZVOUS

I have a rendezvous with Life,
In days I hope will come,
Ere youth has sped, and strength of mind,
Ere voices sweet grow dumb.
I have a rendezvous with Life,
When Spring's first heralds hum.

COUNTEE CULLEN

YEARNING

So long as life continues as life, it will never lose its yearning to be more than it is.

WILLIAM PEPPERELL MONTAGUE

THE ROAD

The road winds up the hill to meet the height;
Beyond the locust hedge it curves from sight—
And yet no man would foolishly contend
That where he sees it not, it makes an end.

EMMA CARLETON

MEN AND RIVERS

Men are like rivers. The water is alike in all of them; but every river is narrow in some places and wide in others; here swift and there sluggish, here clear and there turbid; cold in winter and warm in summer. The same may be said of men. Every man bears within himself the germs of every human quality, displaying all in turn; and a man can often seem unlike himself—yet he still remains the same man.

LEO TOLSTOY

What we need is to take the gas and hot air out of the real business of living, and send it sizzling off in sky-rockets for the entertainment of our idle hours.

MARJORIE BARSTOW GREENBIE

For life alone is creator of life,
And closest contact with the human world
Is like a lantern shining in the night
To light me to a knowledge of myself.

AMY LOWELL

TO LIVE DELIBERATELY

I went [to Walden Pond] because I wished to live deliberately, to front only the essential facts of life, and see if I could not learn what it had to teach, and not, when I came to die, discover that I had not lived. I did not wish to live what was not life, living is so dear; nor did I wish to practise resignation, unless it was quite necessary. I wanted to live deep and suck out all the marrow of life.

HENRY DAVID THOREAU

HIGH DESTINY

Everyone shares the responsibility in the future. But this responsibility can materialize into a constructive effort only if people realize the full meaning of their lives, the significance of their endeavors and their struggles, and if they keep their faith in the high destiny of Man.

LECOMTE DU NOÜY

LIFE

Let me but live my life from year to year,
 With forward face and unreluctant soul;
 No hurrying to, nor turning from, the goal;
Not mourning for the things that disappear
In the dim past, nor holding back in fear
 From what the future veils; but with a whole
 And happy heart, that pays its toll
To Youth and Age, and travels on with cheer.

So let the way wind up the hill or down,
 O'er rough or smooth, the journey will be
  joy:
 Still seeking what I sought when but a boy,
New friendship, high adventure, and a crown,
My heart will keep the courage of the quest,
And hope the road's last turn will be the best.

HENRY VAN DYKE

PERSONALITY

Every good that enters the world enters through an individual—a conscious, reasonable, moral man; and it depends on the quality of the man what measure of good he brings. The world moves by personality.

ANDREW MARTIN FAIRBAIRN

EYES TO SEE

What a large volume of adventures may be grasped within this little span of life by him who interests his heart in everything, and who, having eyes to see what time and chance are perpetually holding out to him as he journeyeth on his way, misses nothing he can fairly lay his hands on.

LAURENCE STERNE

Wonders are many, and none is more wonderful than Man.

SOPHOCLES

A dull autobiography has never been written.

LESLIE STEPHEN

'Tis life, whereof our nerves are scant,
Oh life, not death, for which we pant;
More life, and fuller, that I want.

ALFRED TENNYSON

A GREAT AWARENESS

I think the artist is a specially privileged person, because always he sees the world spread out like a stage before him, a play being enacted for his own special benefit. He approaches it objectively, with all his senses sharpened, filled with "a great awareness"— a sensitivity like that of a human camera, to make a record of it. He looks not for those things which are the same or similar to his own past experiences, but for differences; he forgets himself and identifies himself with the new scene and its activities.

LOIS LENSKI

NEW LIFE

A stone thrown into a pond creates waves which are practically imperceptible before they reach the shore. A shout thrown into the air re-echoes for a few moments, then dies away forever. But the life of Jesus, sacrificially thrown into the lives of His disciples, kindled there a new life that has never died away.

WALTER MARSHALL HORTON

GRACE AT EVENING

Be with us, Lord, at eventide;
　Far has declined the day,
Our hearts have glowed
Along the road,
　Thou hast made glad our way.

Take Thou this loaf and bless it, Lord,
　And then with us partake;
Unveil our eyes
To recognize
　Thyself, for Thy dear sake.

EDWIN MCNEILL POTEAT

There is more to life than increasing its speed.

MAHATMA GANDHI

From THE ANGLER'S REVEILLE

Then come, my friend, forget your foes and
　leave your fears behind,
And wander out to try your luck with cheerful,
　quiet mind;
For be your fortune great or small, you'll take
　what God may give,
And through the day your heart shall say, 'Tis
　luck enough to live.

HENRY VAN DYKE

Beloved, let us love one another: for love is of God; and every one that loveth is born of God, and knoweth God.

If we love one another, God dwelleth in us, and his love is perfected in us.

God is love; and he that dwelleth in love dwelleth in God, and God in him.

And this commandment have we from him, That he who loveth God love his brother also.   I JOHN 4:7, 12, 16, 21

SACRAMENT

Love is not passion, love is not pride,
Love is a journeying side by side;
Not of the breezes, nor of the gale,
Love is the steady set of the sail.

Deeper than ecstasy, sweeter than light,
Born in the sunshine, born in the night;
Flaming in victory, stronger in loss,
Love is a sacrament made for a cross.

SWINGING DOOR

There is only one place of refuge on this planet
for any man—that is in another man's heart.
To love is to make of one's heart a swinging
door.

HOWARD THURMAN

He prayeth best, who loveth best
All things both great and small;
For the dear God who loveth us,
He made and loveth all.

SAMUEL T. COLERIDGE

MIRACLES

To have faith is to create;
To have hope is to call down blessing;
To have love is to work miracles.

MICHAEL FAIRLESS

Love feels no burdens,
thinks nothing of trouble,
attempts what is above its strength,
pleads no excuse of impractibility—
for it thinks all things lawful
for itself if possible.

THOMAS A KEMPIS

PRAYER BY A BRIDE AND GROOM

Our gracious heavenly Father, who givest the supreme gift of love to Thy children, we thank Thee for each other. We thank Thee for all who love us and who have given so much of themselves to make us happy. We thank Thee for the love that has bound our hearts and lives together and made us husband and wife.

As we enter upon the privileges and joys of life's most holy relationship and begin together the great adventure of building a Christian home, we thank Thee for all the hopes that make the future bright. Teach us the fine art of living together unselfishly that, loving and being loved, blessing and being blessed, we may find our love ever filled with a deeper harmony as we learn more perfectly to share it through the years.

Help us to keep the candles of faith and prayer always burning in our home. Be Thou our Guest at every meal, our Guide in every plan, our Guardian in every temptation.

None can know what the future holds. We ask only that we may love, honor, and cherish each other always, and so live together in faithfulness and patience that our lives will be filled with joy and the home which we have this day established become a haven of blessing and a place of peace.

WESLEY H. HAGER

INSCRIPTION ON A SUNDIAL

Time flies,
Suns rise,
And shadows fall.
Let time go by.
Love is forever over all.

LEARNING TO LOVE

Is life not full of opportunities for learning love? Every man and woman every day has a thousand of them. The world is not a playground; it is a schoolroom. Life is not a holiday, but an education. And the one eternal lesson for us all is how better we can love. What makes a man a good artist, a good sculptor, a good musician? Practice. What makes a man a good man? Practice. Love is not a thing of enthusiastic emotion. It is a rich, strong, manly, vigorous expression of the whole Christian character—the Christlike nature in its fullest development. And the constituents of this great character are only to be built up by ceaseless practice.

HENRY DRUMMOND

Give all to love;
Obey thy heart;
Friends, kindred, days,
Estate, good fame,
Plans, credit and the Muse—
Nothing refuse.

RALPH WALDO EMERSON

MARRIAGE

Two persons inspired by the same ideals,
animated by the same important tasks,
fully sharing their joys and sorrows,
giving all their best to each other—
united in one super-individual "we" in life-
    enjoyment and creativity,
        and in service to each other, to their fam-
        ilies,
    their community, and humanity at large.

PITIRIM SOROKIN

TRUE LOVE

I think true love is never blind,
But rather brings an added light,
An inner vision, quick to find
The beauties hid from common sight.

No soul can ever clearly see
Another's highest, noblest part,
Save through the sweet philosophy
And loving wisdom of the heart.

PHOEBE CARY

Let me not to the marriage of true minds
Admit impediments. Love is not love
Which alters when it alteration finds,
Or bends with the remover to remove.
O' no! it is an ever-fixèd mark,
That looks on tempests, and is never shaken;
It is the star to every wandering bark,
Whose worth's unknown, although his height
    be taken.
Love's not Time's fool, though rosy lips and
    cheeks
Within his bending sickle's compass come;
Love alters not with his brief hours and weeks,
But bears it out even to the edge of doom:
    If this be error, and upon me prov'd,
    I never writ, nor no man ever lov'd.

WILLIAM SHAKESPEARE

The Christian faith does not consist in the belief that we are saved, but in the belief that we are loved.

PIERRE VINET

LOVE-WISE

Now who can take from us what we have
    known—
    We that have looked into each other's eyes?
    Though sudden night should blacken all the
      skies,
The day is ours, and what the day has shown.
What we have seen and been, hath not this
    grown
    Part of our very selves? We, made love-wise,
    What power shall slay our living memories,
And who shall take from us what is our own?

RICHARD WATSON GILDER

A part of kindness consists in loving people
more than they deserve.

JOSEPH JOUBERT

DIRECTION

Love does not consist in gazing at each other
(one perfect sunrise gazing at another!) but in
looking outward together in the same direction.

ANTOINE DE SAINT-EXUPÉRY

Love is a good above all others, which alone
    maketh every burden light.
Love is watchful, and whilst sleeping still
    keeps watch; though fatigued is not weary;
    though pressed is not forced.
Love is sincere, gentle, strong, patient, faith-
    ful, prudent, long-suffering, manly.
Love is circumspect, humble, upright; not
    weary, not fickle, nor intent on vain things;
    sober, chaste, steadfast, quiet, and guarded
    in all the senses.

THOMAS A KEMPIS

SOURCE

It is not a question of how much we know,
how clever we are, nor even how good; it all
depends upon the heart's love. External actions are the results of love, the fruit it bears;
but the source, the root, is in the deep of the
heart.

FRANÇOIS FÉNELON

MARRIAGE

Going my way of old,
Contented more or less,
I dreamt not life could hold
Such happiness.

I dreamt not that love's way
Could keep the golden height,
Day after happy day,
Night after night.

W. W. GIBSON

HEART OF LOVE

There is beauty in the forest,
When the trees are grown and fair;
There is beauty in the meadow,
When wild flowers scent the air;
There is beauty in the sunlight
And the soft blue beams above:
Oh, the world is full of beauty,
When the heart is full of love!

Two shall be born a whole wide world apart
And one day out of darkness they shall stand
And read life's meaning in each other's eyes.

TRUE LOVE

True love is but a humble, low-born thing,
And hath its food served up in earthenware;
It is a thing to walk with, hand in hand,
Through the everydayness of this work-day
    world,
Baring its tender feet to every roughness,
Yet letting not one heart-beat go astray
From beauty's law of plainness and content—
A simple, fireside thing, whose quiet smile
Can warm earth's poorest hovel to a home.

JAMES RUSSELL LOWELL

Hell is not to love any more.

GEORGE BERNANOS

LINKED LIVES

In all your thoughts, and in all your acts, in
every hope and in every fear, when you soar
to the skies and when you fall to the ground,
always you are holding the other person's
hand.

A. A. MILNE

From SUSSEX

God gave all men all earth to love,
    But since our hearts are small,
Ordained for each one spot should prove
    Belovèd over all;
That, as He watched Creation's birth,
    So we, in godlike mood,
May of our love create our earth
    And see that it is good.

RUDYARD KIPLING

This is the miracle that happens every time to
those who really love: the more they give,
the more they possess of that precious nourish-
ing love from which flowers and children have
their strength and which could help all human
beings if they would take it without doubting.

RAINER MARIA RILKE

LOVE'S MIRACLE

Upon the marsh mud, dank and foul,
    A golden sunbeam softly fell,
And from the noisome depths arose
    A lily miracle.

Upon a dark bemired life
    A gleam of human love was flung,
And lo, from that ungenial soil
    A noble life upsprung.

L. M. MONTGOMERY

Love communicates
an immense value
to our smallest actions.

AUGUSTE SAUDREAU

THE GIFT

A wise lover
values not so much
the gift of the lover
as the love of the giver.

THOMAS A KEMPIS

Memories

For I have received of the Lord that which also I delivered unto you, That the Lord Jesus the same night in which he was betrayed took bread:

And when he had given thanks, he brake it, and said, Take, eat: this is my body, which is broken for you: this do in remembrance of me.

After the same manner also he took the cup, when he had supped, saying, This cup is the new testament in my blood: this do ye, as oft as ye drink it, in remembrance of me.

For as often as ye eat this bread, and drink this cup, ye do shew the Lord's death till he come. I CORINTHIANS 11:23-26

OLD RUGS

Her rugs are worn, yet she explains,
    That though thick new ones would be nice,
It's more like home while she retains
    The old. New rugs at any price
Could not reveal the paths of shoes,
    From babyhood through college days,
Whose footprints have thinned down the blues
    And scuffed the golds to burlap maize.
Alone now in her house she hugs
    Thoughts of dear distant ones, and sees
In all her faded, footworn rugs
    The mark of heart-bright memories.

JEAN CARPENTER MERGARD

CHOOSING MEMORIES

It is easier to make memories than to unmake
them. It is easier to remember than to forget.
Indeed, it is quite impossible to be sure we
have forgotten—anything. And since memory
remains, we would do well to look at what we
choose to make our memories.

RICHARD L. EVANS

When saving for old age, be sure to put away a
few pleasant thoughts.

THE COIN

Into my heart's treasury
    I slipped a coin
That time cannot take
    Nor a thief purloin—
Oh better than the minting
    Of a gold-crowned king
Is the safe-kept memory
    Of a lovely thing.

SARA TEASDALE

KEEP SOME GREEN MEMORY ALIVE

I shall keep some cool green memory in my
    heart
To draw upon should days be bleak and cold.
I shall hold it like a cherished thing apart
To turn to now or when I shall be old:
Perhaps a sweeping meadow, brightly green,
Where grasses bend and the winds of heaven
    blow
Straight from the hand of God, as cool and
    clean
As anything the heart of man can know.

Or it may be this green remembered tree
That I shall turn to if the nights be long,
High on a hill, its cool boughs lifting free,
And from its tip, a wild bird's joyous song.
A weary city dweller to survive
Must keep some cool green memory alive.

GRACE NOLL CROWELL

Memory is not just the imprint of the past time
upon us; it is the keeper of what is meaningful
for our deepest hopes and fears.

ROLLO MAY

We have committed the Golden Rule to memory; now let us commit it to life.

EDWIN MARKHAM

RIGHT OF FRANCHISE

Memory becomes a transcendent thing in the
libraries of the world. Men who have been
dead for centuries exercise the right of the
franchise through their books.

LYNN HAROLD HOUGH

WHISPERING VOICES

There is no disgrace in being homesick. At times I have felt the tugging of those invisible fingers and heard the whispering of those voices.

For I have seen the hills of Scotland moist with mist; have seen the fir trees marching down to the loch-sides; have seen the sheep on the hills and the heather in bloom; have heard the skirling of the pipes down the glen and the gurgling of the burn over the rocks and the familiar music of the kettle on the hob; have seen pictures that will never fade and sounds that will never die away.

I have longed for the northland, to see again the low stone houses, the swelling hills, the white tails of the waterfalls.

I have wanted to hear again the gentle low voices of the women and the music of the Gaelic tongue; to smell the delicate fragrance of bluebells in the spring and the rhododendron; to hear the mavis sing and the lark.

I have wanted to see the long twilights, to look out over the waters of the Firth, and be grateful to God that there was still more of Scotland beyond.

PETER MARSHALL

GRATEFUL MEMORIES

Like a bird singing in the rain, let grateful memories survive in time of sorrow.

ROBERT LOUIS STEVENSON

There are few greater treasures to be acquired in youth than great poetry—and prose—stored in the memory. At the time one may resent the labor of storing. But they sleep in the memory and awake in later years, illuminated by life and illuminating it.

RICHARD W. LIVINGSTONE

DO YOU REMEMBER?

Whether your childhood was sad or happy as you look back upon it, there is one thing about it that is true. There were moments of intense and complete joy, which for the instant left nothing to be desired. It may have been your first new dress, or new suit; the thing about which you had dreamed for, oh, so many days was actually yours! Perhaps it was the first time you received a letter through the mail. It may have been your first time to visit a circus to see live tigers, lions, elephants, and big, big snakes. Perhaps it was the time when your mother let you mix the dough for the bread or sent you on your first errand in the next block alone. Your greatest moment of fullness may have come when, for the first time, you were conscious that your mother loved you—that swirling sense of sheer ecstasy when you were completely aware of another's love. Do you remember?

HOWARD THURMAN

SOMETIMES

Across the fields of yesterday
    He sometimes comes to me,
A little lad just back from play—
    The lad I used to be.

And yet he smiles so wistfully
    Once he has crept within,
I wonder if he hopes to see
    The man I might have been.

THOMAS S. JONES, JR.

KIND WORDS

O the kind words we give shall in memory live
And sunshine forever impart;
Let us oft speak kind words to each other;
Kind words are sweet tones of the heart.

JOSEPH L. TOWNSEND

 Music

Make a joyful noise unto the Lord, all ye lands.

Serve the Lord with gladness: come before his presence with singing.

Know ye that the Lord he is God: it is he that hath made us, and not we ourselves; we are his people, and the sheep of his pasture.

Enter into his gates with thanksgiving, and into his courts with praise: be thankful unto him, and bless his name.

For the Lord is good; his mercy is everlasting; and his truth endureth to all generations. PSALM 100:1-5

MUSIC

Let me go where'er I will
I hear a sky-born music still:
It sounds from all things old,
It sounds from all things young,
From all that's fair, from all that's foul,
Peals out a cheerful song.

It is not only in the rose,
It is not only in the bird,
Not only where the rainbow glows,
Nor in the song of woman heard,
But in the darkest, meanest things
There alway, alway something sings.

'Tis not in the high stars alone,
Nor in the cups of budding flowers,
Nor in the red-breast's mellow tone,
Nor in the bow that smiles in showers,
But in the mud and scum of things
There alway, alway something sings.

RALPH WALDO EMERSON

THE MASTER PLAYER

An old, worn harp that had been played
Till all its strings were loose and frayed,
Joy, Hate, and Fear, each one essayed
To play. But each in turn had found
No sweet responsiveness of sound.

Then Love the Master-Player came
With heaving breast and eyes aflame;
The harp he took all undismayed,
Smote on its strings, still strange to song,
And brought forth music sweet and strong.

PAUL LAURENCE DUNBAR

COMMUNION

Some of the loftiest aspirations of the human soul are reserved to those who have the great gift of musical expression, for they thereby lift themselves out of a material world and enter a spiritual one. In holding communion with the great composers, who were surely instruments in the hands of a Divine Power, we are enabled to express something of the Infinite. Whether I play in public in the midst of thousands or in the privacy of my own room, I forget everything except my music. Whenever I am lifted out of the material plane and come in touch with another, a holier world, it is as if some hand other than mine were directing the bow over the strings.

FRITZ KREISLER

SONG

There will be no song on our lips if there be no anguish in our hearts.

KARL BARTH

INSPIRATION

You ask me where I get my ideas. That I cannot tell you with certainty. They come unsummoned, directly, indirectly—I could seize them with my hands—out in the open air, in the woods, while walking, in the silence of the nights, at dawn, excited by moods which are translated by the poet into words, by me into tones that sound and roar and storm about me till I have set them down in notes.

LUDWIG VAN BEETHOVEN

JOYOUS RESPONSE

A friend once asked the great composer Haydn why his church music was always so full of gladness. He answered: "I cannot make it otherwise. I write according to the thoughts I feel. When I think upon my God, my heart is so full of joy that the notes dance and leap from my pen; and since God has given me a cheerful heart, it will be pardoned me that I serve Him with a cheerful spirit."

HENRY VAN DYKE

THE MASTER'S TOUCH

At the end of dinner each evening in his jungle Hospital in Lambaréné, Dr. Albert Schweitzer would fold his napkin, announce the number of the hymn to be sung, get up and walk over to the upright piano on the other side of the room. He would arrange the hymn carefully on the music stand, study it for a moment, then start to play.

The piano must have been at least fifty years old. The keyboard was badly stained; large double screws fastened the ivory to each note. The volume pedal was stuck. One or more strings were missing on at least a dozen keys. The felt covering the hammers was worn thin and produced pinging effects.

When I saw Dr. Schweitzer sit down at the piano and prop up the hymnbook, I winced. Here was one of history's greatest interpreters of Bach, a man who could fill any concert hall in the world. The best grand piano ever made would be none too good for him. But he was now about to play a dilapidated upright virtually beyond repair. And he went at it easily and with the dignity that never leaves him.

The amazing and wondrous thing was that the piano seemed to lose its poverty in his hands. Whatever its capacity was to yield music was now being fully realized. The tinniness and chattering echoes seemed subdued. It may be that this was the result of Schweitzer's intimate acquaintance with the piano, enabling him to avoid the rebellious keys and favoring only the co-operative ones. Whatever the reason, his being at the piano strangely seemed to make it right.

NORMAN COUSINS

GOD IS AT THE ORGAN

God is at the organ;
 I can hear
A mighty music echoing,
 Far and near.

God is at the organ
 And the keys
Are storm-strewn billows,
 Moorlands, trees.

God is at the organ,
 I can hear
A mighty music, echoing
 Far and near.

EGBERT SANDFORD

The nightingale has a lyre of gold
The lark's is a clarion call,
And the blackbird plays but a boxwood flute,
But I love him best of all.

WILLIAM ERNEST HENLEY

168

Nature

And God said, Let the earth bring forth grass, the herb yielding seed, and the fruit tree yielding fruit after his kind, whose seed is in itself, upon the earth: and it was so.

And the earth brought forth grass, and herb yielding seed after his kind, and the tree yielding fruit, whose seed was in itself, after his kind: and God saw that it was good.   GENESIS 1:11-12

GOOD COMPANY

Today I have grown taller from walking with
  the trees,
The seven-sister poplars, who go softly in a
  line;
And I think my heart is whiter from its parley
  with a star
That trembled out at nightfall and hung above
  the pine.
The call note of a redbird from the cedars in
  the dusk
Woke his happy note within me to an answer
  free and fine,
And a sudden angel beckoned from a column
  of blue smoke—
Lord, who am I that they should stoop: these
  holy folk of Thine?

KARLE WILSON BAKER

THE GARDEN

The kiss of the sun for pardon,
  The song of the birds for mirth—
One is nearer God's heart in a garden
  Than anywhere else on earth.

DOROTHY FRANCES GURNEY

From VESTIGIA

I took a day to search for God,
And found Him not. But as I trod
  By rocky ledge, through woods untamed,
  Just where one scarlet lily flamed,
I saw His footprint in the sod.

Then suddenly, all unaware,
Far off in the deep shadows, where
  A solitary hermit thrush
  Sung through the holy twilight hush—
I heard His voice upon the air.

BLISS CARMAN

PRAYER

O God, we thank Thee for this universe, our
  great home; for its vastness and its riches,
  and for the manifoldness of the life which
  teems upon it and of which we are part.
We praise Thee for the arching sky and the
  blessed winds, for the driving clouds and
  the constellations on high.
We praise Thee for the salt sea and the running water, for the everlasting hills, for the
  trees, and for the grass under our feet.
We thank Thee for our senses by which we
  can see the splendor of the morning, and
  hear the jubilant songs of love, and smell the
  breath of the springtime.
Grant us, we pray Thee, a heart wide open to
  all this joy and beauty, and save our souls
  from being so steeped in care or so darkened
  by passion that we pass heedless and unsee-
  ing when even the thorn-bush by the wayside is aflame with the glory of God.

WALTER RAUSCHENBUSCH

EARTH'S EYE

A lake is the landscape's most beautiful and
expressive feature. It is earth's eye, looking
into which the beholder measures the depth
of his own nature.

HENRY DAVID THOREAU

In the concert of nature it is hard to keep in
tune with oneself if one is out of tune with
everything.

GEORGE SANTAYANA

Nature is painting for us, day after day, pictures of infinite beauty if only we have the
eyes to see them.

JOHN RUSKIN

A PRAYER IN SPRING

Oh, give us pleasure in the flowers today;
And give us not to think so far away
As the uncertain harvest; keep us here
All simply in the springing of the year.

Oh, give us pleasure in the orchard white,
Like nothing else by day, like ghosts by night;
And make us happy in the happy bees,
That swarm dilating round the perfect trees.

And make us happy in the darting bird
That suddenly above the bees is heard,
The meteor that thrusts in with needle bill,
And off a blossom in mid air stands still.

For this is love and nothing else is love,
The which it is reserved for God above
To sanctify to what far ends He will,
But which it only needs that we fulfill.

ROBERT FROST

PRAYER

Lord, make me sensitive to the sight
Of swallows in their graceful flight;
Let each dip, each swoop, each glide
Forever in my heart abide.

A darkened steeple against the sky,
A firefly's gleam where shadows lie,
Lightning that splits the sky apart—
Let each of Thy miracles pierce my heart!

Then, though blindness be my curse,
The wonders of this universe
Will be so mirrored in my soul,
I'll not need eyes to make me whole.

BARBARA MARR

SUNSET

But beauty seen is never lost,
God's colors all are fast;
The glory of this sunset heaven
Into my soul has passed.

JOHN GREENLEAF WHITTIER

Oh, the splendor of the universe! For many of us autumntime is the most glorious of all the year.

God has dipped His paint brush in His palette of colors and splashed the hills and woods and fields with robes of saffron and crimson and gold and yellow and brown and scarlet.

The maples and chestnuts and oaks vie with one another in autumnal beauty. The sumac dazzles the eye with brilliant scarlet. The sunsets are too gorgeous for human description.

In this amazing garden of beauty our lips involuntarily sing forth the praises of the psalmist: "Bless Jehovah, O my soul; and all this is within me, bless his holy name."

CHARLES KINGSLEY

Generations of mankind have discovered that gardening is work for philosophers, and that the daily planting and weeding will make a philosopher out of him who never was before. I mean philosopher in the true sense, not simply a placid soul who can accept life without protest, but a mind awakened, fertile, discriminating.

JOHN ERSKINE

Who loves a garden still his Eden keeps,
Perennial pleasures plants, and wholesome
    harvests reaps.

BRONSON ALCOTT

INTRINSIC VALUE

Beauty breaks through not only at a few
highly organized points, it breaks through
almost everywhere. Even the minutest things
reveal it as well as do the sublimest things,
like the stars. Whatever one sees through the
microscope, a bit of mould, for example, is
charged with beauty. Everything from a dew-
drop to Mount Shasta is the bearer of beauty.
And yet beauty has no function, no utility. Its
value is intrinsic, not extrinsic. It is its own
excuse for being. It greases no wheels, it bakes
no puddings. It is a gift of sheer grace, a gratuitous largesse. It must imply behind things a
Spirit that enjoys beauty for its own sake and
that floods the world everywhere with it.
Wherever it can break through, it does break
through, and our joy in it shows that we are
in some sense kindred to the giver and revealer
of it.

RUFUS M. JONES

CONVICTION

A crumpled rose-leaf, a gleam in the water lit
up by sunset, a child's happy smile, waken in
me the conviction that, as I am looking out
upon Nature, so there is Another gazing on
me.

WILLIAM BARRY

STOREHOUSE

If I were to name the three most precious resources of life, I should say books, friends,
and nature; and the greatest of these, at least
the most constant and always at hand, is
nature. Nature we have always with us, an
inexhaustible storehouse of that which moves
the heart, appeals to the mind, and fires the
imagination—health to the body, a stimulus to
the intellect, and joy to the soul. To the scientist, nature is a storehouse of facts, laws,
processes; to the artist she is a storehouse of
pictures; to the poet she is a storehouse of
images, fancies, a source of inspiration; to the
moralist she is a storehouse of precepts and
parables; to all she may be a source of knowledge and joy.

JOHN BURROUGHS

Nothing is more beautiful than the loveliness
of the woods before sunrise.

GEORGE WASHINGTON CARVER

I believe a leaf of grass is no less than the
    journey-work of the stars,
And the pismire is equally perfect, and a grain
    of sand, and the egg of the wren,
And the tree-toad is a chef-d'oeuvre for the
    highest,
And the running blackberry would adorn the
    parlors of heaven,
And the narrowest hinge in my hand puts to
    scorn all machinery,
And the cow crunching with depress'd head
    surpasses any statue,
And a mouse is miracle enough to stagger
    sextillions of infidels.

WALT WHITMAN

From SILVER POPLARS

God wrote His loveliest poem on the day
He made the first tall silver poplar tree,
And set it high upon a pale-gold hill
For all the new enchanted earth to see.

And then God took the music of the winds,
And set each leaf aflutter and athrill—
Today I read His poem word by word
Among the silver poplars on the hill.

GRACE NOLL CROWELL

VACATION PRAYER

Loving Father, who didst make this earth so fair, open our eyes to see its wonders and our hearts to feel its beauty. In our days of refreshment and recreation, draw us nearer to Thee through the things which Thou hast made. May the joy of Thy sunshine, the quiet of Thy forests, the murmur of Thy streams, and the steadfast strength of Thine everlasting hills teach us the deep secret of Thy peace.

Renew in us faith and courage, physical strength and spiritual vision, that we may know ourselves to be safely held in Thy strong hands.

From this life, so near to Nature's heart, may we drink in new strength to help us reach the restless hearts of men. May we go back to the world and its duties, stronger, simpler, sweeter, and thus become more worthy messengers of Him who saw His Father's goodness in the sparrow's flight and His Father's love in the beauty which clothes the lilies of the field.

HUGH L. BURLESON

TREES

I think that I shall never see
A poem lovely as a tree.

A tree whose hungry mouth is pressed
Against the earth's sweet-flowing breast;

A tree that looks at God all day,
And lifts her leafy arms to pray;

A tree that may in summer wear
A nest of robins in her hair;

Upon whose bosom snow has lain;
Who intimately lives with rain.

Poems are made by fools like me,
But only God can make a tree.

JOYCE KILMER

GOD OF THE OPEN AIR

By the faith that the wild flowers show when they bloom unbidden,
By the calm of a river's flow to a goal that is hidden,
By the strength of the tree that clings to its deep foundation,
By the courage of birds' light wings on the long migration—
Wonderful Spirit of trust that abides in Nature's breast!
Teach me how to confide, and live my life, and rest.

HENRY VAN DYKE

MAGNANIMITY

As spring comes we become more aware of the magnanimity of Nature, a sort of elemental big-heartedness and inclusive impartiality that is a reflection of the character of God. Spring sunshine will not fall on beautiful, graceful birch trees alone, but upon the less lovable scrub pine, alders, and willows, too. April showers will not pick and choose, playing favorites with the daffodils and crocuses, and shunning objectionable dandelions and lowly violets, blessing the arbutus and avoiding the bloodroot and wild strawberry. The great sun will warm the acres of saint and sinner alike. Warm rains will beat with equal benefit upon the gardens of the grateful and the grumbling

HAROLD E. KOHN

WINGS

The little cares of every day,
  The tiny humdrum things,
May bind my feet when I would stray,
  But still my heart has wings
While red geraniums are pressed
  Against my window glass,
And low above my green-sweet hill
  The gypsy wind clouds pass!

THE MANUSCRIPTS OF GOD

And nature, the old nurse, took
  The child upon her knee,
Saying, "Here is a story book
  My father hath writ for thee.
Come, wander with me," she said,
  "In regions yet untrod
And read what is still unread
  In the manuscripts of God."

HENRY WADSWORTH LONGFELLOW

"Let trees be made, for earth is bare,"
  Spake the Voice of the Lord in thunder:
The roots ran deep and trees were there,
  And earth was full of wonder.

ARTHUR GUITERMAN

When I heard the learn'd astronomer,
When the proofs, the figures, were ranged in
  columns before me,
When I was shown the charts and diagrams, to
  add, divide, and measure them,
When I sitting heard the astronomer where he
  lectured with much applause in the lecture-
  room,
How soon unaccountable I became tired and
  sick,
Till rising and gliding out I wander'd off by
  myself,
In the mystical moist night-air, and from time
  to time,
Look'd up in perfect silence at the stars.

WALT WHITMAN

The man who has seen the rising moon break out of the clouds at midnight has been present like an archangel at the creation of light and of the world.

RALPH WALDO EMERSON

TO A DANDELION

Dear common flower, that grow'st beside the
  way,
Fringing the dusty road with harmless gold.

JAMES RUSSELL LOWELL

GOLDEN SIGHT

He was glad to see Hoppy,
His knobby-skinned friend
Who lived in his garden
Three summers on end.

But folks used to wonder
Why he would consort
With this ugly creature
Whose touch left a wart!

Yet he knew a beauty
That none of the rest
Of all living beings,
Save Hoppy, possessed.

His eyes are the secret,
You'll see if you're bold,
That his are the only ones
God made of gold.

RALPH W. SEAGER

THE RHODORA

In May, when sea-winds pierced our solitudes,
I found the fresh Rhodora in the woods,
Spreading its leafless blooms in a damp nook,
To please the desert and the sluggish brook.
The purple petals, fallen in the pool,
Made the black water with their beauty gay;
Here might the red-bird come his plumes to
  cool,
And court the flower that cheapens his array.
Rhodora! if the sages ask thee why
This charm is wasted on the earth and sky,
Tell them, dear, that if eyes were made for
  seeing,

Then Beauty is its own excuse for being:
Why wert thou there, O rival of the rose!
I never thought to ask, I never knew;
But, in my simple ignorance, suppose
The self-same Power that brought me there
  brought you.

RALPH WALDO EMERSON

From THE UNUTTERABLE BEAUTY

God, give me speech, in mercy touch my lips,
I cannot bear Thy Beauty and be still,
Watching the red-gold majesty that tips
The crest of yonder hill,
And out to sea smites on the sails of ships,

That flame like drifting stars across the deep,
Calling their silver comrades from the sky,
As long and ever longer shadows creep,
To sing their lullaby,
And hush the tired eyes of earth to sleep.

Thy radiancy of glory strikes me dumb,
Yet cries within my soul for power to raise
Such miracles of music as would sum
Thy splendour in a phrase,
Storing it safe for all the years to come.

G. A. STUDDERT-KENNEDY

LIVING WITH NATURE

The man who lives with Nature, understands her moods and adapts himself to her ways, is by this very conformity molded to a certain largeness and nobility of soul, saved from certain petty sins, and finds courage, sincerity, and perseverance rising up within him to match the elemental forces of the mountains or the sea, with which his life is interwoven.

ALBERT W. PALMER

Overcoming

The Lord is my shepherd; I shall not want.

He maketh me to lie down in green pastures: he leadeth me beside the still waters.

He restoreth my soul: he leadeth me in the paths of righteousness for his name's sake.

Yea, though I walk through the valley of the shadow of death, I will fear no evil: for thou art with me; thy rod and thy staff they comfort me.

Thou preparest a table before me in the presence of mine enemies: thou anointest my head with oil; my cup runneth over.

Surely goodness and mercy shall follow me all the days of my life: and I will dwell in the house of the Lord for ever.   PSALM 23:1-6

ARE YE ABLE?

Able to suffer without complaining,
To be misunderstood without explaining;
Able to endure without a breaking,
To be forsaken without forsaking;
Able to give without receiving,
To be ignored without any grieving;
Able to ask without commanding,
To love despite misunderstanding;
Able to turn to the Lord for guarding,
Able to wait for His own rewarding?

BRENTON THOBURN BADLEY

PRAYER

Give me, O God, the understanding heart—
The quick discernment of the soul to see
Another's inner wish, the hidden part
Of him that, wordless, speaks for sympathy.

GEORGIA HARKNESS

God will not permit any troubles to come
upon us, unless He has a specific plan by which
great blessing can come out of the difficulty.

PETER MARSHALL

TEST OF CHARACTER

There is no more searching test of the human
spirit than the way it behaves when fortune is
adverse and it has to pass through a prolonged
period of disappointing failures. Then comes
the real proof of the man. Achievement, if a
man has the ability, is a joy; but to take hard
knocks and come up smiling, to have your
mainsail blown away and then rig a sheet on
the bowsprit and sail on—this is perhaps the
deepest test of character.

HARRY EMERSON FOSDICK

COLORS

Your living is determined not so much by
what life brings to you as by the attitude you
bring to life; not so much by what happens to
you as by the way your mind looks at what
happens. Circumstances and situations do
color life, but you have been given the mind
to choose what the color shall be.

JOHN HOMER MILLER

Afflictions are but the shadow of God's wings.

GEORGE MACDONALD

INSCRIPTION

All that which pleases is
but for a moment

All that which troubles is
but for a moment

That only is important
which is eternal

MILAN CATHEDRAL

The man who removes a mountain begins by
carrying away small stones.

CHINESE PROVERB

ARITHMETIC

Count your garden by the flowers,
Never by the leaves that fall;
Count your days by golden hours,
Don't remember clouds at all.
Count your nights by stars, not shadows,
Count your years with smiles, not tears,
Count your blessings, not your troubles,
Count your age by friends, not years.

INNER LIGHT

So many things that now seem like fixed stars were born of fierce struggle and apparent defeat. Lincoln believed that he had done a poor job after he delivered the Gettysburg Address, and Keats died believing that his name would not be remembered. Beethoven wrote his greatest music after he became deaf, and Milton his greatest poetry after he became blind. The people who are worth knowing are the people who never gave up. From the outside, to their own friends, many of them seemed ordinary enough people; but each of them held a kind of special light inside himself.

MARCHETTE CHUTE

POSSIBILITY

Put forth thy hand in God's name. Know that the word "impossible," where truth and mercy, and the everlasting voices of nature order, has no place in the brave man's dictionary. That, when all men have said, "impossible," and tumbled noisily elsewhither, and thou alone art left, then first thy time and possibility have come. It is for thee now. Do thou that, and ask no man's counsel but thine own only and God's. Brother, thou hast possibility within thee for much. The possibility of writing on the eternal skies the record of an heroic life.

MERTON S. RICE

Mankind is a weaver who from the wrong side works on the carpet of time. The day will come when he will see the right side and understand the grandeur of the pattern he with his own hands has woven through the centuries without anything but a tangle of strings.

ALPHONSE DE LAMARTINE

COUNSEL

It is not by regretting what is irreparable that true work is to be done, but by seeking the best of what we are. It is not by complaining that we have not the right tools, but by using well the tools we have. The manly and wise way is to look your disadvantages in the face, and see what can be made out of them.

FREDERICK W. ROBERTSON

GOD'S DELAYS

God's delays are not denials,
　He has heard your prayer,
He knows all about your trials,
　He knows your every care.

God's delays are not denials,
　Help is on the way,
He is watching o'er life's dials,
　Bringing forth the day.

God's delays are not denials,
　You will find Him true;
Working through the darkest trials,
　What is best for you.

GRACE E. TROY

Once I knew the depth where no hope was and darkness lay on the face of all things. Then love came and set my soul free. Once I fretted and beat myself against the wall that shut me in. My life was without a past or future, and death a consummation devoutly to be wished. But a little word from the fingers of another fell into my hands that clutched at emptiness, and my heart leaped up with the rapture of living. I do not know the meaning of the darkness, but I have learned the overcoming of it.

HELEN KELLER

BACKBONE

Each one of us should do something every day that we do not want to do but know we should do, to strengthen our backbone and put iron in our soul.

HENRY HITT CRANE

BASIC RULES FOR DAILY LIVING

1. Take twenty minutes by yourself at the beginning of each day.
2. Live above small troubles by losing yourself in big, worthwhile interests.
3. Grow every day; life is a game; keep your eye on the ball, rather than on the scoreboard.
4. Have power to see things through; keep remembering that most accomplishments are three-fourths drudgery, and one-fourth joy.
5. Alternate your interests. It is better to be busy than bored. Balance your life with work, play, love, and worship.
6. Be gracious to others; do kind deeds beyond the call of duty; remember that every person is fighting a battle.
7. Talk over your problems with others—with confiding friends, your doctor of medicine, your minister, your God.
8. Work and co-operate with God, praying that God will do something *through* you rather than *for* you.

THOMAS S. KEPLER

SUNSHINE AND RAIN

If all the skies were sunshine,
Our faces would be fain
To feel once more upon them
The cooling plash of rain.

HENRY VAN DYKE

If what shone afar so grand
Turns to ashes in thy hand,
On again! the victory lies
In the struggle, not the prize.

LUCK

Do I believe in luck? I should say I do! It's a wonderful force. I have watched the successful careers of too many lucky men to doubt its existence and its efficacy. You see some fellow reach out and grab an opportunity that the other fellows standing around had not realized was there.

He calls into play his breadth of vision. He sees the possibilities of the situation, and has the ambition to desire them, and the courage to tackle them. He intensifies his strong points, bolsters his weak ones, cultivates those personal qualities that cause other men to trust him and to co-operate with him. He sows the seeds of sunshine, of good cheer, of optimism, of unstinted kindness. He gives freely of what he has, both spiritual and physical things. He thinks a little straighter; works a little harder and a little longer; travels on his nerve and his enthusiasm; he gives such service as his best efforts permit. He keeps his head cool, his feet warm, his mind busy.

He doesn't worry over trifles, plans his work ahead, and then sticks to it, rain or shine. He talks and acts like a winner, for he knows in time he will be one. And then—luck does all the rest.

HIDDEN TREASURES

The spirit of man is stronger than anything that can happen to it.

ROBERT FALCON SCOTT

WAITING PERIODS

The art of waiting is not learned at once. The child must wait until he is old enough to have a bicycle, the young man until he is old enough to drive a car, the medical student must wait for his diploma, the young couple for savings to buy a new home.

HOWARD WHITMAN

COURAGE

Courage shall leap from me, a gallant sword
To rout the enemy and all his horde,
Cleaving a kingly pathway through despair.

ANGELA MORGAN

The human will, that force unseen,
The offspring of a deathless soul,
Can hew the way to any goal,
Though walls of granite intervene.

ELLA WHEELER WILCOX

THE LADDER OF ST. AUGUSTINE

The heights by great men reached and kept,
Were not attained by sudden flight,
But they, while their companions slept,
Were toiling upward in the night.

HENRY WADSWORTH LONGFELLOW

ASSURANCE

We can do without reward in this life;
we can do without glory;
we can do without a crutch and without a
    spur—
but we cannot do without the assurance that
    as we struggle for fine things the struggle
    is a real one and a fight that counts.

JOHN BAILLIE

PATTERN

Not till the loom is silent
    And the shuttles cease to fly,
Shall God unroll the canvas
    And explain the reason why
The dark threads are as needful
    In the weaver's skillful hand
As the threads of gold and silver
    In the pattern He has planned.

PERSPECTIVE

If Winter comes, can Spring be far behind?

PERCY BYSSHE SHELLEY

Happiness is not mostly pleasure; it is mostly victory.

HARRY EMERSON FOSDICK

FRIENDLY FORCES

What is required of us is that we love the difficult and learn to deal with it. In the difficult are the friendly forces, the hands that work on us.

RAINER MARIA RILKE

LIFE-ENGAGING DIFFICULTIES

There is no happiness except as we take on life-engaging difficulties. The mortal flaw in the advertised version of happiness is in the fact that it purports to be effortless. We demand difficulty even in our games. We demand it because without difficulty there can be no game. A game is a way of making something hard for the fun of it. The fun is in winning within the rules. No difficulty, no fun.

JOHN CIARDI

Praise ye the Lord. Praise God in his sanctuary: praise him in the firmament of his power.

Praise him for his mighty acts: praise him according to his excellent greatness.

Praise him with the sound of the trumpet: praise him with the psaltery and harp.

Praise him with the timbrel and dance: praise him with stringed instruments and organs.

Praise him upon the loud cymbals: praise him upon the high sounding cymbals.

Let every thing that hath breath praise the Lord. Praise ye the Lord.

PSALM 150:1-6

PSALM OF A CITY MAN

I will lift up mine eyes unto the skyscrapers—
From whence shall my help come?
My help comes from the Lord,
Higher and greater than them all!
Deeper than the rocks on which their towering
structure rests,
And far above their upmost thrust, is the glory
of His truth;
Brighter than the sun reflected from a million
windows,
More brilliant than the myriad lights that
illumine them by night,
God's mercy shines!

Even in the rush of trade and the crush of
traffic
He will guide the feet of those who follow in
His way;
From the lust of passion and the lure of
possession
He will protect their spirit!
And wherever they move among the masses
of men,
Ministering to the cause of human need,
Where hearts are blinded and hopes are
blighted,
The Eternal will bless their going out and
their coming in—
Today, tomorrow, and forever!

H. VICTOR KANE

The praise that comes of love does not make
us vain, but humble rather.

JAMES M. BARRIE

GREAT AND SIMPLE JOYS

Let us praise and thank God in gladness and
humility for all great and simple joys:
For the gift of wonder and the joy of discovery, and for the constant newness of life;
For children and the joy of innocency, for the
sanctities of family life, and for all that our
friendships bring us;
For the fruits of sympathy and sorrow, for the
gift of humor and gaiety of heart, and for
the joy of work attempted and achieved;
For the gifts of science and invention, for
singers and all musicians, for poets and
craftsmen, for those who work in form and
color to increase the beauty of life, for the
consecration of art in the service of God,
and for all things that help us to see the
beauty of holiness;
For the grace of Christ in common people, their
forbearance and generosity, their good temper, their courage, and their kindness, and
for all humble lives of service.

BREAK IN THE CLOUDS

There is always sunshine somewhere for which
I praise God — the sunshine that brightens
other lives when mine is shrouded in gloom.
Glory to Thee, my God, for the gladness of
little children, for the joy of mothers, for the
bliss of lovers. The radiance of their hearts is
from Thy touch because in the joy of Thy creation Thou rejoicest. And I praise Thee, my
God, that in my unhappiest days there are
breaks in the clouds through which I see the
blue beyond and the glorious sun of Thy compassionate love. Even a moment of light gives
me new hope and new courage.

CHARLES H. BRENT

CAN I BE SILENT?

Doth not all nature around me praise God? If I were silent, I should be an exception to the universe. Doth not the thunder praise Him as it rolls like drums in the march of the God of armies? Do not the mountains praise Him when the woods upon their summits wave in adoration? Does not the lightning write His name in letters of fire? Hath not the whole earth a voice? And shall I, can I, silent be?

CHARLES H. SPURGEON

We adore Thee, God, because Thou hast empowered man to create beauty. Our every sense is conscious of beauty in

the graceful column,
the sound of a tuneful violin,
the touch of soft linen,
the odor of choice perfume,
the flavor of good food.

All show beauty to the sensitive soul.

MARIE WELLES CLAPP

From VENI CREATOR

Lord of my heart's elation,
Spirit of things unseen,
Be thou my aspiration
Consuming and serene!

Be thou my exaltation
Or fortitude of mien,
Lord of the world's elation
Thou breath of things unseen!

BLISS CARMAN

PRAISE AND THANKS

For spring and autumn, sun and rain,
The blessedness of work-filled days,
For blooming rose and garnered grain,
Take, Lord, my praise.

For firelight flickers through the gloom,
For frostbound streams, for grassy
banks,
For love-filled heart and book-filled room,
Accept my thanks.

GEORGE BURT LAKE

THE ONE THOUSANDTH PSALM

O God, we thank Thee for everything!

For the sea and its waves, blue, green, and gray and always wonderful;

For the beach and the breakers and the spray and the white foam on the rocks;

For the blue arch of heaven; for the clouds in the sky, white and gray and purple;

For the green of the grass; for the forests in their spring beauty; for the wheat and corn and rye and barley;

For the brown earth turned up by the plow; for the sun by day and the dews by night.

We thank Thee for all Thou hast made and that Thou hast called it good.

For all the glory and beauty and wonder of the world;

For the glory of springtime, the tints of the flowers and their fragrance;

For the glory of summer flowers, the roses and cardinals and clethra;

For the glory of the autumn, the scarlet and crimson and gold of the forest;

For the glory of winter, the pure snow on the shrubs and trees.

We thank Thee that Thou hast placed us in the world to subdue all things to Thy glory,

And to use all things for the good of Thy children.

We thank Thee! We enter into Thy work and go about Thy business.

EDWARD EVERETT HALE

Prayer

After this manner therefore pray ye: Our Father which art in heaven, Hallowed be thy name.

Thy kingdom come. Thy will be done in earth, as it is in heaven.

Give us this day our daily bread.

And forgive us our debts, as we forgive our debtors.

And lead us not into temptation, but deliver us from evil: For thine is the kingdom, and the power, and the glory, for ever. Amen.

MATTHEW 6:9-13

THE SURPRISE

So joyously, at answered prayer,
The heart leaps up from its despair,
It must indeed have been afraid
God wasn't listening when it prayed.

ELAINE V. EMANS

The function of prayer is to set God at the center of attention.

ALBERT EDWARD DAY

RESULTS OF PRAYING

Increased physical buoyancy,
greater intellectual vigor,
moral stamina,
better human relations, and
complete and harmonious assembly
    of body, mind, and spirit
    which gives the frail human reed
    its unshakable strength.

ALEXIS CARREL

Prayer is the soul's sincere desire,
    Uttered or unexpressed;
The motion of a hidden fire,
    That trembles in the breast.

Prayer is the burden of a sigh,
    The falling of a tear;
The upward glancing of an eye,
    When none but God is near.

JAMES MONTGOMERY

We must alter our lives in order to alter our hearts, for it is impossible to live one way and pray another.

WILLIAM LAW

Prayer is the world in tune.

HENRY VAUGHAN

"O God," I cried, and that was all. But what are the prayers of all the universe more than expansions of that one cry? It is not what God can give us, but God that we want.

GEORGE MACDONALD

ANSWERS

God may not always answer prayers, but he always answers people.

PRAYER

Grant me, O Lord, to know what I ought to know,
to love what I ought to love,
to praise what delights Thee most,
to value what is precious in Thy sight,
to hate what is offensive to Thee.
Do not suffer me to judge according to the sight of my eyes,
nor to pass sentence according to the hearing of the ears of ignorant men;
but to discern with a true judgment between things visible and spiritual,
and above all, always to inquire what is the good pleasure of Thy will.

THOMAS A KEMPIS

Prayer is the ascent of the mind to God.

JEREMY TAYLOR

Prayer is the Godward reach of a man's soul.

LYNN JAMES RADCLIFFE

DEFINITIONS OF PRAYER

Prayer helps to form the "steel of spirituality" within the soul.

Prayer imparts a peace within "as high as the mountain, as deep as the sea"—creating a Christlike serenity of soul.

Prayer generates courage within, and I stand erect, taller of soul, and converse with God, listening to the whisperings of His will, and learn the great lesson of life, that this world is merely a place to grow souls in, and that this life is only the introduction to life eternal.

Prayer and faith, inseparable companions, plant a garden in the soul, and in this wondrous garden roses bloom not only in December but all the year round.

Prayer is the time-exposure of the soul to the highest that we know.

Prayer sinks a shaft deep into our lives where the real and lasting values of life abide.

Prayer lights a candle in the soul, by whose radiant light we discover the God-shaped space in our heart, reserved for Him in our creation.

Prayer is a battlefield on which the issues of life are determined.

Prayer takes away dimness from the soul and clarifies our vision.

Prayer is a spiritual gymnasium in which we exercise and practice for godliness.

Prayer is essential to a full-flowing of the spiritual life. The soul deprived of the experience and inspirations of prayer is like a plant that comes to the point of blossoming but never blooms.

Prayer is being "in the secret place with Jesus" —a place of spiritual retreat and of soul-refreshment.

Prayer imparts what we may call a tang to spiritual life. We are admonished to be the salt of the earth, and prayer furnishes the salt.

Prayer is a trellis, supporting the vines and flowers of the spirit as they climb heavenward, consisting of love, joy, peace, longsuffering, gentleness, faith, meekness, temperance.

Prayer helps us in building a "Cathedral of Character" in the soul, building it of things spiritual, which have survival value, and which we can carry into the eternal life with us.

Prayer is a cleansing process, washing our thoughts, feelings, motives, and will, purifying the entire being including the heart, thus enabling us to see God, for without purity no one can see God.

Prayer is the greatest spiritual asset in the world.

V. L. CRAWFORD

THE GOLDEN CENSER

Eternal Love, we have no good to bring Thee,
No single good of all our hands have
wrought,
No worthy music have we found to sing Thee,
No jeweled word, no quick upsoaring
thought.

And yet we come; and when our faith would
falter,
Show us, O Love, the quiet place of prayer;
The golden censer and the golden altar,
And the great angel waiting for us there.

AMY CARMICHAEL

THE LORD'S PRAYER

I cannot say *Our* if I live in a watertight spiritual compartment.

I cannot say *Father* if I do not demonstrate the relationship in daily living.

I cannot say *which art in heaven* if I am so occupied with the earth that I am laying up no treasures there.

I cannot say *hallowed be Thy name* if I, who am called by His name, am not holy.

I cannot say *Thy kingdom come* if I am not doing all in my power to hasten its coming.

I cannot say *Thy will be done* if I am questioning, resentful of, or disobedient to His will for me.

I cannot say *on earth, as it is in heaven* if I am not prepared to devote my life here to His service.

I cannot say *give us this day our daily bread* if I am living on past experience or if I am an under-the-counter shopper.

I cannot say *forgive us our trespasses, as we forgive them that trespass against us* if I harbor a grudge against anyone.

I cannot say *lead us not into temptation* if I deliberately place myself in a position to be tempted.

I cannot say *deliver us from evil* if I am not prepared to fight it in the spiritual realm with the weapon of prayer.

I cannot say *Thine is the kingdom* if I do not accord the King the disciplined obedience of a loyal subject.

I cannot say *Thine is the power* if I fear what men may do or what my neighbors may think.

I cannot say *Thine is the glory* if I am seeking glory for myself.

I cannot say *forever and ever* if my horizon is bounded by the things of time.

THE WATCHMAN-EXAMINER

THREE THINGS

I know three things must always be
    To keep a nation strong and free:
One is a hearthstone bright and dear
    With busy, happy loved ones near;
One is a ready heart and hand
    To love and serve and keep the land;
One is a worn and beaten way
    To where the people go to pray.

So long as these are kept alive,
    Nation and people will survive;
God, keep them always, everywhere—
    The home, the heart, the place of prayer.

PRAYER

O God, help us
to be generous in our opinions of others,
to be considerate of all we meet,
to be patient with those with whom we work,
to be faithful to every trust,
to be courageous in the face of danger,
to be humble in all our living,
to be prayerful every hour of the day,
to be joyous in all life's experience,
and to be dependent upon Thee for strength in facing life's uncertainties.

WALLACE FRIDY

Humanity is never so beautiful as when praying for forgiveness or else forgiving another.

JEAN PAUL RICHTER

GOD'S WILL

I know not by what methods rare,
But this I know: God answers prayer.
I know not if the blessing sought
Will come in just the guise I thought.
I leave my prayer to Him alone
Whose will is wiser than my own.

ELIZA M. HICKOK

BEGINNING

Prayer begins where human capacity ends.

NORMAN VINCENT PEALE

CO-OPERATION

Prayer is the divinely appointed means by which man co-operates with God in order to receive spiritual power.

JOHN SUTHERLAND BONNELL

A GRACE

Reveal Thy Presence now, O Lord,
    As in the Upper Room of old;
Break Thou our bread, grace Thou our board,
    And keep our hearts from growing cold.

THOMAS TIPLADY

ANSWERS

No prayer ever rises in vain. It is as inevitably answered as is the call of gravitation to matter. Prayer and its answer belong to an established, immovable order, and work according to recognized law. If prayer is manifestly and magnificently answered, we marvel; whereas we should marvel if it is not abundantly answered.

CHARLES H. BRENT

Prayer moves the Hand which moves the world.

JOHN A. WALLACE

God answers prayer; sometimes when hearts
    are weak,
    He gives the very gifts believers seek;
But often faith must learn a deeper rest,
    And trust God's silence, when He does not
    speak;
For He whose name is Love will send the best:
    Stars may burn out nor mountain walls
    endure,
But God is true; His promises are sure
    To those who seek.

MYRA GOODWIN PLANTZ

Prayer is not a substitute for work: it is the secret spring and indispensable ally of all true work—the clarifying of work's goal, the purifying of its motives, and the renewing of its zeal.

GEORGE A. BUTTRICK

Pray and hurl your life after your prayers.

HARRY EMERSON FOSDICK

BENEDICTION

The sun be warm and kind
To you,
The darkest night, some star
Shine through.
The dullest morn
A radiance brew.
And when dusk comes—
God's hand
To you.

ELEANOR POWERS

A SHEAF OF FAMILIAR AND FAVORITE PRAYERS

I

Oh God, I ask not for easier tasks. I ask for stronger aptitudes and greater talents to meet any tasks which may come my way. Help me to help others so that their lives may be made easier and happier. Strengthen my confidence in my fellow men in spite of what they may do or say. Give me strength to live according to the Golden Rule, enthusiasm to inspire those around me, sympathy to help lighten the burdens of those who suffer, and a spirit of joy and gladness to share with others.

HARRY S. BULLIS

II

Our heavenly Father,
we adore Thee,
whose name is love,
whose nature is compassion,
whose presence is joy,
whose word is truth,
whose spirit is goodness,
whose holiness is beauty,
whose will is peace,
whose service is perfect freedom,
and in knowledge of whom
    standeth our eternal life.

III

O Thou who art the light of the minds that
   know Thee,
the life of the souls that love Thee,
and the strength of the hearts that serve Thee;

help us so to know Thee that we may truly
   love Thee,
so to love Thee that we may fully serve Thee,
whom to serve is perfect freedom.

IV

A PAGE'S ROAD SONG
(13th century)

   Jesu,
   If Thou wilt make
Thy peach trees bloom for me,
And fringe my bridle path both sides
   with tulips, red and free,
If Thou wilt make Thy skies as blue
   As ours in Sicily,
And wake the little leaves that sleep
   On every bending tree—
I promise not to vexen Thee
That Thou shouldst make eternally
     Heaven my home;
     But right contently,
A singing page I'll be
   Here, in Thy springtime,
   Jesu.

WILLIAM ALEXANDER PERCY

V

O our God, we believe in Thee, we hope in Thee, and we love Thee because Thou hast created us, redeemed us, and dost sanctify us. Increase our faith, strengthen our hope, and deepen our love, that, giving ourselves up wholly to Thy will, we may serve Thee faithfully all the rest of our life. And we pray that finally we may be found worthy through Thy grace to inherit life eternal.

VI

O Holy Spirit of God, abide with us;
inspire all our thoughts;
pervade our imaginations;
suggest all our decisions;
order all our doings.
Be with us in our silence and in our speech,
in our haste and in our leisure,
in company and in solitude,
in the freshness of the morning and in the weariness of the evening;
and give us grace at all times humbly to rejoice in Thy mysterious companionship.

JOHN BAILLIE

VII

O Thou who art the Way, the Truth, and the Life, we lift our hearts to Thee. Guide us in the Way this day, enlighten us with the Truth, and grant us the more abundant Life which Thou alone canst give. This we ask, not that we may selfishly get good or glory for ourselves, but that we may do good unto others and so glorify Thy name.

HOWARD B. GROSE

VIII

Give us, O Lord, steadfast hearts, which no unworthy thought can drag downwards; unconquered hearts, which no tribulation can wear out, upright hearts, which no unworthy purpose may tempt aside. Bestow upon us also, O Lord our God, understanding to know Thee, diligence to seek Thee, wisdom to find Thee, and a faithfulness that may finally embrace Thee.

THOMAS AQUINAS

IX

Our Father, who hast set a restlessness in our hearts, and made us all seekers after that which we can never fully find.

Forbid us to be satisfied with what we make of life.

Draw us from base content, and set our eyes on far-off goals.

Keep us at tasks too hard for us, that we may be driven to Thee for strength.

Deliver us from fretfulness and self-pity.

Make us sure of the goal we cannot see, and of the hidden good in the world.

Open our eyes to simple beauty all around us, and our hearts to the loveliness men hide from us because we do not try enough to understand them.

Save us from ourselves, and show us a vision of a world made new.

PRAYERS NEW AND OLD

X
From THANKS FROM EARTH TO HEAVEN

Holy Poet, I have heard
Thy lost music, Thy least word;
Not Thy beauty's tiniest part
Has escaped this loving heart!

While the great world goes its way
I watch in wonder all the day,
All the night my spirit sings
For the loveliness of things.

JOHN HALL WHEELOCK

Serving

After that he poureth water into a basin, and began to wash the disciples' feet, and to wipe them with the towel wherewith he was girded.

After he had washed their feet . . . he said unto them, Know ye what I have done to you?

Ye call me Master and Lord: and ye say well; for so I am.

If I then, your Lord and Master, have washed your feet; ye also ought to wash one another's feet.

For I have given you an example, that ye should do as I have done to you.

Verily, verily, I say unto you, The servant is not greater than his lord; neither he that is sent greater than he that sent him.   John 13:5, 12-16

SERVICE

There are strange ways of serving God;
You sweep a room or turn a sod,
And suddenly, to your surprise,
You hear the whirr of seraphim,
And find you're under God's own eyes
And building palaces for Him.

HERMANN HAGEDORN

The greatest pleasure I know is to do a good action by stealth and have it found out by accident.

CHARLES LAMB

PRAYER

O Father, may it never be said of us that
    having come to an open door, we closed it;
having come to a lighted candle, we quenched
    it;
having heard the voice of a neighbor begging
    bread, we made denial, speaking of our own
    case.

JEAN MC KENZIE

It is high time that the ideal of success should be replaced by the ideal of service.

ALBERT EINSTEIN

JERUSALEM TO JERICHO

As we travel life's earthly road from Jerusalem to Jericho may we be good Samaritans to all who need us, cheering, healing, and fortifying them with true neighborliness, vitalizing all the relations of life with an unselfish love, remembering that love is the strongest force in the world.

GEORGE W. TRUETT

The service we render to others is really the rent we pay for our room on this earth. It is obvious that man is himself a traveller; that the purpose of this world is not "to have and to hold" but "to give and to serve." There can be no other meaning.

WILFRED T. GRENFELL

EXERCISE

There is no exercise better for the heart than reaching down and lifting people up.

JOHN ANDREW HOLMER

SOMETHING OF YOURSELF

You simply give to others a bit of yourself—
    a thoughtful act,
    a helpful idea,
    a word of appreciation,
    a lift over a rough spot,
    a sense of understanding,
    a timely suggestion.
You take something out of your mind,
garnished in kindness out of your heart, and
put it into another fellow's mind and heart.

CHARLES H. BURR

No one knocks
at my door
who is not
sent by God.

The quality of mercy is not strain'd,
It droppeth as the gentle rain from heaven
Upon the place beneath. It is twice bless'd:
It blesseth him that gives and him that takes.

WILLIAM SHAKESPEARE

A WOMAN'S WAY

When her teen-age daughter
Has a broken heart,
A woman sets to baking
A luscious cherry tart.

When her son's team loses,
When his dog is dead,
A woman bakes a chocolate cake
Or spicy gingerbread.

When the crops are scanty,
When the bills are high,
A woman smiles her brightest
And bakes an apple pie.

Sympathy for sorrow,
Solace for mistakes,
Go into the mixing
When a woman bakes.

JANE MERCHANT

SWINGING DOOR

Human need in all of its dimensions is the swinging door into the innermost life of another.

HOWARD THURMAN

Love ever gives,
Forgives, outlives,
And ever stands
With open hands.
And, while it lives,
It gives.
For this is Love's prerogative—
To give and give and give.

JOHN OXENHAM

Only the hands that give away the flowers of their plucking retain the fragrance thereof.

CHINESE PROVERB

There is something gloriously unselfish about a brook. One might almost think that it is this unselfish character of the brook that makes it such a happy thing. It lopes laughingly through low-lying swamps, by the side of a deeply rutted road, then through a culvert and out among groves of cedars and past delicate birches. It dashes gleefully under fences, past the spire-like sentinels of balsam and spruce and the miscellany of poplar, black ash, beech, and maple. Other companionable little creeks join the brook as it skips and runs toward the patiently waiting lake.

A brook is going somewhere. It is water-on-a-mission. About to present itself to other waters at its destination, it never neglects little wayside opportunities. On its way to make its final offering, it gaily gives itself all along the way. Deer drink of its refreshing coolness with a deep content. Boys of seven years and of seventy prod its pools and eddies with their lures and return home at day's end with the brook's gift of speckled trout. Fish, crustaceans, mollusks, and water insects are given a home in its swirling currents and tranquil pools. From its birth in bubbling springs to its arrival at its final goal the brook is selfless and a happy appearing thing.

HAROLD E. KOHN

Know well that a hundred holy temples of wood and stone have not the value of one understanding heart.

ZOROASTRIAN SCRIPTURES

DAY WELL SPENT

If you sit down at set of sun
And count the acts that you have done,
    And, counting, find
One self-denying deed, one word
That eased the heart of him who heard—
    One glance most kind,
That fell like sunshine where it went—
Then you may count that day well spent.

GEORGE ELIOT

THE SUBSTITUTE

He is the person who waits upon the bench
with his hand upon his knee, watches every
play, listens to all the cheers, always hoping
to get in.

He watches his teammates execute plays which
he has helped to work, during practice, to
perfection.

For months he's had the lowly place of sub-
merging himself in loyal desire that teamwork might be made complete, and yet he
has not heard his name in the crowd's ac-
claim.

The crowd sees him waiting for his chance, the
chance perhaps that will never come, but
nevertheless he gives his best.

He is content when thousands laud his teammates, but let us remember that successful
teams were never built without the "sub"
who prays, hopes, works, and waits.

He who comes to do good knocks at the gate;
he who loves finds the door open.

RABINDRANATH TAGORE

The tree gives shade even to him who cuts off
his boughs.

SRI CHAITANYA

LAMPS

I met a stranger in the night
    Whose lamp had ceased to shine;
I paused and let him light
    His lamp from mine.

A tempest came up in the night
    And shook the world about;
And when the wind was gone,
    My lamp was out.

But back to me that stranger came,
    His lamp was glowing fine;
He held the precious flame,
    And lighted mine.

I am only one,
But still I am one.
I cannot do everything,
But still I can do something;
And because I cannot do everything
I will not refuse to do the something that I
can do.

EDWARD EVERETT HALE

SALUTE TO THE TREES

Many a tree is found in the wood
And every tree for use is good:
Some for the strength of the gnarled root,
Some for the sweetness of flower and fruit,
Some for shelter against the storm,
And some to keep the hearthstone warm;
Some for the roof, and some for the beam,
And some for a boat to breast the stream—
In the wealth of the wood since the world
    began
The trees have offered their gifts to man.

HENRY VAN DYKE

PRAYER

O heavenly Father, who hast filled the world with beauty: open, we beseech Thee, our eyes to behold Thy gracious hand in all Thy works; that rejoicing in Thy whole creation, we may learn to serve Thee with gladness.

BOOK OF COMMON PRAYER

No man or woman of the humblest sort can really be strong, gentle, pure, and good without the world being better for it, without somebody being helped and comforted by the very existence of that goodness.

PHILLIPS BROOKS

A child's kiss
Set on thy sighing lips shall make thee glad;
A poor man served by thee shall make thee
rich;
A sick man helped by thee shall make thee
strong;
Thou shalt be served thyself by every sense
Of service which thou renderest.

ELIZABETH BARRETT BROWNING

Education is good only as it helps people to enrich and fulfill their lives, both in leading toward personal joy and in leading toward the extension of one's talents into modes of helping other people.

HAROLD TAYLOR

THE FOUR-WAY TEST

1. Is it the truth?
2. Is it fair to all concerned?
3. Will it build good will and better friendships?
4. Will it be beneficial to all concerned?

ROTARY INTERNATIONAL

Question not, but live and labor
  Till your goal be won,
Helping every feeble neighbor,
  Seeking help from none;
Life is mostly froth and bubble,
  Two things stand like stone:
Kindness in another's trouble,
  Courage in your own.

ADAM LINDSAY GORDON

Be an opener of doors for such as come after thee, and do not try to make the universe a blind alley.

RALPH WALDO EMERSON

PRAYER FOR SERVICE

Let me, O Lord, have always one for whom
To do the humble tasks of everyday . . .
The tender, life-warm things, O grant me this,
You who served men a holy, human way!
When morning comes, let there be one to rouse
And one for whom, through all the light-crisp
  hours,
To sweep and sew and dust and bake and fill
Rooms with good cheer, a garden with glad
  flowers.
When stars shine high above our neighbor
  trees,
Outside this quiet, ruffly-curtained place,
Grant me at least one form to be tucked in . . .
One hand to touch, one kiss-awaiting face.
How much more radiantly day breaks; how
  much
More lightly all the laughing hours will tread;
How hushed the night for one who serves
  with love,
You know who poured men wine and broke
  them bread.

VIOLET ALLEYN STOREY

Stewardship

Jesus sat over against the treasury, and beheld how the people cast money into the treasury: and many that were rich cast in much.

And there came a certain poor widow, and she threw in two mites, which make a farthing.

And he called unto him his disciples, and said unto them, Verily I say unto you, That this poor widow hath cast more in, than all they which have cast into the treasury:

For all they did cast in of their abundance; but she of her want did cast in all that she had, even all her living.   Mark 12:41-44

MEDIUMS OF EXCHANGE

These are our mediums of exchange: time, talents, energy, space, influence, possessions, and money.

Time. For what are we spending it?

Talents. To what are we devoting them?

Energy. For what are we consuming it?

Space. To what are we allotting it?

Influence. Toward what is it being lent?

Possessions. For what are we using them?

Money. For what are we exchanging it?

These are not only important questions. They are character-revealing questions. They are destiny-determining questions.

J. WINSTON PEARCE

Every charitable act is a stepping-stone toward heaven.

HENRY WARD BEECHER

SHARING

The roses red upon my neighbor's vine
Are owned by him, but they are also mine.
His was the cost and his the labor, too;
But mine and his their loveliness to view.
They bloom for me, and are for me as fair
As for the man who gives them all his care.
Thus I am rich, because a good man grew
A rose-clad vine for all his neighbor's view.
I know from this that others plant for me,
And what they own my joy may also be.
So why be selfish when so much that's fine
Is grown for you upon your neighbor's vine?

A. L. GRUBER

THE PERFECT GIFT

To love is to want to give and above all give oneself. A perfect love is the perfect gift of oneself without thought of reward or return.

R. H. J. STEUART

REVELATION

The soul of a man is in his gifts, because they are a part of a man's life. Money is life. It is the honest reward for honest labor. It is the symbol of a man's strength. It is the evidence of his talent. Truly, it is a part of his life. Thus, when a man gives, he gives a part of his life. This, then, is the deeper meaning of stewardship—to give, to share, to surrender—knowing that in it all the soul of a man shall be revealed.

ARNOLD H. LOWE

The problem with our giving is that we give the widow's mite, but not with the widow's spirit.

We give Thee but Thine own,
Whate'er the gift may be;
All that we have is Thine alone,
A trust, O Lord, from Thee.

May we Thy bounties thus
As stewards true receive,
And gladly, as Thou blessest us,
To Thee our first-fruits give.

WILLIAM WALSHAM HOW

GIVING

To give a little from a shining store,
Is that to give? To give and feel no loss,
Is that to give as Christ gave on the Cross?
To share the crumbs of happiness we gain
With those who weep apart, to give our best
Of healing sympathy to hearts in pain,
To give our labor when we fain would rest,
This is the charity men knew when He
First breathed that word by starlit Galilee.

WILLIAM F. KIRK

———

Our money is ourselves. It is our very life, our daily work, our time and strength and skill, our very life blood minted into coin. When we hold our money in our hands we are holding so many minutes and hours and days of our life, just so much of our vital force as has been expended in its acquisition, so much of our toil and time. When we give we are literally giving our life for our fellow men, to help, to heal, and to save them. Giving is in reality the laying down of our lives for the brethren—losing our lives for Christ's sake that we may find them in a larger fellowship with Christ in the world's redemption. As we thus realize that our money-giving is self-giving, our stewardship merges into a glorious partnership not only with Christ but also with all those who in any way are at work forwarding the Kingdom.

GUY MORRILL

———

WHEN LIFE IS DONE

I'd like to think when life is done
That I had filled a needed post,
That here and there I'd paid my fare
With more than idle talk and boast;

That I had taken gifts divine,
The breath of life and manhood fine,
And tried to use them now and then
In service for my fellow men.

EDGAR A. GUEST

———

WHAT MONEY CANNOT BUY

Money cannot buy real friendship. Friendship must be earned.

Money cannot buy the glow of good health. Right living is the secret.

Money cannot buy a clear conscience. Square dealing is the price tag.

Money cannot buy happiness. Happiness is a mental attitude and one may be as happy in a cottage as in a mansion.

Money cannot buy sunsets, singing birds, and the music of the wind in the trees. These are as free as the air we breathe.

Money cannot buy character. Character is what we are when we are alone with ourselves in the dark.

———

DEDICATION

Laid on Thine altar, O my Lord divine,
Accept this gift today for Jesus' sake;
I have no jewels to adorn Thy shrine,
No far-famed sacrifice to make;
But here within my trembling hand I bring
This will of mine, a thing that seemeth small.
But Thou alone, O Lord, canst understand
How when I yield Thee this, I yield mine all.

Thanksgiving

O give thanks unto the Lord, for he is good: for his mercy endureth for ever.

Oh that men would praise the Lord for his goodness, and for his wonderful works to the children of men!

For he satisfieth the longing soul, and filleth the hungry soul with goodness.

Let them sacrifice the sacrifices of thanksgiving, and declare his works with rejoicing.   PSALM 107:1, 8-9, 22

THANKSGIVING STREET

Keep gratitude alive in your heart. Try living on "Thanksgiving Street." Reckon up your mercies and you will feel an inner kindling of soul. People will be glad at the sight of you. And who knows? Perhaps even the heart of the infinite Giver of every good and perfect gift will rejoice.

AARON N. MECKEL

———

Give thanks to God
   And humbly pray
To serve Him well
   This new-born day.

Give thanks to God
   For friends and flowers,
For sunny days
   And cooling showers.

Give thanks to God,
   Fill well your part;
Let love divine
   Possess your heart.

Give thanks to God,
   His bounty see;
Be still and know,
   And grateful be.

GRENVILLE KLEISER

———

Two kinds of gratitude: the sudden kind
We feel for what we take, the larger kind
We feel for what we give.

EDWIN ARLINGTON ROBINSON

WONDER

Wonder is the attitude of admiration for life's beauty, perfection, and subtlety.

Wonder is the attitude of awe in the presence of life's vastness and power.

Wonder is the attitude of reverence for the infinite values and meanings of life, and of marveling over God's purpose and patience in it all.

Thus wonder leads to the birth of constructive imagination and vision, and soon issues in the more triumphant verbs I see and I believe.

GEORGE WALTER FISKE

———

THANK YOU, GOD

When you say to me "Thank you," remember I could not have done for you what I did had it not been for what hundreds of other people have done for me. Neither could they have done for me what they did had it not been for what thousands of other people had done for them. And so the thing goes on in infinite time and space. Therefore, when you say "Thank you," you really meant to say "Thank You, God."

RICHARD C. CABOT

———

A POET'S GRACE

O Thou, who kindly doth provide
   For ev'ry creature's want!
We bless the God of Nature wide
   For all Thy goodness lent.
And if it please Thee, heavenly Guide,
   May never worse be sent;
But, whether granted or denied,
   Lord, bless us with content.

ROBERT BURNS

HIS WORK OF CREATION

Among the many acts of gratitude we owe to God, it may be accounted one to study and contemplate the perfections and beauties of His work of creation. Every new discovery must necessarily raise in us a fresh sense of the greatness, wisdom, and power of God.

JONATHAN EDWARDS

GRATITUDE

I thank You for these gifts, dear God,
    Upon Thanksgiving Day—
For love and laughter and the faith
    That bids me kneel to pray.

For life that lends me happiness,
    And sleep that gives me rest;
These are the gifts that keep my heart
    Serene within my breast.

Love, laughter, faith and life and sleep,
    We cherish every one—
They carry us along the road
    That leads from sun to sun.

MARGARET E. SANGSTER

When we eat the good bread, we are eating months of sunlight, weeks of rain and snow from the sky, richness out of the earth. We should be great, each of us radiant, full of music and full of stories. Able to run the way clouds do, able to dance like the snow and the rain. But nobody takes time to think that he eats all these things and that sun, rain, snow are all a part of himself.

MONICA SHANNON

PETITION

O Lord, that lends me life,
Lend me a heart replete with thankfulness.

WILLIAM SHAKESPEARE

WE THANK THEE

We thank Thee for life's common things—
The limpid, lovely water springs,
The shining diamond of the dew,
The firmament's transcendent blue;
For the wild rose whose fragile cup
In field and hedge is lifted up;

For love's sweet smile upon us bent;
For baby faces innocent;
For helpless hands that reach and sue
And make us patient, kind, and true;
For youthful hearts unworn and bold,
That keep our own from growing old.

We thank Thee for life's homely ways,
The discipline of working days;
For hearts made tenderer by trial,
For the stern teaching of denial;
For pain that keys the quivering chord;
For joy and grief, we thank Thee, Lord.

MARY E. BUTTS

An easy thing, O Power Divine,
To thank Thee for these gifts of Thine:
For summer's sunshine, winter's snow,
For hearts that kindle, thoughts that glow;
But when shall I attain to this—
To thank Thee for the things I miss?

THOMAS W. HIGGINSON

Today

This is the day which the Lord hath made; we will rejoice and be glad in it.

PSALM 118:24

THE UPWARD ROAD

I will follow the upward road today,
I will keep my face to the light;
I will think high thoughts as I go my way,
I will do what I know is right;
I will look for the flowers by the side of the
    road,
I will laugh and love and be strong,
I will try to lighten another's load,
This day as I fare along.

MARY S. EDGAR

RESOLUTION

To live with all my might while I do live and
never to lose one moment of time.

JONATHAN EDWARDS

The present is always determined by the past,
and always we are free to determine the future.

H. J. FORMAN

PRAYER

O God, I saw Thee push the black bolts back
today and set ajar the Gates of Dawn, and the
Spirit of Morning coming through at once was
everywhere. The golden torrent of her hair she
shook wide and free and lightly tiptoed up the
sky, while all her trailing skirts spread glory.
She blew a whisper through the woodland and
it broke in song; she glanced along the streams
and they mirrored heaven; she ran across the
lawns, through gardens enamel-petalled and
aroma-drunk. They stood unutterably still and
rich, as if their soul had come. Glorious God,
I saw Thy Morning, and it seemed like resurrection to a life once dead in trespasses and
sins.

OSWALD W. S. MC CALL

From COMMON DAYS

No day is common.—I have walked them
    through
And found the quick surprises of their hours:
Some lovely, unexpected thing to do,
Some plain path's sudden blossoming with
    flowers.
And always through my labor I have found
Reward so rich, so full of Love's sweet praise,
I tread them softly, they are hallowed ground,
There are no common days.

GRACE NOLL CROWELL

MORNING PRAYER

Here, Lord, is my life.
I place it on the altar today.
Use it as You will.

ALBERT SCHWEITZER

THE PRESENT IS YOURS

There are many fine things which you mean to
do some day, under what you think will be
more favorable circumstances. But the only
time that is surely yours is the present. Hence
this is the time to speak the word of appreciation and sympathy, to do the generous deed, to
forgive the fault of a thoughtless friend, to
sacrifice self a little more for others. Today is
the day in which to express your noblest qualities of mind and heart, to do at least one
worthy thing which you have long postponed,
and to use your God-given abilities for the en-
richment of some less fortunate fellow traveler. Today you can make your life significant
and worthwhile. The present is yours to do
with it as you will.

GRENVILLE KLEISER

OPPORTUNITY

Today is, for all that we know, the opportunity and occasion of our lives. On what we do or say today may depend the success and completeness of our entire life-struggle. It is for us, therefore, to use every moment of today as if our very eternity were dependent on its words and deeds.

HENRY CLAY TRUMBULL

DESIGNERS OF DESTINY

Time's wheel spins on, twisting from nature's
  distaff
The threads upon her spindle.
These strands, in turn, in life's great loom
  Yield changing personal patterns.

These we are. 'Tis interesting at times
To view the fashion of the weaving
  And see whereto we tend.

Such survey of the self doth profit oft
While yet the loom weaves on.
The weavers we, the woven too,
  Designers of our destiny.

DAYS

Some days my thoughts are just cocoons—all
  cold and dull and blind,
They hang from dripping branches in the grey
  woods of my mind;
And other days they drift and shine—such
  free and flying things!
I find the gold-dust in my hair, left by their
  brushing wings.

KARLE WILSON BAKER

MORNING CALL

To be seeing the world made new every morning, as if it were the morning of the first day, and then to make the most of it for the individual soul as if it were the last day, is the daily curriculum of the mind's desire.

JOHN H. FINLEY

TIME PASSES QUICKLY

There is nothing we can do about time except to see that, as far as possible, it passes fruitfully. If in passing it lays up its store of good deeds done, noble ambitions clung to heroically, and kindness and sympathy scattered with a lavish hand, there will always be given to it a permanence and enduring quality that nothing can take away.

Take time to look: it is the price of success.
Take time to think: it is a source of power.
Take time to play: it is the secret of perennial youth.
Take time to read: it is the source of wisdom.
Take time to be friendly: it is the way to happiness.
Take time to laugh: it is the music of the soul.

Are you in earnest? Seize this very minute:
What you can do, or dream you can, begin it;
Boldness has genius, power, and magic in it.
Only engage and the mind grows heated;
Begin and then the work will be completed.

JOHANN WOLFGANG VON GOETHE

I WILL NOT HURRY

I will not hurry through this day!
Lord, I will listen by the way,
To humming bees and singing birds,
To speaking trees and friendly words;
And for the moments in between
Seek glimpses of Thy great Unseen.

I will not hurry through this day;
I will take time to think and pray;
I will look up into the sky,
Where fleecy clouds and swallows fly;
And somewhere in the day, maybe
I will catch whispers, Lord, from Thee!

RALPH SPAULDING CUSHMAN

ONE STEP OF TRIUMPH

My feet shall never stand on Everest's peak,
Nor smudge the sands of undiscovered shore.
My ears shall never hear the waters roar
Where jungle rivers fall in Mozambique.
For me, no stratospheric flights; I seek
No depths uncharted to the ocean floor.
These will come to others who explore
The geographic goals of which they speak.
Still, I have known the high discovery,
Moments when exultation held my hand,
And these have come in no exotic land,
While just one step from my back porch will
    show
A world and year unsearched, that beckons me
To cast first print in New Year's printless
    snow.

RALPH W. SEAGER

TIME WELL SPENT

Spend your time in nothing which you know
    must be repented of;
in nothing on which you might not pray for
    the blessing of God;
in nothing which you could not review with a
    quiet conscience on your dying bed;
in nothing which you might not safely and
    properly be found doing if death should
    surprise you in the act.

RICHARD BAXTER

MARK OF THE CHRISTIAN

Starting afresh patiently and in good cheer
and hope is the mark of the Christian. One of
the helpful definitions of Christianity is this:
the Christian life is a series of new beginnings.

JOHN B. COBURN

TIME

It is worth while to be wise in the use of time.
In the eternal life there is no waste of years.
It is with time that we purchase everything
that life has of good. The most reckless spendthrift in the world is the one who squanders
time. Money lost may be regained, friendships
broken may be renewed, houses and lands
may be sold or buried or burned, but may be
bought or gained or built again. But what
power can restore the moment that has passed,
the day whose sun has set, the year that has
been numbered with the ages gone?

ANNA R. BROWN LINDSAY

NOW

To each man's life there comes a time supreme,
One day, one night, one morning, or one noon,
One freighted hour, one moment opportune,
One space when fate goes tiding with the
    stream.
Happy the man who, knowing how to wait,
Knows also how to watch, and work, and
    stand
On life's broad deck alert, and on the prow
To seize the passing moment big with fate,
From opportunity's extended hand
When the great clock of destiny strikes
    "Now."

If we're thoughtful just this minute,
    In whate'er we say or do,
If we put a purpose in it,
    That is honest through and through,
We shall gladden life, and give it
    Grace to make it all sublime;
For though life is long, we live it
    Just this minute at a time.

The future that we study and plan for begins
today.

CHESTER O. FISCHER

PRECIOUS POSSESSION

You wake up in the morning, and lo! your
purse is magically filled with twenty-four
hours of the unmanufactured tissue of the universe of your life. It is yours. It is the most
precious of possessions. No one can take it
from you. It is unstealable. And no one receives either more or less than you receive.

ARNOLD BENNETT

MY HOUR

Happy the man, and happy he alone,
He who can call today his own;
He who, secure within, can say,
"Tomorrow, do thy worst, for I have lived
    today.
Be fair or foul, or rain or shine,
The joys I have possessed, in spite of fate, are
    mine.
Not heaven itself upon the past has power,
But what has been, has been, and I have had
    my hour."

HORACE

ATTITUDE

Your attitude toward life in general
is reflected in your response
to the dawn of a new day.

J. N. GEHMAN

Some people wait for the coming Monday before putting forth renewed efforts. Others
wait for the beginning of a new month, and
still others for the turn of the season, or the
year. But in my own experience I have found
that the best time for a renewal of effort, indeed the greatest of all periods of time for anything, is today.

VASH YOUNG

ADVANTAGE

Men spend their lives in anticipations, in de-
termining to be vastly happy at some period
or other, when they have time. But the present
time has one advantage over every other: it is
our own.

CHARLES CALEB COLTON

Trust

Eye hath not seen, nor ear heard, neither have entered into the heart of man, the things which God hath prepared for them that love him.

I Corinthians 2:9

THIS IS FAITH

The anchored trust that at the core of things
Health, goodness, animating strength flow
    from exhaustless springs;
That no star rolls unguided down the rings of
    endless maze,
That no feet tread an aimless path through
    wastes of empty days;
That trusts the everlasting Voice, the glad
    calm Voice that saith
That order grows from chaos, and that life is
    born from death;
That from the wreck of rending stars behind
    the storm and scathe,
There dwells a heart of central calm—and
    this, and this is faith!

NO NEED

Where there is faith, there is love;
Where there is love, there is peace;
Where there is peace, there is God;
And where there is God, there is no need.

LEO TOLSTOY

The imperturbable splendor and grandeur of
    the universe;
the imperious command of the highest;
the beauty of nature without and that far more
    mysterious whisper of beauty within;
the glory of many human lives;
the face of Jesus Christ;
the tale of human history;
the enveloping Presence which speaks per-
    sonally to each man one by one—
these and others are the varied strands woven
    into the fabric of a rich and worthy cer-
    tainty.

HENRY PITNEY VAN DUSEN

From THE MARSHES OF GLYNN

As the marsh-hen secretly builds on the watery
    sod,
Behold I will build me a nest on the greatness
    of God:
I will fly in the greatness of God as the marsh-
    hen flies
In the freedom that fills all the space 'twixt the
    marsh and the skies:
By so many roots as the marsh-grass sends in
    the sod
I will heartily lay me a-hold on the greatness
    of God:
Oh, like to the greatness of God is the great-
    ness within
The range of the marshes, the liberal marshes
    of Glynn.

SIDNEY LANIER

From VOYAGERS

When outward bound we boldly sail
    And leave the friendly shore,
Let not our hearts of courage fail
    Before the voyage is o'er.
We trust in Thee, whate'er befall;
Thy sea is great, our boats are small.

When homeward bound we gladly turn,
    O bring us safely there,
Where harbour-lights of friendship burn
    And peace is in the air.
We trust in Thee, whate'er befall;
Thy sea is great, our boats are small.

HENRY VAN DYKE

SALUTATION

Peace be in thy home
　And in thy heart,
Or if thou roam
　Earth's highways wide,
The Lord be at thy side,
　To bless and guide.

THE SEAMAN'S PSALM

The Lord is my Pilot; I shall not drift. He
　lighteth me across the dark waters; he steer-
　eth me in deep channels; he keepeth my log.
He guardeth me by the star of holiness for his
　name's sake.
Yea, though I sail mid the thunders and tem-
　pests of life I will dread no danger, for thou
　art near me.
Thy love and thy care they shelter me.
Thou preparest a harbor before me in the
　homeland of Eternity.
Thou anointest the waves with oil; my ship
　rideth calmly.
Surely sunlight and starlight shall favor me on
　the voyage I take, and I will rest in the port
　of my God forever.

JAMES ROGERS

WINGS

Lord of all growing things,
By such sweet, secret influences as those
That draw the scilla through the melting
　snows,
And bid the fledgling bird trust untried wings,
When quick my spirit grows,
Help me to trust my wings.

O Thou in all Thy might so far,
　In all Thy love so near,
Beyond the range of sun and star,
　And yet beside us here.

FREDERICK L. HOSMER

PERFECT TRUSTING

I cannot understand
The why and wherefore of a thousand things;
The burdens, the annoyances, the daily stings,
　I cannot understand;
　But I can trust,
For perfect trusting, perfect comfort brings.
　I cannot see the end.
The hidden meaning of each trial sent,
The pattern into which each tangled thread is
　　bent,
　I cannot see the end;
　But I can trust,
And in God's changeless love I am content.

PILGRIMS TO EVEREST

That where the safe ways end,
Known and unknown divide,
God's great uncharted passes upward tend,
Where the Spirit of man undaunted is un-
　denied,　　·
And beyond the last campfire man has Faith
　for friend,
And beyond all guidance the courage of God
　for Guide.

HORACE SHIPP

It is a greater compliment to be trusted than to
be loved.

GEORGE MACDONALD

218

Be ready always to give an answer to every man that asketh you a reason of the hope that is in you.   I Peter 3:15

CHRIST AS A MISSIONARY

Christ was a home missionary in the house of Lazarus.

He was a foreign missionary when the Greeks came to Him.

A city missionary when He taught in Samaria and Jerusalem.

A Sunday school missionary when He opened up the Scriptures and set men to studying the Word of God.

A children's missionary when He took them in His arms and blessed them.

A missionary to the poor when He opened the eyes of the blind beggar.

A missionary to the rich when He opened the spiritual eyes of Zaccheus.

Even on the Cross Christ was a missionary to the robber.

His last command was the missionary commission.

AMOS R. WELLS

To be glad instruments of God's love in this imperfect world is the service to which man is called.

ALBERT SCHWEITZER

LITTLE LIGHTS

God, bless each little light that burns
In an unexpected place . . .
An altar in a darkened church . . .
Or in a sad, sad face.

God, bless each little light and fan
Its flame and keep it bright.
There is so much of darkness that
We need each little light.

VIOLET ALLEYN STOREY

NEVER GIVE UP

We are sowing seed. Some indeed may fall on beaten paths and some among thorns, but it is our business to keep on sowing. We are not to stop sowing because some of the soil looks unpromising.

We are holding a light. We are to let it shine! Though it may seem but a twinkling candle in a world of blackness, it is our business to let it shine.

We are blowing a trumpet. In the din and noise of battle the sound of our little trumpet may seem to be lost, but we must keep sounding the alarm to those who are in danger.

We are kindling a fire. In this cold world full of hatred and selfishness our little blaze may seem to be unavailing, but we must keep our fire burning.

We are striking with a hammer. The blows may seem only to jar our hands as we strike, but we are to keep on hammering.

We have bread for a hungry world. The people may seem to be so busy feeding on other things that they will not accept the Bread of Life, but we must keep on giving it, offering it to the souls of men.

We have water for famishing people. We must keep standing and crying out, "Ho, every one that thirsteth, come ye to the waters."

We must persevere. We must never give up.

BILLY GRAHAM

MESSENGER

You want to be your Lord's messenger to your neighbor? To be that your love must instinctively seize on and love what is lovable in your neighbor.

H. F. B. MACKAY

WHAT PRICE DISCIPLESHIP?

Matthew is supposed to have suffered martyrdom by being put to death by a halberd, a slender ax for splitting helmets, in a city of ancient Ethiopia.

Mark was dragged through the streets of Alexandria, Egypt, till he died.

Luke was hanged upon an olive tree in Greece.

John miraculously escaped death when put into a caldron of boiling oil at Rome. He afterwards died a natural death at Ephesus.

James the Great was beheaded at Jerusalem.

James the Less was thrown from a pinnacle or wing of the temple, stoned, and finally beaten to death with a fuller's club.

Philip was hanged up against a pillar at Hierapolis, a city of Phrygia.

Bartholomew was put to death by the command of a barbarous king in Armenia.

Andrew was bound to a cross, whence he preached to the people till he expired.

Thomas was run through the body by a lance in the East Indies.

Jude was cruelly put to death in Persia.

Simon Zelotes was crucified by the Druids in Britain.

Matthias was stoned and then beheaded.

Bring me my bow of burning gold!
Bring me my arrows of desire!
Bring me my spear! O clouds unfold!
Bring me my chariot of fire!

I will not cease from mental fight,
Nor shall my sword sleep in my hand,
Till we have built Jerusalem
In England's green and pleasant land.

WILLIAM BLAKE

THE BEST OF AMERICA

The greatest thing to come out of America has been the American missionary effort: the quiet, selfless men and women who left the comfort and security of their homeland to bring the gospel of Christianity to less favored nations. In hundreds of far-off places these obscure missionaries have been far more effective ambassadors than any of the money-men or the agricultural experts or the industrial technicians. And why? Because they represent the best of the original American dream: the selflessness, the idealism, the belief that all men are brothers under the Fatherhood of God.

CHARLES MALIK

O God, who dost prefer before all temples the upright heart and pure, and who dost instruct us in all truth: we know that if we walk with Thee what in us is dark Thou wilt illumine; what is low, raise and support; what is shallow, deepen; so that every chapter of our lives will witness to Thy power, and justify the ways of God to men.

WESTMINSTER ABBEY PRAYER

THEIR COMING

God's best gifts come quietly, like the silent growth of crops or the flowering of a garden, like marsh marigolds lifting yellow heads beside the brook or the hushed resurrection of faith in a soul where it had seemed to die. No ear can hear their coming—the cautious steps of mature thoughts in the mind of a growing child, the advent of a holy and lasting love in the heart of a man or a maid, or the approach of a prodigal son to the Father's house.

HAROLD E. KOHN

SYMBOLISMS

O Earth! Thou hast not any wind that blows
Which is not music; every weed of thine
Pressed rightly flows in aromatic wine:
And every humble hedgerow flower that
grows,
And every little brown bird that doth sing,
Hath something greater than itself, and bears
A living word to every living thing,
Albeit holds the message unawares.
All shapes and sounds have something which
is not
Of them: a spirit broods amid the grass;
Vague outlines of the Everlasting Thought
Lie in the melting shadows as they pass;
The touch of an Eternal Presence thrills
The fringes of the sunset and the hills.

RICHARD REALF

The wayside pool reflects the fleeting clouds
as exactly as does the mighty ocean.

PETITION

Give me not pallid ease—
Give me races to run,
Mountains to climb,
Burdens to lift;
Give me not nations to rule—
Give me people to love,
Worlds to serve,
And God to know.

C. WARD CRAMPTON

No doctrine of the Christian religion is worth
preserving which cannot be verified in daily
life.

JOHN WATSON

MISSIONARY BOOK

Every book in the New Testament was written
by a foreign missionary.

Every epistle in the New Testament that was
written to a church was written to a foreign
missionary church.

Every letter in the New Testament that was
written to an individual was written to the
convert of a foreign missionary.

Every book in the New Testament that was
written to a community of believers was
written to a general group of foreign missionary churches.

The one book of prophecy in the New Testament was written to the seven foreign missionary churches in Asia.

The only authoritative history of the early
Christian church is a foreign missionary
journal.

The disciples were called Christians first in a
foreign missionary community.

The language of the books in the New Testament is the missionary language.

The map of the early Christian world is the
tracings of the missionary journeys of the
apostles.

The problems which arose in the early church
were largely questions of missionary pro-
cedure.

Of the twelve apostles chosen by Jesus every
apostle except one became a missionary.

According to the apostles the missionary is the
highest expression of the Christian life.

WILLIAM ADAMS BROWN

EXPRESSION

The great-heartedness of religion craves expression and must be expressed.

L. P. JACKS

223

SERVICE TO HUMANITY

While at the university and while enjoying the happiness of being able to study and even to produce some results in science and art, I could not help thinking continually of others who were denied that happiness by their material circumstance or their health. Then one brilliant summer morning there came to me, as I awoke, the thought that I must not accept this happiness as a matter of course, but must give something in return for it. Proceeding to think the matter out at once with calm deliberation, while the birds were singing outside, I settled with myself before I got up, that I would consider myself justified in living till I was thirty for science and art, in order to direct myself from that time forward to the service of humanity. In addition to outward, I now had inward happiness.

ALBERT SCHWEITZER

PREPARATION

Whatever God gives you to do, do it as well as you can. This is the best possible preparation for what he may want you to do next.

GEORGE MACDONALD

DESTINY

Whom God elects for service great
  May humbly let the years slip by,
And never guess how truly straight
  To glory all his pathways lie.

Man's final purpose none can see,
  Or step by step chart man's career,
And through the veil of destiny
  Discover why God sent him here.

Yet, when the hour requires the man
  To bear great burdens and be wise,
By ways that only God can plan
  Full-fit for duty he shall rise.

Oh, call it destiny or fate,
  Or Providence that guides us here,
But him God holds for service great,
  When he is needed, will appear.

EDGAR A. GUEST

AWAKENING

Suddenly, we know not how, a sound
Of living streams, an odor, a flower crowned
With dew, a lark upspringing from the sod,
And we awake. O joy and deep amaze,
Beneath the everlasting hills we stand,
We hear the voices of the morning seas,
And earnest prophesyings in the land,
While from the open heaven leans forth at gaze
The encompassing great cloud of witnesses.

EDWARD DOWDEN

From THE VOICE

The silent beauty of the stars,
The cold blue magic of the sea,
The glistening dewdrops on a lawn,
Become the voice
Of God to me.

The murmuring waves upon the beach,
The stately silhouetted tree,
The captive loveliness of dawn,
Become the voice
Of God to me.

JOHNSTONE G. PATRICK

Work

Let thy work appear unto thy servants, and thy glory unto their children.

And let the beauty of the Lord our God be upon us: and establish thou the work of our hands upon us; yea, the work of our hands establish thou it. PSALM 90:16-17

MY COMPANION

Here in my workshop where I toil,
    Till heart and hands are well-nigh spent;
Out on the road where the dust and soil
    Fall thick on garments worn and rent;
Or in the kitchen where I bake
    The bread the little children eat—
He comes, His hand of strength I take,
    And every lowly task grows sweet.

THE WATCHMAN-EXAMINER

PRAYER

Almighty God, we thank Thee for the job of this day. May we find gladness in all its toil and difficulty, in its pleasure and success, and even in its failure and sorrow. We would look always away from ourselves, and behold the glory and the need of the world that we may have the will and the strength to bring the gift of gladness to others; that with them we may stand to bear the burden and heat of the day and offer Thee the praise of work well done.

CHARLES LEWIS SLATTERY

THE MASTER WORD OF LIFE

The word which is the open sesame to every
    portal,
the great equalizer in the world,
the true philosopher's stone which transmutes
    all the base metal of humanity into gold;
the word which makes the stupid bright, the
    bright brilliant, and the brilliant steady;

the word in the heart which makes all things
    possible and without which all is vanity and
    vexation;
the word which brings hope to the youth, con-
    fidence to the middle-aged, repose to the
    aged—
that master word is work.

W. ROBERTSON NICOLL

GLORIFYING GOD

It is not only prayer that gives God glory but work.

Smiting on an anvil, sawing a beam, white-washing a wall, driving horses, sweeping, scouring, everything gives God some glory if being in His grace you do it as your duty.

To go to communion worthily gives God great glory, but to take food in thankfulness and temperance gives Him glory too.

To lift up the hands in prayer gives God glory, but a man with a dungfork in his hand, a woman with a sloppail, give Him glory too.

He is so great that all things give Him glory if you mean they should.

GERARD MANLEY HOPKINS

GIFT

Let us ask ourselves as we arise each morning, What is my work today? We do not know where the influence of today will end. Our lives may outgrow all our present thoughts and outdazzle all our dreams. God puts each fresh morning, each new chance of life, into our hands as a gift, to see what we will do with it.

ANNA R. BROWN LINDSAY

Work is love made visible.

KAHLIL GIBRAN

PETITION

O grant me this—
In all my work,
Lord, of Thy best!—
High thought in true word drest,
To cheer, to lift,
To comfort the depressed,
To lighten darkness,
To bring rest
To souls distrest.
In all my work, O manifest
Thy will!
So shall the work be blest.

JOHN OXENHAM

PILGRIMS OF THE SEA

Ships have something more in them than the
    timbers of which they are made.
Human thought and human labor and human
    love;
the designer's clever conception,
the builder's patient toil,
the explorer's daring venture,
the merchant's costly enterprise,
the sailor's loyal affection,
the traveller's hopes and fears—
all the manifold sympathies of humanity—
inform the silent pilgrims of the sea with a
    human quality.

HENRY VAN DYKE

God gives the birds their food, but He does
not throw it into their nests.

GREEK PROVERB

From TWO TRAMPS IN MUD TIME

But yield who will to their separation,
My object in living is to unite
My avocation and my vocation
As my two eyes make one in sight.
Only where love and need are one,
And the work is play for mortal stakes,
Is the deed ever really done
For Heaven and the future's sakes.

ROBERT FROST

People are constantly warned not to overdo. It
is only by overdoing sometimes that we learn
how much we can do.

MARJORIE BARSTOW GREENBIE

There are two changeless sources of solid happiness: first, the belief in God and, second, the
habit of hard work toward useful ends.

FRANCES E. WILLARD

There is no truer and more abiding happiness
than the knowledge that one is free to go on
doing, day by day, the best work one can do.

ROBIN G. COLLINGWOOD

TINY PUSHES

I long to accomplish a great and noble task,
but it is my chief duty to accomplish tasks as
though they were great and noble. The world
is moved along, not only by the mighty shoves
of its heroes, but also by the aggregate of the
tiny pushes of each honest worker.

HELEN KELLER

Happiness includes chiefly the idea of satisfaction after full honest effort. No one can possibly be satisfied and no one can be happy who feels that in some paramount affair he has failed to take up the challenge of life.

ARNOLD BENNETT

FARMERS

I watch the farmers in their fields
　And marvel secretly.
They are so very calm and sure,
　They have such dignity.

They know such simple things so well,
　Although their learning's small,
They find a steady, brown content
　Where some find none at all.

And all their quarrelings with God
　Are soon made up again;
They grant forgiveness when He sends
　His silver, tardy rain.

Their pleasure is so grave and full
　When gathered crops are trim,
You know they think their work was done
　In partnership with Him.

WILLIAM ALEXANDER PERCY

Man must work. He may work grudgingly or he may work gratefully; he may work as a man, or he may work as a machine. There is no work so rude that he may not exalt it; no work so impassive that he may not breathe a soul into it; no work so dull that he may not enliven it.

HENRY GILES

MOTTO
My work is bigger than myself.

JEAN MARTIN CHARCOT

To find one's work is to find one's place in the world.

RICHARD C. CABOT

AN EMPLOYER'S PRAYER
Dear Lord, please help me
to accept human beings as they are, not yearn
　for perfect creatures;
to recognize ability and encourage it;
to understand shortcomings and make allow-
　ances for them;
to work patiently for improvement and not to
　expect too much too quickly;
to appreciate what people do right, not just
　criticize what they do wrong;
to be slow to anger and hard to discourage;
to have the hide of an elephant and the pa-
　tience of Job;
in short, Lord, please help me to be a better
　boss!

Take off your hats to your yesterdays;
Take off your coats for your tomorrows.

Unless a man undertakes more than he possibly can do he will never do all he can do.

HENRY DRUMMOND

Almighty God doesn't call any man or woman to a trivial or unimportant life work. If you can't see your job as being somehow vital and meaningful to mankind, change it or get out of it.

JOHN OLIVER NELSON

ON MY WAY TO WORK

Dear Lord, excuse my heavy boots,
  My dungarees and cap;
I'm praying on my way to work,
  For I'm a working chap.

The bus is just ahead, but, Lord,
  I've surely time to pray
For strength to be a better man
  Than I was yesterday.

Blessed is the man who has some congenial work, some occupation in which he can put his heart, and which affords a complete outlet to all the forces there are in him.

JOHN BURROUGHS

Civilization develops only where considerable numbers of men work together for common ends.

GEORGE FOOT MOORE

Happiness depends chiefly on our cheerful acceptance of routine, on our refusal to assume, as many do, that daily work and daily duty are a kind of slavery.

LE BARON RUSSELL BRIGGS

From MORITURI SALUTAMUS

Shall we sit idly down and say
The night hath come; it is no longer day?
The night hath not yet come; we are not quite
Cut off from labor by the failing light;
Something remains for us to do or dare;
Even the oldest tree some fruit may bear.

HENRY WADSWORTH LONGFELLOW

WORK OF ART

Anything that one does, from cooking a dinner to governing a state, becomes a work of art if motivated by the passion for excellence and done as well as it can be. A man who does his job in that spirit will be the one who gets the most satisfaction out of life.

L. P. JACKS

There is always somebody or something to work for; and while there is, life must be, and shall become, worth living.

LE BARON R. BRIGGS

SIMPLE GOODNESS

Goodness is richer than greatness. It lifts us nearer to God. It is manifested according to our abilities, within our sphere. Every day I bless God that the great necessary work of the world is so faithfully carried on by humble men in narrow spaces and by faithful women in narrow circles, performing works of simple goodness.

EDWIN HUBBELL CHAPIN

There is no future in any job. The future lies in the man who holds the job.

GEORGE W. CRANE

If you want to be not only successful, but personally, happily, and permanently successful, then do your job in a way that puts lights in people's faces. Do that job in such a way that, even when you are out of sight, folks will always know which way you went by the lamps left behind.

KENNETH MC FARLAND

World Horizons

Go ye therefore, and teach all nations, baptizing them in the name of the Father, and of the Son, and of the Holy Ghost:

Teaching them to observe all things whatsoever I have commanded you: and, lo, I am with you alway, even unto the end of the world.

MATTHEW 28:19-20

PRAYER

Heavenly Father, by whom all men were
    created as one species,
and who by accidents of climate, geography,
    and environment
became separated into races, colors, and
    creeds:
help us to perceive the basic oneness we were
    born to realize.
Forgive our tendency to transform prejudice
    into principle,
or to think that sentimental gestures
are equivalent to brotherly devotion.

RALPH S. MEADOWCROFT

Happiness to be true must be oriented on
landmarks much greater than one's own little
personal joys and gratifications.

DAGOBERT D. RUNES

Strange stirrings of hope and expectation are
moving across the world. It is possible that
we may be on the fringe of a new and marvelous epoch.

RUFUS M. JONES

BROTHERS

I honor the land that gave me birth,
    I thrill with joy when the flag's unfurled,
But the gift she gives of supremest worth,
    Is the brother's heart for all the world;
So come, ye sons of the near and far,
    Teuton and Latin, Slav and Jew,
For brothers beloved of mine ye are—
    Blood of my blood in a world made new.

GEORGE E. DAY

APPROACH

I do not believe there is a problem in this country or the world today which could not be
settled if approached through the teaching of
the Sermon on the Mount.

HARRY S. TRUMAN

WORLD TEAM

We are members of a world team. We are part-
ners in a grand adventure. Our thinking must
be world-wide.

WENDELL WILLKIE

UNITED FAMILY

Our idea of God's power depends upon our
idea of God's purpose, and we cannot have a
clear conception of his power until we perceive with heart and mind that the purpose of
God is brotherhood, the creation of "Man,"
in the making of a united family of human
beings.

G. A. STUDDERT-KENNEDY

NEIGHBORHOOD

When the world seems large and complex, we
need to remember that great world ideals all
begin in some home neighborhood.

KONRAD ADENAUER

RESPONSIBILITY

We are all of us fellow passengers on the same
planet, and we are all of us equally responsible for the happiness and well-being of the
world in which we happen to live.

HENDRIK WILLEM VAN LOON

PRACTICAL OBJECTIVE

The twentieth century will be chiefly remembered by future generations not as an era of political conflicts or technical inventions but as an age in which human society dared to think of the welfare of the whole human race as a practical objective.

ARNOLD TOYNBEE

A man's feet should be planted in his country, but his eyes should survey the world.

GEORGE SANTAYANA

From THE PRESENT CRISIS

New occasions teach new duties; Time makes
    ancient good uncouth;
They must upward still, and onward, who
    would keep abreast of Truth;
Lo, before us gleam her camp-fires! we our-
    selves must Pilgrims be,
Launch our Mayflower, and steer boldly
    through the desperate winter sea,
Nor attempt the Future's portal with the Past's
    blood-rusted key.

JAMES RUSSELL LOWELL

God has written one line of His thought upon every people.

GIUSEPPE MAZZINI

A THOUSAND WORLDS

I feel more and more every day, as my imagination strengthens, that I do not live in this world alone, but in a thousand worlds.

JOHN KEATS

PRAYER

Lord, lift us out of private-mindedness and give us public souls to work for Thy Kingdom by daily creating that atmosphere of brotherhood by a happy temper, a friendly mind, and a generous heart, which alone can bring in the great peace to Thy honor and the comfort of mankind.

CHARLES H. BRENT

The best bridges of understanding between minds are built out of the best materials those minds possess.

HARRY A. *and* BONARO W. OVERSTREET

SIGHT

The real voyage of discovery
consists not in seeking
new landscapes,
but in having new eyes,
in seeing the universe
with the eyes of another,
of a hundred others,
in seeing the hundred universes
that each of them sees.

MARCEL PROUST

Now man has taken the ball of earth and made it a little thing.

CARL SANDBURG

From A NEW EARTH

God grant us wisdom in these coming days,
And eyes unsealed, that we clear visions see
In that new world that He would have us build,
To Life's ennoblement and His high ministry.

JOHN OXENHAM

THE TUFT OF FLOWERS

I went to turn the grass once after one
Who mowed it in the dew before the sun.

The dew was gone that made his blade so keen
Before I came to view the leveled scene.

I looked for him behind an aisle of trees;
I listened for his whetstone on the breeze.

But he had gone his way, the grass all mown,
And I must be, as he had been—alone,

'As all must be,' I said within my heart,
'Whether they work together or apart.'

But as I said it, swift there passed me by
On noiseless wing a bewildered butterfly,

Seeking with memories grown dim o'er night
Some resting flower of yesterday's delight.

And once I marked his flight go round and
    round,
As where some flower lay withering on the
    ground.

And then he flew as far as eye could see,
And then on tremulous wing came back to me.

I thought of questions that have no reply,
And would have turned to toss the grass to
    dry;

But he turned first, and led my eye to look
At a tall tuft of flowers beside a brook,

A leaping tongue of bloom the scythe had
    spared
Beside a reedy brook the scythe had bared.

The mower in the dew had loved them thus,
By leaving them to flourish, not for us,

Nor yet to draw one thought of ours to him,
But from sheer morning gladness at the brim.

The butterfly and I had lit upon,
Nevertheless, a message from the dawn,

That made me hear the waking birds around,
And hear his long scythe whispering to the
    ground,

And feel a spirit kindred to my own;
So that henceforth I worked no more alone;

But glad with him, I worked as with his aid,
And weary, sought at noon with him the
    shade;

And dreaming, as it were, held brotherly
    speech
With one whose thought I had not hoped to
    reach.

Men work together,' I told him from the
    heart,
Whether they work together or apart.'

ROBERT FROST

Albert Schweitzer's aim is not to dazzle an age but to awaken it, to make it comprehend that moral splendor is part of the gift of life, and that each man has unlimited strength to feel human oneness and to act upon it. He has proved that although a man may have no jurisdiction over the fact of his existence, he can hold supreme command over the meaning of existence for him.

NORMAN COUSINS

BLESSED COMMUNITY

As the sap flows through the branches of the vine and vitalizes the whole organism so that it bursts into the beauty and glory of foliage and blossoms and finally into fruit, so through the lives of men and women, inwardly responsive and joyously receptive, the life of God as Spirit flows, carrying vitality, awakening love, creating passion for goodness, kindling the fervor of consecration and producing that living body, that organism of the Spirit, that "blessed community," which continues through the centuries the revelation of God as love and tenderness and eternal goodness.

RUFUS M. JONES

UNITY

Providence has distributed His gifts, spread them around so that no man is a full man apart from other men. God took the whole man and broke him up into fragmentary men so that they would have to unite their gifts through brotherhood to produce civilization.

NEWELL DWIGHT HILLIS

IN SUCH AN AGE

To be alive in such an age!
With every year a lightening page,
Turned in the world's great wonder-book,
Whereon the leaning nations look,
Where men speak strong for brotherhood,
For peace and universal good;
When miracles are everywhere,
And every inch of common air
Throbs a tremendous prophecy
Of greater marvels yet to be.
O, Thrilling Age!
O, Willing Age!

ANGELA MORGAN

HEARTH AND HOME

Go where he will, the wise man is at home,
His hearth the earth—his hall the azure dome;
Where his clear spirit leads him, there's his road,
By God's own light illumined and foreshowed.

RALPH WALDO EMERSON

The devotee of democracy
adopts a lifelong
assignment in
human relationships.

GORDON W. ALLPORT

The universe is too great a mystery for there to be only one single approach to it.

SYMMACHUS

Philosophy is at bottom homesickness—the longing to be at home everywhere.

NOVALIS

THE GOAL

We are standing in the great dawn of a day they did not know,
On a height they only dreamed of, toiling darkly far below;
But our gaze is toward a summit, loftier, airier, mist-encurled,
Soaring skyward through the twilight from the bases of the world.
Up and up, achieving, failing, weak in flesh but strong in soul.
We may never live to reach it—ah, but we have seen the goal!

ODELL SHEPARD

Worship

I was glad when they said unto me, Let us go into the house of the Lord.

PSALM 122:1

We took sweet counsel together, and walked unto the house of God in company.

PSALM 55:14

Worship the Lord in the beauty of holiness.

PSALM 29:2

WORSHIP

God made my cathedral
    Under the stars;
He gave my cathedral
    Trees for its spires;
He hewed me an altar
    In the depth of a hill;
He gave for a hymnal
    A rock-bedded rill;
He voiced me a sermon
    Of heavenly light
In the beauty around me—
    The calmness of night;
And I felt as I knelt
    On the velvet-like sod
I had supped of the Spirit
    In the Temple of God.

RUTH FURBEE

————

Worship is the exposing of the whole person
    to reality.
Worship is the entire self's response to God,
    requiring a unity of mind, will, and feelings.
Worship entails work, but work cannot take
    its place.
Worship demands thought, but no thinking
    can substitute for it.
Worship engenders emotion, but no feeling as
    such is ever worship.
Worship is the rooting of life in reality; it is
    man's exposing himself to the rightness of
    God; it is finding God real and religion rich
    for every need.
Worship is finding meaning in life within the
    depths of eternity.

NELS F. S. FERRÉ

EMPIRE

There is not a man
That lives who hath not known his God-like
    hours
And feels not what an empire we inherit.

————

COMMONPLACES

Unless we can touch and feel God in the commonplaces, He is going to be a very infrequent and unfamiliar guest. For life is made up of very ordinary experiences. Now and again a novelty leaps into the way, but the customary tenor is seldom broken. The ordinary stars shine upon us night after night; only occasionally does a comet come our way. Look at some of the daily commonplaces: health, sleep, bread and butter, work, friendship, a few flowers by the wayside, the laughter of children, the ministry of song, the bright day, the cool night. If I do not perceive God in these things, I have a very unhallowed and insignificant world.

JOHN HENRY JOWETT

————

To worship is to quicken the conscience by the
    holiness of God,
to feed the mind with the truth of God,
to purge the imagination by the beauty of God,
to open the heart to the love of God,
to devote the will to the purpose of God.

WILLIAM TEMPLE

————

As a plant upon the earth, so man rests upon the bosom of God; he is nourished by unfailing fountains, and draws at his need inexhaustible power.

RALPH WALDO EMERSON

THE SNOWDROP

Close to the sod
   There can be seen
A thought of God
   In white and green.

Unmarred, unsoiled,
   It cleft the clay,
Serene, unspoiled,
   It views the day.

It is so holy
   And yet so lowly.
Would you enjoy
   Its grace and dower

And not destroy
   The living flower?
Then you must, please,
   Fall on your knees.

        ANNA BUNSTON DE BARY

If you would wish to know how the Almighty feels toward us, listen to the beating of your own heart, and add to it infinity.

        JEAN BAPTISTE LACORDAIRE

LAMP-LIGHTS

God loves man's lamp-lights better than His own great stars.

        RABINDRANATH TAGORE

SUPREMELY WORTHFUL

Religion is devotion to what one holds to be supremely worthful not only for himself but for all human living.

        HENRY NELSON WIEMAN

HOLY PLACES

Wherever souls of men have worshiped, there
   Is God: where old cathedrals climb the sky,
Or shining hillsides lift their heads on high,
   Or silent woodland spaces challenge prayer,
Or inner chambers shut the heart from care;
   Where broken temples of old faiths now lie
Forgotten in the sun, or swallows cry
   At dusk about some crossroads chapel, bare
Alike of bells and beauty; where saints walked
   Of old with speaking presences unseen,
Or dreaming boys with quiet voices talked
   In pairs last night on some still college green;
Where Moses' Sinai flamed, or Jesus trod
   The upward way apart: there, *here*, is God!

        HERBERT D. GALLAUDET

And all the windows of my heart
   I open to the day.

        JOHN GREENLEAF WHITTIER

From A FOREST HYMN

My heart is awed within me when I think
Of the great miracle that still goes on,
In silence, round me.

        WILLIAM CULLEN BRYANT

Whatever the thing may be—
if it humbles us,
if it gives us a vision of duty,
if it exalts us,
if it sends us back into the busy world with a
   steadying hand upon us,
and if, above all, it makes us aware of God—
it is worship.

        BOYNTON MERRILL

ACKNOWLEDGMENTS

(see additional acknowledgments on page iv)

HAROLD MATSON COMPANY for extract from *Life Starts Today* by Evelyn Wells.

McGRAW-HILL BOOK COMPANY for extract from *Toward Better Personal Adjustment* by Harold W. Bernard, copyright © 1957 by McGraw-Hill Book Company; extracts from *The Arts of Leisure* by Marjorie Barstow Greenbie, copyright 1935 by Marjorie Barstow Greenbie; extract from *Life Begins at Forty*, copyright 1932 by McGraw-Hill Book Company.

MUSIC CORPORATION for "Trees" by Joyce Kilmer.

W. W. NORTON & COMPANY, INC., for extracts from *Life and Language in the Old Testament* by Mary Ellen Chase, copyright 1955 by W. W. Norton & Company, Inc.; quotation by Eleanor Shipley Duckett in *Roads to Knowledge*, ed. by W. A. Neilson; *The Biological Basis of Human Nature* by Herbert Spencer Jennings; *Man's Search for Himself* by Rollo May, copyright 1954 by W. W. Norton & Company, Inc.; *The Mind Goes Forth* by Harry A. and Bonaro W. Overstreet, copyright © 1956 by W. W. Norton & Company, Inc.

PUTNAM'S & COWARD-McCANN for extract from *Lay Thoughts of a Dean* by William Ralph Inge; extract from *The Ivory Door* by A. A. Milne; "Symbol" from *Ships in Harbor* by David Morton.

FLEMING H. REVELL COMPANY for extracts from *In Quest of God's Power* and *When the Heart Is Hungry* by Charles L. Allen; *Christmas in Our Hearts* and *When Christmas Came to Bethlehem* by Charles L. Allen and Charles L. Wallis; *Mr. Jones, Meet the Master* by Peter Marshall; *Love Is Something You Do* by Frederick B. Speakman; *The Road to the Cross* by Herbert F. Stevenson.

CHARLES SCRIBNER'S SONS for extracts from *A Diary of Private Prayer* by John Baillie; *The Lord's Prayer* by Ernest F. Scott; *God in These Times* by Henry Pitney Van Dusen; *Six Days of the Week* by Henry van Dyke; extract from "Thanks from Earth to Heaven" from *Dust and Light* by John Hall Wheelock.

SIMON AND SCHUSTER, INC., for extract from *Peace of Mind* by Joshua Loth Liebman, copyright 1946 by Joshua Loth Liebman.

THE VIKING PRESS for extracts from *Dobry* by Monica Shannon, copyright 1934 by The Viking Press, © 1962 by Monica Shannon.

WESTMINSTER PRESS for extract from *The Spiritual Legacy of John Foster Dulles*, edited by Henry Pitney Van Dusen, copyright © 1960 by W. L. Jenkins.

WHITESIDE, INC., PUBLISHERS, for extracts from *Reflections of the Spirit* by Winnifred Wygal, copyright 1948 by Whiteside, Inc.

YALE UNIVERSITY PRESS for extracts from *Becoming* by Gordon W. Allport.

Acknowledgment is made to the following for permission to reprint materials as indicated:

ASSOCIATION PRESS for extract from *Every Occupation a Christian Calling* by John Oliver Nelson; "Creed of a Good Neighbor" by Joseph Fort Newton in *Treasury of the Christian Faith*, ed. by Stanley I. Stuber.

BETTER HOMES & GARDENS for extracts by Howard Whitman, copyright by Meredith Publishing Company.

THE CHRISTIAN CENTURY FOUNDATION for "Be Still and Know" by Mary Hallet, copyright 1933.

CHRISTIAN HERALD ASSOCIATION for extracts by Edgar A. Guest, Edgar DeWitt Jones, and Clementine Paddleford in *Fifty Years of Christmas*, copyright 1951 by the Christian Herald Association; V. L. Crawford in *Christian Herald*.

CRESSET PRESS for "For Sleep, or Death" from *Urania* by Ruth Pitter.

DOHNAVUR FELLOWSHIP for poems by Amy Carmichael.

THE FINE EDITIONS PRESS for "To My Little Son" from *Garnet Ring* by Julia Johnson Davis.

THE FIRST PENNSYLVANIA BANKING AND TRUST COMPANY for "Per Aspera" by Florence Earle Coates.

JOHN HANCOCK MUTUAL LIFE INSURANCE COMPANY for "Their Boyhood Was Made in America" by Louis Redmond.

HARPER & ROW, PUBLISHERS, for extracts from *Letters to God and the Devil* by Edward Scribner Ames; *Things That Matter* by Charles H. Brent; *More Than We Are* by Margueritte Harmon Bro; *Not Minds Alone* by Kenneth Irving Brown; *Finding God in a New World* by William Adams Brown; "Let Us Keep Christmas" from *Apples of Gold* by Grace Noll Crowell; "To Those Who Are Content" from *Facing the Stars* by Grace Noll Crowell; "Country Churches" from *Flame in the Wind* by Grace Noll Crowell; "Common Days" and "I Have Found Such Joy" from *Light of the Years* by Grace Noll Crowell; "Denominations" from *This Golden Summit* by Grace Noll Crowell; "Silver Poplars" from *White Flame* by Grace Noll Crowell; *Doctor Schweitzer of Lambaréné* by Norman Cousins; "I Have a Rendezvous with Life" from *Color* by Countee Cullen; *Autobiography of Prayer* and *Dialogue and Destiny* by Albert Edward Day; "Faith" by S. E. Kiser and "Give Thanks to God" by Grenville Kleiser from *Enriching Worship; From the Crossroads, From within These Walls, May Peace Be with You,* and *Tonic for Our Times* by Richard L. Evans; *Christian Faith and Higher Education* and *Making Religion Real* by Nels F. S. Ferré; *The Eternal Legacy from an Upper Room* by Leonard Griffith; *Creative Prayer* by Emily Herman; *Our Eternal Contemporary* by Walter Marshall Horton; *The Man Christ Jesus* by John Knox; *The Hand of God* by Oswald W. S. McCall; "At Little Virgil's Window," "The Christ of the Andes," "The New Trinity," and "Quatrain" from *Poems of Edwin Markham*, ed. by Charles L. Wallis; *The Great Realities* by Samuel H. Miller; *What Is Christianity?* by Charles Clayton Morrison; "The Christ," "Credo," "The Cross at the Crossways," "The Cross Roads," "The Day—The Way," "The Key," "Love Ever Gives," "A New Earth," "Petition," and "Sanctuary" from *The Selected Poems of John Oxenham,* ed. by Charles L. Wallis; *Seeing the Invisible* by Harold Cooke Phillips; "Barabbas Speaks" and "Grace at Evening" from *Over the Sea, the Sky* by Edwin McNeill Poteat; *Hearing the Unheard* by Merton S. Rice; *This I Remember* by Eleanor Roosevelt; *For We Have This Treasure, Love Is a Spendthrift,* and *Who Goes There?* by Paul Scherer; "I Thank Thee" by Robert Davis from *Social Hymns; Work and Contemplation* by Douglas V. Steere; *The Best of G. A. Studdert-Kennedy; Deep Is the Hunger,* *Disciplines of the Spirit,* and *The Inward Journey* by Howard Thurman; *Alternative to Futility, The Common Ventures of Life, The Logic of Belief,* and *Your Other Vocation* by Elton Trueblood; quotations from William Adams Brown, Charles G. Blanden, Grace Noll Crowell, Oliver Huckel, William F. Kirk, Boynton Merrill, John R. Moreland, J. Richard Sneed, and James Wallingford in *Worship Resources for the Christian Year,* ed. by Charles L. Wallis.

HARVARD UNIVERSITY PRESS and THE COMMONWEALTH FUND for extract from *Mental Health in Modern Society* by Thomas A. C. Bennie and Luther E. Woodward.

THE HORN BOOK, INC., for extract by Lois Lenski in *Newbery Medal Books: 1922-1955.*

HYMN SOCIETY OF AMERICA for "A Grace" by Thomas Tiplady.

THE JEWISH THEOLOGICAL SEMINARY OF AMERICA for quotation from "The Eternal Light" program.

LIVERIGHT PUBLISHING CORPORATION for extract from *The Story of Mankind* by Hendrik Willem van Loon, copyright © renewed 1954.

LONGMANS, GREEN & COMPANY, LTD., for extract from *The Triumph of Life* by William Barry.

DAVID McKAY COMPANY, INC., for extract from *Human Destiny* by Lecomte du Noüy.

JULIAN MESSNER, PUBLISHERS, for extract from *The Complete Life* by John Erskine.

WILLIAM MORROW AND COMPANY, INC., for extract from *Emotional Problems and What You Can Do About Them* by William Terhune.

OXFORD UNIVERSITY PRESS, INC., for extract from *Christian Education in a Democracy* by Frank E. Gaebelein.

OXFORD UNIVERSITY PRESS, LTD., for extract from *Note-Books and Papers of Gerard Manley Hopkins,* edited by Humphrey House.

PHILOSOPHICAL LIBRARY, INC., for extracts from *A Dictionary of Thoughts* by Dagobert D. Runes.

THE PILGRIM PRESS for "For the Things That Are Always" from *While the Earth Remaineth* by Jeanette E. Perkins.

RAND McNALLY & COMPANY for poems by Ella Wheeler Wilcox.

HENRY REGNERY COMPANY, PUBLISHERS, for poems by Edgar A. Guest.

SATURDAY REVIEW for quotations from John Ciardi, Norman Cousins, and William Rose Benét.

SOCIETY OF AUTHORS for quotations from George Bernard Shaw.

THESE TIMES for "The Surprise" by Elaine V. Emans; "His Ways" by Esther Guyot; "Old Rugs" by Jean Carpenter Mergard; quotation from Norval F. Pease.

UNITED CHURCH PRESS for "Easter Morning" from *Tribute to Jesus* by Edgar Daniel Kramer.

THE WATCHMAN-EXAMINER for "This Is Our House of Prayer" by Thomas John Carlisle; "Sharing" by A. L. Gruber; "Sunday Service" by Thelma Ireland; "Young Minister" by Ruth M. Parks; quotations from Beulah Hughes and J. Winston Pearce.

ZION'S HERALD for quotation from Wesley H. Hager.

Acknowledgment is made to the following for permission to reprint the poetry indicated:

Richard Armour for "Everyday Madonna"; Joseph Auslander for "Gifts without Season"; Leslie Savage Clark for "Eden and Gethsemane," "Encounter with Eternity," "In the Time of Trouble," and "The Way"; estate of Thomas Curtis Clark for "The Search"; Grace Noll Crowell for "Good Books"; E. P. Dickie for "Three Things There Are"; Mrs. Robert Freeman for "Beyond the Horizon" by Robert Freeman; Ethel Romig Fuller for "Confession"; Winfred Ernest Garrison for "The Book"; Hermann Hagedorn for "The Mother in the House" and "Service"; Hannah Kahn for "An Old Church"; H. Victor Kane for "Psalm of a City Man"; Elinor Lennan for "Prayer for a Play House"; Adelaide Love for "Alchemy"; Barbara Marr for "Prayer"; estate of James J. Metcalfe for "God's Children" and "However Much I Have to Do"; Madeleine Sweeney Miller for "Who Builds the Church?"; Charlotte Baker Montgomery for "Days" and "Good Company" by Karle Wilson Baker; estate of Christopher Morley for "To a Child"; Ida Norton Munson for "Easter Light" and "Journeys"; Ella H. Meyer for poems by Angela Morgan; William J. Parker for "Discovery" by Helen Baker Parker; Johnstone G. Patrick for "The Voice"; LeRoy Pratt Percy for "Farmers" and "A Page's Road Song" by William Alexander Percy; Daniel A. Poling for "Prayer"; May Richstone for "Lucky the Lad"; Margaret E. Sangster for "A Bit of the Book," "Gratitude," and "A Mother's Prayer"; Mrs. Lew Sarett for "God Is at the Anvil" by Lew Sarett; W. S. Scott for "Dawn" by Frederick George Scott; Ralph W. Seager for "Golden Sight," "No Manger for Easter," "One Step in Triumph," "Spring Belongs with Easter," "Spring Wealth," and "The Wisest of the Wise"; Odell Shepard for "In the Dawn"; Eleanor Slater for "Petition"; Hilda W. Smith for "The Carpenter of Galilee"; Eleanor B. Stock for "The Prayer of the Quest"; Hildegard Hoyt Swift for "The Teacher"; Gilbert Thomas for extract from "The Cup of Happiness"; Nancy Byrd Turner for "The Christmas Star" and "The Fellowship of Prayer"; B. Y. Williams for "Prayer" and "Your House of Happiness"; Dorothy Clarke Wilson for "The Christ of the World's Highway"; Leland Foster Wood for "The Main Aims."

Acknowledgment is made to the following persons for permission to reprint material from their writings:

Theodore F. Adams, Florence E. Allen, Brooks Atkinson, Leonard Bernstein, John Sutherland Bonnell, John Mason Brown, George A. Buttrick, Marchette Chute, John B. Coburn, Henry Hitt Crane, Will Durant, Harry Emerson Fosdick, Gordon Lynn Foster, Edwin Osgood Grover, Herschel H. Hobbs, J. Edgar Hoover, Lynn Harold Hough, Helen Keller, Lin Yutang, Arnold H. Lowe, Ralph S. Meadowcroft, John Homer Miller, Samuel H. Miller, Guy Morrill, Richard M. Nixon, Harry A. Overstreet, Norman Vincent Peale, Leo Politi, Nathan Pusey, John A. Redhead, Archibald Rutledge, Joseph R. Sizoo, Ralph W. Sockman, Pitirim Sorokin, James S. Stewart, Harold Taylor, Harry S. Truman, and Robert Ulich.

INDEX OF PROSE AUTHORS AND SOURCES

Abbott, Lyman 97
Abélard, Peter 34
Adams, Theodore F. 28, 109
Adenauer, Konrad 233
Adler, Felix 86
Agassiz, Louis 4
Alcott, Bronson 123
Allen, Charles L. 100
Allen, Florence E. 72
Allen, James 122, 124, 142
Allport, Gordon W. 62, 236
Ames, Edward Scribner 66
Aquinas, Thomas 194
Augustine, St. 18, 66

Bacon, Francis 14
Baillie, John 182, 194
Balfour, Arthur James 27
Barrie, James M. 71, 185
Barry, William 173
Barth, Karl 167
Baxter, Richard 213
Beck, Alan 111
Beecher, Henry Ward 18, 203
Beethoven, Ludwig van 167
Benét, William Rose 132
Bennett, Arnold 144, 214, 229
Benson, Arthur Christopher 81, 82, 111, 141
Bergson, Henri 138
Bernard, Harold W. 79
Bernstein, Leonard 76
Bethune, Mary McLeod 50
Black, Hugh 79, 80
Boddy, William H. 42

Bonnard, Abel 79
Bonnell, John Sutherland 192
Book of Common Prayer 200
Book of Days for Christmas, A 3
Bowie, Walter Russell 113
Bowring, John 19
Brent, Charles H. 85, 185, 192, 234
Briggs, Le Baron Russell 123, 128, 230
Bright, William 56
Bro, Marguerite Harmon 114
Brooks, Phillips 55, 109, 123, 200
Brown, John Mason 144
Brown, Kenneth Irving 144
Brown, William Adams 68, 223
Bryan, William Jennings 86
Bullis, Harry S. 193
Bunyan, John 23
Burleson, Hugh L. 174
Burns, C. Delisle 124
Burns, Robert 87
Burr, Charles H. 197
Burroughs, John 173, 230
Butler, Samuel 19
Butterfield, Herbert 87
Buttrick, George A. 192
Byrd, Richard E. 51

Cabot, Richard C. 91, 105, 207, 229
Carlyle, Thomas 85, 124
Carrel, Alexis 189

Carver, George Washington 173
Chang Chao 151
Channing, William Ellery 17, 30, 146
Chapin, Edwin Hubbell 131, 230
Charcot, Jean Martin 229
Chase, Mary Ellen 7
Chesterton, Gilbert Keith 51, 76, 135
Christmas in Our Hearts 38
Chute, Marchette 180
Ciardi, John 182
Cicero, Marcus Tullius 82
Clapp, Marie Welles 186
Claudel, Paul 85
Coburn, John B. 213
Coleridge, Samuel T. 20
Collingwood, Robin G. 228
Colton, Charles Caleb 50, 214
Connor, Ralph 124
Conwell, Russell H. 93
Cousins, Norman 141, 168, 235
Crane, Frank 150
Crane, George W. 230
Crane, Henry Hitt 45, 181
Crawford, V. L. 190
Crowe, Charles M. 65
Chrysostom, St. John 81

Day, Albert Edward 93, 189
Day, Clarence 145
de Beauvoir, Simone 149
de la Mare, Walter 92
Dell, William 4
Dewey, John 122

Dickens, Charles 37, 137
Douglas, Norman 138
Draxe, Thomas 56
Drummond, Henry 30, 158, 229
Dulles, John Foster 26
Dunningham, Lewis L. 3
Durant, Will 118, 151
Dwight, Timothy 138

Eckhart, Johannes 87, 151
Edman, Irwin 50
Edwards, Jonathan 208, 211
Einstein, Albert 137, 197
Eliot, George 91, 105
Eliot, Samuel A. 124
Emerson, Ralph Waldo 20, 67, 138, 175, 200, 239
Enriching Worship 222
Erasmus, Desiderius 30
Erskine, John 35, 172
Eternal Light, The 127
Evans, Richard L. 13, 75, 81, 109, 110, 114, 163

Fénelon, Francois 159
Ferré, Nels F. S. 111, 132, 239
Finley, John H. 212
Fischer, Chester O. 214
Fiske, George Walter 207
Forman, H. J. 211
Fosdick, Harry Emerson 24, 122, 179, 182, 192
Foster, Gordon Lynn 75
Francis of Assisi, St. 17
Fridy, Wallace 191

Fromm, Erich 61
Frost, Robert 151

Gaebelein, Frank E. 144
Galileo 4
Gandhi, Mahatma 154
Gehman, J. N. 214
Gibran, Kahlil 228
Giles, Henry 229
Gilliatt, D. H. 30
Glover, Carl A. 98
Glover, T. R. 142
Goethe, Johann Wolfgang von 49, 102, 105
Goethe's Mother 3
Graham, Billy 24, 221
Grayson, David 51, 52, 91, 145
Greenbie, Marjorie Barstow 153, 228
Grenfell, Wilfred T. 197
Griffith, Leonard 68
Grose, Howard B. 194
Grover, Edwin Osgood 141
Guest, Edgar A. 37

Hale, Edward Everett 199
Hand, Learned 106
Hare, August W. 94
Hare, Julius Charles 24
Harnack, Adolph 99
Heim, Karl 67
Henson, Hensley 127
Herman, Emily 128
Hidden Treasures 181
Hilton, James 145
Hinkle, Beatrice 123
Hobbs, Herschel H. 57
Holmer, John Andrew 197
Holmes, Oliver Wendell 46, 76, 121
Hopkins, Gerard Manley 227
Horace 214
Horton, Walter Marshall 154
Hough, Lynn Harold 163
Hughes, Beulah 41
Huckel, Oliver 66
Hugo, Victor 8
Hunt, John 76
Hyde, William De Witt 121

Inge, William Ralph 20
Ingelow, Jean 17

Jacks, L. P. 8, 223, 230
James, William 88, 142
John XXIII, Pope 76
Johnson, Lionel 105
Johnson, Samuel 141
Jones, Edgar De Witt 36
Jones, Rufus M. 71, 75, 122, 173, 233
Jordan, William George 138
Jowett, John Henry 62, 239

Keats, John 234
Keller, Helen 10, 180, 228
Kempis, Thomas a 30, 87, 157, 159, 160, 189
Kennedy, Charles Rann 44
Kepler, Thomas S. 181
Kerr, Sophie 151
Kierkegaard, Søren 117
King, W. L. Mackenzie 13
Kingsley, Charles 102, 172
Kleiser, Grenville 211
Knox, John 29

Kohn, Harold E. 29, 49, 110, 175, 198, 222

Lacordiare, Jean Baptiste 240
Lamartine, Alphonse de 180
Lamb, Charles 8, 197
Landor, Walter Savage 81
Lao-Tzu 92
Larcom, Lucy 117
Law, William 189
Lecky, William H. 124
Lessing, Gotthold 145
Liebman, Joshua Loth 49, 85
Lin Yutang 143
Lincoln, Abraham 88
Lindsay, Anna R. Brown 79, 213, 227
Link, Henry C. 43
Livingstone, Richard W. 106, 164
Lowe, Arnold H. 203
Lubbock, John 17

MacArthur, Douglas 124
Macdonald, George 68, 87, 179, 189, 224
Mackay, H. F. B. 221
Maclaren, Alexander 30, 86
MacOdrum, Alastair 3
Malik, Charles 27, 152, 222
Maltby, W. Russell 26
Markham, Edwin 97, 163
Marshall, Peter 33, 131, 164, 179
Masefield, John 145
May, Rollo 92, 163
Mayer, Frederick 146
Mazzini, Giuseppe 234
McCall, Oswald W. S. 122, 211
McDowell, William F. 25
McFarland, Kenneth 230
McKenzie, Jean 197
Meadowcroft, Ralph S. 233
Meckel, Aaron N. 207
Merrill, Boynton 41, 240
Milan Cathedral 179
Miles, Catherine 127
Miller, John Homer 179
Miller, Samuel H. 28, 61
Milne, A. A. 160
Mitchell, Donald Grant 112
Montague, William Pepperell 152
Moore, George Foot 230
Morley, Christopher 143
Morrill, Guy 204
Morrison, Charles Clayton 41
Morrison, George H. 65
Mulock, William 138
Munger, T. T. 99

Nelson, John Oliver 229
Newton, Joseph Fort 34, 58, 82
Nicoll, W. Robertson 227
Nixon, M. MacNeile 123
Not Minds Alone 143
Noüy, Lecomte du 153
Novalis 236

Ogdon, William S. 51
O'Reilly, John Boyle 75
Osler, William 122
Oursler, Fulton 7
Outlook, The 19
Overstreet, Bonaro W. 234
Overstreet, Harry A. 75, 234

Paddleford, Clementine 35
Palmer, George Herbert 151
Panin, Ivan 117
Pascal, Blaise 51, 86
Peacock, Thomas Love 20
Peale, Norman Vincent 37, 117, 192
Pearce, J. Winston 203
Pease, Norval F. 14
Pell, Edward Leigh 92
Peloubet, Francis N. 101
Penn, William 56
Phelps, William Lyon 4, 23, 29
Phillips, Harold Cooke 66
Pitkin, Walter D. 94
Politi, Leo 13
Pratt, James Bissett 29
Prayers New and Old 194
Proust, Marcel 234
Pure in Heart, The 138

Radcliffe, Lynn James 189
Rader, William 80
Rauschenbusch, Walter 171
Redhead, John A. 72
Redmond, Louis 93
Renan, Ernest 25
Rennie, Thomas A. C. 94
Rhoades, Winfred 152
Rice, Merton S. 180
Richardson, Norman E. 8
Richter, Jean Paul 55, 191
Rilke, Rainer Maria 160, 182
Robertson, Frederick W. 30, 180
Roosevelt, Eleanor 118
Roosevelt, Franklin D. 72
Roosevelt, Theodore 110
Rotary International 200
Runes, Dagobert D. 4, 233
Ruskin, John 20, 171
Rutherford, Samuel 57

Saint-Exupéry, Antoine de 44, 159
Sandburg, Carl 234
Santayana, George 72, 171, 234
Sargent, Malcolm 71
Saudreau, Auguste 160
Scharfe, Howard C. 58
Scherer, Paul 55
Schweitzer, Albert 123, 128, 146, 211, 221, 224
Scott, Ernest F. 93
Scott, Robert Falcon 181
Seeley, John Robert 26
Shannon, Monica 208
Shelley, Percy Bysshe 138, 182
Sheppard, Dick 27
Sherrill, Henry Knox 65
Sizoo, Joseph R. 26, 33, 150
Slattery, Charles Lewis 227
Smith, Elizabeth Oakes 71
Smith, Roy L. 135
Smith, T. V. 131
Smuts, Jan Christian 9, 20
Sneed, J. Richard 10
Socrates 91
Sophocles 154
Sorokin, Pitirim 158
Soule, L. H. 135
South, Robert 65, 81
Speakman, Frederick B. 67, 101
Speer, Robert E. 24
Spencer, Herbert 14
Spurgeon, Charles H. 186

Sri Chaitanya 199
Steinmetz, Charles P. 146
Stephen, Leslie 154
Sterne, Laurence 154
Steuart, R. H. J. 203
Stevenson, Herbert F. 67
Stevenson, Robert Louis 79, 164
Stewart, James S. 10, 56, 67
Stidger, William L. 92
Studdert-Kennedy, G. A. 233
Symmachus 236

Tagore, Rabindranath 199, 240
Taylor, Harold 200
Taylor, Jeremy 189
Teacher's Treasury of Stories 146
Temple, William 239
Teresa, St. 190
Terhune, William 80
These Times 113
Thoreau, Henry David 123, 153, 171
Thurman, Howard 105, 137, 149, 157, 164, 198
Tittle, Ernest Fremont 42
Toynbee, Arnold 234
Tolstoy, Leo 153, 217
Tomkins, Floyd W. 65
Traherne, Thomas 98
Trueblood, Elton 75, 109, 132
Truett, George W. 35, 197
Truman, Harry S. 233
Trumbull, Henry Clay 212
Twelve Baskets Full 127

Ulich, Robert 132
Underhill, Evelyn 19, 85

Van Dusen, Henry Pitney 217
van Dyke, Henry 34, 50, 79, 106, 168, 228
Van Loon, Hendrik Willem 233
Vaughan, Henry 189
Vinet, Pierre 158

Wallace, John A. 192
Wallingford, James 33
Walton, Izaak 61
Watchman-Examiner, The 87, 191, 227
Watson, John 56, 58, 223
Webster, Daniel 87
Weil, Simone 98
Wells, Amos R. 221
Wells, Evelyn 145
Wells, H. G. 29
When Christmas Came to Bethlehem 35, 37
White, Ellen G. 113
Whitehead, Alfred North 121, 127
Whitman, Howard 182
Whitman, Walt 72, 94
Wieman, Henry Nelson 240
Wilbur, Ray Lyman 93
Willard, Frances E. 228
Willkie, Wendell 233
Wilson, Woodrow 13
Winter, William 98
Wister, Owen 4
Woodward, Luther E. 94
Worsdell, Edward 141
Wright, Ronald Selby 76
Wygal, Winnifred 17, 149

Young, Vash 214

POETRY INDEX
This index includes first lines, titles, and poets.

A bit of the Book in the morning 8
A child's kiss 200
A cold coming we had of it 36
A good book is a wonder-thing 146
A ray of sun—from sparkling window high 42
A well-kept garden filled with flowers 143
Able to suffer without complaining 179
Across the fields of yesterday 164
Alchemy 35
Alcott, Bronson 173
All beauty whispers to the listening heart 88
Although God loves the whole wide world 112
An easy thing, O Power Divine 208
An old, worn harp that had been played 167
And all the windows of my heart 240
And Christ Is Crucified Anew 58
And He was only thirty-three 68
And nature, the old nurse, took 175
And not by eastern windows only 131
And should my soul be torn with grief 8
And so I find it well to come 61
And so the Word had breath, and wrought 28
And the Word Was Made Flesh 33
Angels Unaware 75
Angler's Reveille, The (extract) 154
Another Lincoln (extract) 92
Are Ye Able 179
Are you in earnest? Seize this very minute 212
Arithmetic 179
Armour, Richard 113
As I Go on My Way 127
As the marsh-hen secretly builds on the watery sod 217
Association with the Lord can bring 27
At Daybreak 62
Awakening 224

Barabbas Speaks 57
Badley, Brenton Thoburn 179
Baker, Karle Wilson 171, 212
Be Still and Know That I Am God 88
Be sure that on Life's common street 87
Be with us, Lord, at eventide 154
Because upon the first 67
Believing the Best 4
Benediction 192
Benson, Louis F. 38

Best, Susie M. 98
Best Treasure, The 81
Best Wind, The 138
Beyond the Horizon 102
Bigler, Blaine C. 52
Bishop Blougram's Apology (extract) 71
Blake, William 10, 138, 222
Blanden, Charles G. 56
Book, The 10
Bowie, Walter Russell 23
Brainard, Mary Gardner 72
Brewing of Soma, The 86
Bring me my bow of burning gold 222
Brooks, Phillips 66
Brothers 233
Browning, Elizabeth Barrett 200
Browning, Robert 71, 137
Bryant, William Cullen 33
Build thee more stately mansions 93
Builder of Churches 44
Burns, Robert 110, 207
But all the pleasure that I find 51
But beauty seen is never lost 172
But he who gets to Bethlehem 38
But Thee, but Thee, O sovereign Seer of time 25
But yield who will to their separation 228
Butts, Mary E. 208
By the faith that the wild flowers show 174

Calvary and Easter 65
Carleton, Emma 152
Carlisle, Thomas John 44
Carman, Bliss 171, 186
Carmichael, Amy 55, 117, 190
Carruth, William Herbert 86
Cary, Phoebe 158
Celestial Paths 102
Chalmers, Patrick Reginald 106
Chambered Nautilus, The (extract) 93
Children 113
Christ, The 24
Christ be with me, Christ within me 23
Christ bears a thousand crosses now 56
Christ of the Andes, The (extract) 26
Christ of the World's Highway, The 27
Christmas Star, The (extract) 33
Clark, James S. 121
Clark, Leslie Savage 57, 99, 100
Close to the sod 240
Clough, Arthur Hugh 131
Coates, Florence Earle 92
Coffin, Robert P. Tristram 41, 52, 88, 92
Coin, The 163
Coleridge, Samuel T. 157
Come Up Higher 121
Common Days (extract) 211
Confession 110

Coolidge, Susan 65, 91
Count your garden by the flowers 179
Country Churches (extract) 41
Courage shall leap from me 182
Cowper, William 17
Crabbe, George 102
Craftsman 27
Credo (Oxenham) 4
Credo (Robinson) 3
Cross at the Crossways, The 58
Cross Roads, The 94
Crossing the Bar 98
Crowell, Grace Noll 27, 37, 41, 46, 51, 135, 146, 163, 174, 211
Cullen, Countee 152
Cure me with quietness 101
Cushman, Ralph S. 30, 58, 62, 135, 213
Cypress Gardens 49

Daley, Edith 85
Davis, Julia Johnson 94
Davis, Ozora S. 13
Dawn 86
Day, George E. 233
Day Well Spent 199
Days 212
de Bary, Anna Bunston 240
Dear common flower, that grow'st 175
Dear Lord, excuse my heavy boots 230
Death closes all; but something ere 132
Death of the Hired Man, The (extract) 111
Dedication 204
Denominations 46
Designers of Destiny 212
Destiny 224
Dickie, E. P. 56
Dickinson, Emily 49, 117, 142
Discovery 79
Doane, W. C. 101
Dowden, Edward 224
Dream and Dreamer 118
Driscoll, Louise 121
Drop Thy still dews of quietness 86
du Autermont, Harriet 72
Dunbar, Paul Laurence 167
Dyer, Edward 51

Each in His Own Tongue (extract) 86
Each life converges to some center 117
Earth's Common Things (extract) 137
Easter Carol, An 66
Easter Light 67
Easter Morning 67
Edgar, Mary S. 92
Eliot, George 117, 199
Eliot, T. S. 36
Emans, Elaine V. 189
Emerson, Ralph Waldo 158, 167, 176, 236
En Route 113
Encounter with Eternity 100

Eternal Goodness, The (extract) 97
Eternal Love, we have no good 190
Every morning lean thine arms awhile 62
Everyday Madonna 113
Expostulation and Reply (extract) 118

Faith 71
Faith and Doubt 71
Faith and Sight 72
Faith is not merely praying 71
Far Trumpets Blowing (extract) 38
Farjeon, Eleanor 132
Farmers 229
Farrington, Harry Webb 25
Father in Heaven, make me wise 112
Fellowship of Prayer, The 29
Fisher, Aileen 152
Fletcher, Giles 23
Flowers rejoice when night is done 62
Flynn, Charles Edwin 111
For books are more than books 9
For life alone is creator of life 153
For man is a dreamer ever 118
For me 'twas not the truth you taught 26
For resurrection living 99
For Sleep, or Death 101
For spring and autumn, sun and rain 186
For such as you, I do believe 114
Forest Hymn, A (extract) 240
Foss, Sam Walter 79
Freeman, Robert 102
Friend to Man, A 79
Frost, Robert 75, 111, 172, 228, 235
Fuller, Ethel Romig 110
Furbee, Ruth 239

Gallaudet, Herbert D. 240
Garrison, Winfred Ernest 10
Gibran, Kahlil 80
Gibson, W. W. 159
Gifts That Are Mine 38
Gilder, Richard Watson 159
Gillilan, Strickland 127
Give all to love 158
Give me not pallid ease 223
Give me, O God, the understanding heart 179
Give thanks to God 207
Giving 204
Glad that I live am I 19
Go not abroad for happiness 137
Go where he will, the wise man 236
Goal, The (Dickinson) 117
Goal, The (Shepard) 236
God answers prayer; sometimes 192
God, bless each little light 221

God builds no churches 44
God gave all men all earth 160
God, give me speech, in mercy 176
God grant us wisdom in these coming days 234
God is at the anvil 85
God is at the organ 168
God made my cathedral 239
God of the Open Air 174
God who gives the bird its anguish 88
God will not change 87
God wrote His loveliest poem 174
God's Children 112
God's delays are not denials 180
God's Love 62
God's Will 192
Goethe, Johann Wolfgang von 212
Going my way of old 159
Golden Censer, The 190
Golden Sight 176
Good Books 146
Good Company 171
Gordon, Adam Lindsay 200
Grace, A 192
Grace at Evening 154
Grace before Sleep 49
Gratitude 208
Gruber, A. L. 203
Guest, Edgar A. 8, 76, 128, 149, 204, 224
Guilty 14
Guiterman, Arthur 175
Gunsaulus, Frank W. 87
Gurney, Dorothy Frances 171

Hagedorn, Hermann 114, 197
Hale, Edward Everett 186
Hallet, Mary 88
Happiness 19
Happiness is like a crystal 19
Happiest Man, The 20
Happy is he who by love's sweet song 20
Happy is the family 114
Happy the man, and happy he alone 214
Harbour Lights (extract) 99
Harkness, Georgia 179
Hatch, Edwin 100
He came and took me by the hand 97
He is a path, if any be misled 23
He opened a window in the straw 35
He prayeth best, who loveth best 157
He ruffles through his hymnbook 44
He sent men out to preach the living Word 141
He stirs—He moves—in the lifting gloom 66
He treads no more the paths of Galilee 27
He was glad to see Hoppy 176
Hear the voice of the Bard 10
Heart of Love 159
Hearth and Home 236
Heaven 97
Heaven is the place 97
Heir of the Kingdom 'neath the skies 123

Henderson, Daniel 24
Henley, William Ernest 168
Henry Hudson Speaks 118
Her rugs are worn, yet she explains 163
Here in my workshop where I toil 227
Here is the Truth in a little creed 28
Hickok, Eliza M. 192
Higginson, Thomas W. 208
His Ways 85
Hodgson, Ralph 97
Hold fast your dreams 121
Holmes, Oliver Wendell 93, 111
Holy Places 240
Holy Poet, I have heard 194
"Home is the place where 111
Home's not merely four square walls 114
Hosmer, Frederick L. 218
Hosmer, Laurence 33
How, William Walsham 203
How can our minds and bodies be 49
How does the soul grow 91
How hard for unaccustomed feet 99
How restful are unhurried things 51
However much I have to do 52
Hughes, Langston 97
Hymn for a Household 24

I am my neighbor's Bible 10
I believe a leaf of grass is no less 173
I cannot find my way: there is no star 3
I cannot understand 218
I dare not slight the stranger 29
I did not know, till 'neath the rod 98
I do not ask for wealth 52
I do not ask, O Lord 149
I have a rendezvous with Life 152
I have believed the best of every man 4
I have closed the door on doubt 72
I have felt a presence 88
I Have Found Such Joy (extract) 135
I have to live with myself 149
I heard a man explaining 57
I honor the land that gave me birth 233
I know not by what methods rare 192
I know not how that Bethlehem's Babe 25
I know not where His islands lift 97
I know three things must always be 191
I like to spread clean sheets on beds 110
I met a stranger in the night 199
I never cut my neighbor's throat 14
I saw God bare His soul one day 55
I saw His blood upon the rose 56
I saw the mountains stand 121
I see from my house by the side of the road 79

I shall keep some cool green memory 163
I thank Thee for my quiet home 76
I thank You Father for a home to keep 111
I thank You for these gifts, dear God 208
I think that I shall never see 174
I think true love is never blind 158
I took a day to search for God 171
I watch the farmers in their fields 229
I went to turn the grass once after one 235
I will follow the upward road today 211
I will lift up mine eyes unto the skyscrapers 185
I will not hurry through this day 213
I'd like to think when life is done 204
I'd rather see a sermon than hear one any day 128
If all the skies were sunshine 181
If Jesus built a ship 27
If one by one we counted people out 14
If peace be in the heart 50
If we're thoughtful just this minute 214
If what shone afar so grand 181
If you sit down at set of sun 199
If you would have a mind at peace 49
If you'd move to a bygone measure 106
I'll stand beside the keeper of the inn 38
I'm going out to clean the pasture spring 75
I'm nobody! Who are you 49
In May, when sea-winds pierced our solitudes 176
In Memoriam (extract) 28
In Such an Age 236
In the Time of Trouble 99
In your face I sometimes see 94
Inscription 49, 62
Inscription on a Sundial 157
Into my heart's treasury 163
Invitation 97
Ireland, Thelma 44

Jackson, Lydia O. 111
Jesu, if Thou wilt make 193
Jones, Thomas S., Jr. 164
Journey of the Magi 36
Journeys 51
Judean hills are holy 23
Judge not the Lord by feeble sense 17

Kahn, Hannah 105
Kane, H. Victor 185
Keep Some Green Memory Alive 163
Kind Words 164
Kindly Neighbor, The (extract) 76
Kipling, Rudyard 160
Kirk, William F. 204
Kiser, S. E. 71

Kleiser, Grenville 207
Kramer, Edgar Daniel 67

Ladder of St. Augustine, The 182
Laid on Thine altar, O my Lord divine 204
Lake, George Burt 186
Lamps 199
Land of Beyond, The (extract) 117
Lanier, Sidney 25, 217
Last Defile, The 117
Laugh, for the time is brief 17
Lennan, Elinor 193
Leonard, Priscilla 19
Let me go where'er I will 167
Let me not to the marriage of true minds 158
Let me, O Lord, have always one 200
"Let trees be made, for Earth is bare 175
Let Us Keep Christmas (extract) 37
Light looked down and beheld Darkness 33
Like tides on a crescent sea-beach 86
Little Boys in Church 41
Little Lights 221
Little Song of Life, A 19
Lives of great men all remind us 105
Longfellow, Henry Wadsworth 105, 175, 182
Lord God, how full our cup of happiness 18
Lord, make me sensitive to the sight 172
Lord of all growing things 218
Lord of my heart's elation 186
Lord, the newness of this day 87
Love, Adelaide 35
Love ever gives 198
Love is not passion 157
Love's Miracle 160
Love-Wise 159
Lowell, Amy 153
Lowell, James Russell 9, 128, 160, 175, 234
Lucky the lad whose teachers know 143

Main Aims, The 114
Make us Thy mountaineers 117
Man 123
Manger Mouse, The 35
Manuscripts of God, The 175
Many a tree is found in the wood 199
Markham, Edwin 13, 18, 26, 28
Marr, Barbara 172
Marriage 159
Marshes of Glynn, The (extract) 217
Martin, Leona Bolt 143
Marvel, The 38
Masefield, John 17, 132
Master Player, The 167
Matins 62
May the glad dawn 68
McKeehan, Irene Pettit 72
Men go to their garden for pleasure 62
Merchant, Jane 198

Mergard, Jean Carpenter 163
Metcalfe, James J. 52, 112
'Mid all the traffic of the ways 61
Miracle 85
Moment, John J. 81
Montgomery, James 189
Montgomery, L. M. 160
Moody, William Vaughn 88
Moreland, John R. 58
Morgan, Angela 182, 236
Morituri Salutamus (extract) 230
Morley, Christopher 94
Morton, David 55
Mother in the House, The 114
Mother's Prayer, A 112
Munson, Ida Norton 51, 67
Music 167
My altars are the mountains 239
My Companion 227
My faith is all a doubtful thing 55
My feet shall never stand 213
My friends are little lamps 82
My Hour 214
My life shall touch a dozen lives 127
My mother, who boasted of no degree 109
Myself 149
Mystery, The 97

New Earth, A (extract) 234
New occasions teach new duties 234
New Trinity, The 13
No day is common.—I have walked 211
No Manger for Easter 66
No vision and you perish 72
Nobody ever added up 18
Not for one single day 118
Not for us are content, and quiet 132
Not only once, and long ago 58
Not till the loom is silent 182
Not what, but Whom, I do believe 4
Now 214
Now who can take from us what we have known 159
Noyes, Alfred 99

O Christ of Olivet, you hushed 26
O Earth! Thou hast not any wind 223
O Father, may that holy star 33
O God, we thank Thee for every-thing 186
O grant me this 228
O Lord, that lends me life 208
O Son of Man, who walked each day 29
O the kind words we give shall in memory live 164
O Thou in all Thy might so far 218
O Thou, who kindly doth provide 207
Oft as we jog along life's winding way 94
Oh, give us pleasure in the flowers today 172
Oh the sheer joy of it 135
Oh, the wild joys of living 137

Oh! Thou who taught my infant eye 102
Old Church, An 105
Old Rugs 163
On My Way to Work 230
One Step in Triumph 213
One Thousandth Psalm, The 186
Open the door of the heart 75
Orthodox 14
Otherwise 152
Our Brotherhood 13
Our Christ 25
Our families in Thine arms enfold 111
Oxenham, John 4, 24, 58, 61, 94, 98, 109, 118, 198, 228, 234

Page's Road Song, A 193
Parker, Helen Baker 79
Parks, Ruth M. 42
Passion Flower, The 57
Pasture, The 75
Patrick, Johnstone G. 224
Peace be in thy heart 218
Pearse, Mark Guy 14
Per Aspera 92
Percy, William Alexander 193, 229
Perfect Trusting 218
Personal Translation 10
Petition (Crampton) 223
Petition (Oxenham) 228
Pilgrims to Everest 218
Pilot, how far from home 99
Pitter, Ruth 101
Place these gifts on my altar 38
Plantz, Myra Goodwin 192
Plunkett, Joseph Mary 56
Poetry 132
Poet's Grace, A 207
Poling, Daniel A. 149
Poteat, Edwin McNeill 57, 154
Powers, Eleanor 192
Praise and Thanks 186
Prayer (Harkness) 179
Prayer (Holmes) 111
Prayer (Marr) 172
Prayer (Poling) 149
Prayer (van Dyke) 88
Prayer for Service 200
Prayer in Spring, A 172
Prayer is the soul's sincere desire 189
Prayer of a Homemaker 111
Prayer of the Quest, The 91
Present Crisis, The (extract) 234
Presentiment of better things on earth 117
Psalm of a City Man 185
Psalm of Life, The (extract) 105

Quatrain (Blanden) 56
Quatrain (Markham) 28
Question not, but live and labor 200
Quinn, John Robert 109

Realf, Richard 223
Recognition 101
Reese, Lizette Woodworth 19, 99
Requiem 101
Reveal Thy Presence now, O Lord 192
Rhodora, The 176
Richardson, Charles Francis 50
Richstone, May 143

Robinson, Edwin Arlington 3, 207
Rogers, James 218

Sacrament 157
Salutation 218
Salute to the Trees 199
Sanctuary (extract) 61
Sandford, Egbert 168
Sangster, Margaret E. 8, 112, 208
Sarett, Lew 85
Savage, Minot J. 137
Scott, Frederick George 86
Search, The (Clark) 203
Search (Thacker) 113
Seager, Ralph W. 35, 38, 66, 172, 176, 213
Seaman's Psalm 218
Secret, The (extract) 62
Seekers, The (extract) 132
Sense of Him, A 26
Sermons We See (extract) 128
Service 197
Service, Robert W. 117
Shakespeare, William 158, 197, 208
Shall we sit idly down and say 230
Sharing 203
Sheer Joy (extract) 135
Shepard, Odell 236
Shepherd of mortals, here behold 24
Shipp, Horace 218
Silver Poplars (extract) 174
Simmons, Laura 29
Small boys in the church pew grow 41
Smile 18
Smith, Hilda W. 37
Snowdrop, The 240
So I go on, not knowing 72
So joyously, at answered prayer 189
So short the road from Bethlehem 57
Softly I closed the Book 10
Some days my thoughts are just cocoons 212
Some Faith at Any Cost 72
Some seek a heaven for rest 100
Sometimes 164
Starlit Hill, The 30
Stars rise and set, that star 33
Stars and Soul 151
Star-Splitter, The (extract) 14
Stevenson, Robert Louis 101
Stidger, William L. 23, 55
Stock, Eleanor B. 91
Storey, Violet Alleyn 68, 200, 221
Strange Holiness (extract) 88
Stranger, The 81
Studdert-Kennedy, G. A. 135, 176
Suddenly, we know not how 224
Sunday Service 44
Sunset and evening star 98
Surprise, The 189
Sussex (extract) 160
Swain, Charles 114
Swift, Hildegarde Hoyt 141
Symbol 55
Symbolisms 223
Symbols of faith, they lift their reaching spires 41

Take us on the Quest of Beauty 91
Take what God gives 17
Teacher, The 141
Tears 99
Teasdale, Sara 49, 163
Tennyson, Alfred 28, 98, 132, 154
Thank God, a man can grow 92
Thank God! there is always a Land of Beyond 117
Thanks from Earth to Heaven (extract) 194
That man can thank his lucky stars 52
That where the safe ways end 218
The anchored trust that at the core of things 217
The Carpenter of Galilee 37
The common hopes that make us men 13
The cornerstone in Truth is laid 109
The Cross of Calvary 98
The door is on the latch tonight 38
The good intent of God 24
The greatest poem ever known 94
The heights by great men reached 182
The human will, that force un-seen 182
The immortal spirit hath no bars 86
The kiss of the sun for pardon 171
The little cares of every day 175
The Lord is my Pilot 218
The nightingale has a lyre of gold 168
The Northwest Passage 118
The quality of mercy is not strain'd 197
The rainbow of spring is in the air 172
The road winds up the hill 152
The roses red upon my neighbor's vine 203
The silent beauty of the stars 224
The stone is lifted from the tomb 67
The sun be warm and kind 192
The walls which now 105
The whole, wide world turned selfless 35
The world sits at the feet of Christ 30
There are strange ways 197
There are three green eggs 18
There are veins in the hills 81
There is beauty in the forest 159
There is strange holiness around 88
There must be magic 152
There was a night, there was a hill 30
They are the idols of hearts 113
They questioned my theology 14
Things Enough 52
Think you mid all this mighty sun 118
This Is Faith 217
This is our House of Prayer 46
Thomas, Gilbert 18

246

Thou lowly, meek, and lovely flower 57
Three Things 191
Three things must a man possess 13
"Three things there are," said one 56
Thurman, Howard 38
Time flies 157
Time's wheel spins on 212
Tiplady, Thomas 192
'Tis life, where of our nerves are scant 135
To a Dandelion 175
To be alive in such an age 236
To each man's life there comes 214
To give a little from a shining store 204
To make a happy fireside clime 110
To My Little Son 94
To those who are content 51
Today a man discovered gold 79
Today I have grown taller 171
Tomb, thou shalt not hold Him longer 66
Toward Jerusalem 55
Townsend, Joseph L. 164
Treasure Island 106
Trees 174
Trimmed Lamp, The 29
Troy, Grace E. 180

True Love 158
True love is but a humble, low-born thing 160
True Pathos 110
Tuft of Flowers, The 235
Turner, Nancy Byrd 29, 33
Two kinds of gratitude: the sudden kind 207
Two Tramps in Mud Time (extract) 228

Ulysses (extract) 132
Under the wide and starry sky 101
Understanding 98
Unutterable Beauty, The (extract) 176
Upon the marsh mud, dank and foul 160
Upward Road, The 211

Van Dyke, Henry 62, 87, 118, 154, 174, 181, 199, 217
Veni Creator (extract) 186
Vestigia (extract) 171
Voice, The (extract) 224
Voyagers (extract) 217

Way, The 57
We are so foolish about death 101
We are standing in the great dawn 236

We come to God by devious ways 46
We give Thee but Thine own 203
We have sailed seas of vastness 113
We muse on miracles who look 85
We search the world for truth 7
We thank Thee for life's common things 208
What Is Home? 114
What is poetry? Who knows 132
"What is the real good 75
Whatever else Thou sendest me 58
Wheelock, John Hall 194
When Father carved our Christmas bird 113
When her teen-age daughter 198
When I consider Life and its few years 99
When I heard the learn'd astronomer 175
When Life Is Done 204
When life seems just a dreary grind 135
When men go down to the sea in ships 102
When outward bound we boldly sail 217
When Spring comes and the evening robin calls 92
When you go walking down a

street 81
Where Beauty Dwells 143
Wherever souls of men have worshiped 240
Whichever way the wind doth blow 138
Whitman, Walt 173, 175
Whittemore, Elizabeth 82
Whittier, John Greenleaf 7, 30, 61, 86, 97, 102, 172
Who builds the church 46
Who keeps a rendezvous with stars 100
Who loves a garden 173
Whom God elects for service great 224
Wiggin, Kate Douglas 38
Wilcox, Ella 182
Wilkinson, Marguerite 14
Williams, B. Y. 17
Wilson, Dorothy Clarke 27
Wisest of the Wise, The 38
With silence only as their benediction 102
Woman's Way, A 198
Wordsworth, William 88, 118
Worship 239

You shall know Him when He comes 101
Young Minister 42
Your House of Happiness (extract) 17

INDEX OF TOPICS

acceptance 51
action 26, 160
admiration 79
adventure 4, 38, 76, 106, 132, 152, 154, 159
affliction 179
aim 122
Alexander the Great 28
America 93, 106, 222
ancestor 42
anguish 167
anticipation 97, 214
argument 67
art 71
artist 105, 154
aspiration 122, 142, 167
autobiography 154
autumn 172
avocation 228
awakening 62, 224
awareness 154

baby 25, 113
Barabbas 57
barrier 13
beauty 13, 86, 91, 92, 131, 137, 143, 159, 171, 173, 176, 186
Beethoven, Ludwig van 180
beginning 212, 214
believer 4
believing 1-4
Bethlehem 37, 38, 55, 57
Bible 5-10, 45, 223
bird 18, 88, 168, 171, 228
birth 36
blessedness 52, 66, 149
book 8, 9, 106, 142, 143, 145, 146

boy 41, 44, 92, 93, 143
bread 13, 208
bride 157
brook 198
brother 27, 233
brotherhood 11-14, 236
builder 44, 46

Caesar 28
Calvary 25, 30, 55, 56, 57, 58, 65
candle 118, 127
canticle 44
carpenter 30, 37
cathedral 44, 239
caution 82
center 123
certainty 217
character 110, 124, 145, 179
charity 49
Charlemagne 28
cheerfulness 15-20, 35, 137
child 13, 92, 93, 94, 109, 112, 113, 127, 163, 164
choice 72, 91
Christ 4, 10, 21-30, 98, 99, 102, 113, 127, 141, 142, 154, 204, 227, et al.
Christian 42, 213
Christianity 4, 8, 27, 29, 45, 124, 213
Christlikeness 30, 41
Christmas 31-38, 66
church 39-46, 105, 109
circle 87
citizen 110
city 185
claim 13

Columbus, Christopher 106, 124
common 88, 211, 239
communication 75, 88
communion 167
community 43, 236
companion 20, 81
completeness 61
comradeship 76
congregation 127
conscience 122
consecration 62
contemplation 61
contemporary 67, 105
contentment 47-52, 137
contribution 17
conversation 85
conviction 132, 173
Copernicus, Nicolaus 124
cornerstone 3
courage 65, 68, 182
craftsman 27
creation 138
creed 3, 14, 28, 82, 141
Cross 30, 53-58, 98, 204
curiosity 144

darkness 24, 33, 102, 118
death 36, 66, 99, 101, 154
democracy 13, 76, 146, 236
denomination 44, 46
destiny 88, 153, 212, 224
devotion 46, 59-62
difference 81
difficulty 182
discipleship 26, 222, 223
discovery 142, 234
disposition 20

diversity 81
divinity 29
doctrine 29
door 36, 38, 46, 75, 118, 197, 199
doubt 4, 55, 71, 72
dream 118, 121, 122, 143
duty 17, 86

Easter 63-68, 98, 99
Eden 55, 173
education 141, 142, 143, 144, 145, 146, 233
employer 229
enchantment 138
endeavor 123
enjoyment 19, 50, 52
enthusiasm 138
eternity 67, 100, 128
example 26

face 14, 27
faith 20, 43, 49, 55, 57, 68, 69-72, 106, 117, 217
family 19, 109, 111, 112, 114
farmer 229, 235
father 106, 110, 111, 113
fellowship 29, 73-76
fishing 154
flower 57, 62, 174, 175, 176, 240
forgiveness 14
freedom 14
friendship 26, 77-82, 85
frog 49, 176
future 50, 71, 105, 118, 153, 211, 214, 230

Galilee 55
garden 49, 52, 93, 143, 171, 173
generosity 50

genius 145
gentleman 75, 150
Gethsemane 55, 68
gift 35, 38, 160, 203, 204, 222, 227
gladness 19, 168
goal 117, 122, 182, 236
God 3, 4, 7, 9, 25, 45, 58, 83-88, 112, 135, 217, 218, 227, 228, 233, 240, *et al.*
gold 176
Golden Rule 163
Golgotha 58
goodness 137, 230
goodwill 75, 82
grace 17, 49, 154
gratitude 30, 49, 207, 208
greatness 19
groom 157
growth 3, 41, 89-94, 143
guarantee 94
guest 24, 45, 114
guilt 14

hand 81, 160
happiness 14, 17, 18, 19, 20, 29, 50, 51, 97, 111, 114, 117, 135, 137, 138, 150, 159, 182, 204, 214, 229, 233
health 20, 49, 71
heart 37, 38, 50, 58, 75, 114, 121, 124, 159, 167, 204
heaven 19, 24, 56, 58, 95-102, 111, 114, 185, 203
hell 160
heredity 106
heritage 103-106
hero 19, 79
history 24, 29, 30, 57, 87, 105
holiness 23, 46, 55, 240
Holy Spirit 33
home 43, 49, 51, 76, 99, 101, 107-114, 127, 158, 236
homesickness 164, 236
hope 37, 43, 49, 115-118
horizon 102, 141
hospitality 76
house 17, 45, 46, 112, 190
Hudson, Henry 118
humanity 17, 26, 29, 76, 224
humor 17, 19, 71, 82, 143
husband 109

idea 121, 167
ideal 119-124, 137
idealism 121
ignorance 143
immortality 25, 92, 98, 99, 100, 101, 102
Incarnation 24, 30, 33, 34, 57
individual 26, 153
influence 125-128
inscription 23, 49, 61, 62, 91, 100, 128, 157
inspiration 129-132, 167
interdependence 79
invitation 43

Jerusalem 55
journey 35, 36, 51, 94
joy 18, 133-138, 185
Judea 23
judgment 17, 122

Keats, John 180
key 58, 98

kindness 19, 75, 76, 86, 159, 164
Kingdom of God 29, 109, 113
knowledge 91, 146

lake 171
lamp 3, 29, 82, 128, 199, 230, 240
lamplighter 127
laughter 17
learning 139-146
leisure 50, 62, 128
lesson 141
life 3, 13, 19, 43, 45, 51, 66, 122, 137, 147-154
light 3, 7, 13, 24, 33, 35, 62, 98, 102, 118, 153
Lincoln, Abraham 92
listener 88
longing 86
Lord's Prayer 191
love 28, 29, 30, 37, 43, 49, 62, 82, 86, 117, 138, 144, 155-160, 167
loyalty 106
luck 181

Magi 36
man 4, 44, 123, 124, 149, 153, 154, 233
manger 35
marriage 157, 158, 159
medicine 18
memory 49, 93, 109, 159, 161-164
message 88
Milton, John 180
mind 50, 121, 142, 143, 234
minister 42
miracle 35, 85, 157, 160, 173, 240
mirth 18
missionary 221, 222, 223, 224
money 203, 204
morality 14, 132
monogram 35
morning 211, 212
mother 106, 109, 110, 111, 112, 113, 114, 127
motto 114, 229
Mount Everest 76, 213, 218
mountain 121, 174, 179
music 165-168
mouse 35
mystery 65, 86, 97, 146

nation 191, 233
nature 19, 30, 169-176, 186, 239, 240
Nazareth 55
neighbor 10, 13, 14, 76, 79, 82, 203, 233
New Testament 4, 10, 223
nobility 128

obstacles 72
old age 93, 94, 138, 163, 230
Old Testament 7
opportunity 212
optimism 20
ordinary 35
organ 168
overcoming 72, 177-182

Paradise 98
past 50, 94, 105, 106, 118, 211
patience 49, 110, 117
peace 33, 36, 49, 50, 52, 135

people 19, 75, 76
perfection 122
personality 62, 75, 79, 93, 144, 153
philosopher 172
philosophy 236
piano 168
Pilate 56
pioneer 106
play 111
pleasure 121, 172, 204
poetry 132, 142, 164, 174
possibility 117, 180
postman 76
postponement 50
praise 183-186
prayer 29, 46, 61, 62, 157, 180, 187-194, 230
prejudice 13, 26
preparation 141, 224
present 50, 94, 105, 211, 214
problem 118
prophecy 34, 57
prophet 61
purpose 122, 213

quest 88
question 93, 146
quiet 50, 51, 61, 86

rainbow 97
reading 8, 10
reality 143
recipe 35, 49, 146
religion 49, 62, 71, 86, 132, 240
responsibility 87, 153, 233
rest 43, 61
resurrection 65, 66, 67, 68, 99, 100
revelation 61, 203
river 153
road 10, 94
rose 85, 97, 203

sacrament 157
sacrifice 56, 58, 65
saint 19, 62, 87, 128
salvation 224
satisfaction 51, 86, 229
Schweitzer, Albert 168, 235
science 4, 71, 118
Scotland 164
Scott, Walter 82
search 50, 118, 132, 141, 145, 146, 171, 203
searchlight 55
secret 62
security 118
self-examination 51, 91
self-giving 204
self-reliance 82
serenity 51
sermon 41, 128
Sermon on the Mount 233
service 17, 43, 91, 195-200, 224
shadow 23
Shakespeare, William 8, 20, 25
ship 228
sight 72, 234
signpost 58
silence 61, 88, 186
simplicity 52, 135
sinner 41, 56
sky 98, 131
sleep 99, 101
smile 17, 18
Socrates 20, 29

solution 118
song 167
sorrow 164
soul 4, 52, 62, 151
sound 151
spire 41, 44, 118
spring 172, 175, 182
star 33, 35, 44, 85, 131, 175
statistics 7
stewardship 201-204
stranger 14, 29, 81, 199
strength 49
substitute 199
success 230
suffering 58, 71
sundial 18, 157
sunrise 25
symbol 17, 41
sympathy 75, 179

task 228
teacher 27, 141, 142, 143, 144, 145
teamwork 76
tears 99
tenderness 82
testimony 25
thanksgiving 76, 185, 186, 205-208
thought 142, 143, 163, 168
time 117, 212, 213, 214
today 209-214
tomorrow 3, 72, 117, 229
tranquillity 51, 88
translation 10
travel 76, 111, 113, 132
treasure 106, 164, 204
tree 3, 55, 94, 98, 117, 171, 174, 199
trouble 179
trumpet 38
trust 215-218
truth 86, 137, 145, 146
Twain, Mark 93

unbelief 4, 68
understanding 75, 179, 198
university 145
usefulness 51

vacation 174
verbs 72
victory 58, 182
vision 26, 61, 62, 72, 124, 131
vocation 228
voice 30, 224

waiting 182
wall 150
watermelon 86
wealth 49, 52, 172
wife 109, 110, 118
wind 138
window 131, 240
wings 71, 175, 179, 218
wisdom 19, 20, 106, 143
Wise Men 36
wish 71
witness 219-224
wonder 86, 145, 154, 175, 207
Word of God 33, 46
work 225-230, 235
world 20, 61, 88, 97
world horizons 231-236
worship 112, 237-240

yearning 86, 152
youth 68, 92, 106, 122, 128